In & Around
Albany,
Schenectady
& Troy

In & Around
Albany, Schenectady & Troy

by

Susanne Dumbleton & Anne Older

WASHINGTON PARK PRESS
7 Englewood Place
Albany

Washington Park Press
7 Englewood Place
Albany, NY 12203
(518) 465-0169

Acknowledgements

We are indebted to:

The many individuals and groups in the community who responded promptly and fully to our requests for information.

Families and friends who provided enthusiasm and encouragement throughout the undertaking.

The feature writers of the region's newspapers, who continually kept us alert to the changing scene.

Table of Contents

Introduction

The Capital District is an exciting place to visit and a wonderful place to live. There are interesting sites to tour and entertaining things to do throughout the year. The arts flourish, and sports thrive.

In addition, magnificent natural setting and premier cultural attractions lie within range. Mountains, lakes—even the ocean—form the environment residents consider their ordinary frame of reference. Three major cities— Boston, New York, and Montreal—are within easy driving distance.

It is not always simple, however, to discover the assets of the region. No literature discusses the advantages of the area as a whole. Although specialized works describe the architecture or survey the restaurants or narrate the history, none portrays the wide spectrum of opportunity open to the visitor or resident.

In 1980, we wrote IN AND AROUND ALBANY: A GUIDE FOR RESIDENTS, STUDENTS, AND VISITORS to fill that need. It was addressed to all those who wished to partake fully of the many riches offered by the Capital District. It was a composite depiction of the history and the people, a compendium of information about schools, hospitals, transportation, and reference sources, and a comprehensive guide to superior drama, music, art, dance, restaurants, stores, and hotels. It was, in short, an appreciation of the area written for those who were passing through, those who had come to stay, even those who had been here from birth.

This book expands on that first effort. First of all, it takes as its focal point the entire Capital District, treating the three cities—Albany, Schenectady, and Troy—in depth, and highlighting the towns and villages which surround the cities. Second, it takes into account the exciting number of openings and closings, comings and goings during the past five years in the area. Third, while retaining the pertinent information in the previous volume, it adds descriptions of many points of interest not previously discussed, and presents additional ideas for day trips, including favorite places to visit in Boston and New York. Finally, the material in all of the chapters has been updated to insure accuracy.

The Past

The earliest known residents of the Capital District were the Mahican Indians. They lived a simple existence along the banks of the Hudson River. Their chief sat at the peace sachem at Schodack, and Albany served as the great Fire Place of the Mahican where the tribe would gather for social and ceremonial events.

Their neighbors were the Iroquois, a powerful confederation of five nations—Mohawks, Senecas, Onondagas, Oneidas and Cayugas. One hundred years before the coming of white settlers, the Iroquois made war on the Mahicans in hopes of gaining possession of the Hudson Valley. They gradually succeeded, and in 1626, even the Mahicans who had resisted were driven off into the Berkshires—forever.

In 1609, into this region sailed a small ship, the Half Moon, under the command of Henry Hudson. The ship stayed four days (September 19-23) so that the crew could observe the land and test the waters for further navigability. Hudson returned to the Netherlands and gave a favorable report, but nothing developed further for many years. Then in 1624, the Dutch West India Company, anxious to establish a fur trading center, decided to found a permanent settlement in the area. Eighteen families, French-speaking Walloons from the South Netherlands, came up the river and built a fort and houses at what is now the foot of Madison Avenue and Broadway in Albany. This was Fort Orange. The Indians chose to befriend these settlers who were thus free to move about the land without fear of harassment.

The settlement prospered but it did not grow. The Dutch government wanted to strengthen its claim on the area. To encourage immigration, particularly of persons who would develop the land by farming, the Netherlands established a patroon system in 1628 which gave large tracts of land to anyone who would settle 50 adults on the land within 50 years. In this way Kiliaen Van Rensselaer acquired 1250 square miles of land surrounding the Hudson-Mohawk River Valley. The settlers who came for Van Rensselaer at that time—really as indentured servants, for the patroon owner had feudal power over the land—were Swedes, Norwegians, Scots,

Irish, Danes and Germans. These settlers quite naturally wanted to get in on the prosperity of the fur trade, so they clustered their homes around Fort Orange. Squabbles arose and Peter Stuyvesant was summoned from New Amsterdam (New York) to bring peace. He recognized that for the patroon system to work, the new settlers had to be encouraged more actively to develop the land. He thus defined an area around Fort Orange proper as the Place of the Beaver (Beverwyck) and banned patroon settlers from that region. Thus agriculture joined trading as a major activity. The Iroquois, though engaged in their own constant war with the Algonquins, the tribe who had once occupied the region but who had been displaced to Canada and constantly sought to reclaim the land, maintained friendly relations with the European settlers. Indeed they taught the newcomers their considerable skill in farming, tanning, road building, and medicinal herbs.

Across the river, near the confluence of the Hudson and Mohawk Rivers, a Dutch settler named Jean Barensten Wemp in 1659 bought a large tract of land from the Indians. He died shortly thereafter and the land passed to the Vanderheydens and Lansings. This settlement, which was eventually to become Troy, remained a quiet agricultural community for a while.

To the West, meanwhile, in 1651 Arendt Van Curler, also from Holland, purchased 128 square miles from the Mohawks and with fifteen other families established a patroon. They nestled together in houses built beside the confluence of the Mohawk River and the Binne Kill. To define their area and defend themselves against their enemies, the French, the families erected a stockade fence around their homes. There they dwelled in peace and prosperity, farming the land and living simply until 1690. In that year King William's War broke out and on February 8-9 the entire settlement was burned and most residents were either killed or taken captive. The few survivors planned to abandon their land, but several Mohawk Indians, led by one named Lawrence, persuaded them to stay and helped them rebuild on the same land, the area today called the Stockade.

Except for this violent intrusion, the area remained peaceful. Slow growth and moderate prosperity marked all three communities. In spite of the fact that the Dutch surrendered the colony to England in 1664, few English settlers moved north from New Amsterdam (New York City). Thus

Courtesy of The McKinney Library
Albany Institute of History and Art

the power structure remained essentially the same, and strong Dutch influence persisted.

Wars, perhaps more than anything else, brought changes for the three cities. Located at the crossroads of rivers and mountain ranges, the area was the inevitable place of embarkation and debarkation of troops. King Williams' War (1689-1697), Queen Anne's War (1702-1713), King George's War (1744-1748), and the French and Indian War, the conflict which pitted the British and Iroquois against the French and Algonquins (1754-1763), were all fought around or near the cities. Then, of course, came the American Revolution.

Since one third of the Revolution was fought in New York, all of these people lived in quite constant fear of attacks by the British Navy, the British Army, Indians still friendly to the British, or Loyalists.

Former Sage Estate
Albany International

Albany's position in the struggle was pivotal. The British held New York City. The Americans held West Point. Together they crippled vital shipping. The British knew that if they could capture Albany they could easily seize West Point by simultaneous attack from the north and the south and could thus control all movement from Canada to New York City. But they could not take Albany. In 1777 the British Army's campaign was rebuffed at Saratoga. This battle is called the turning point of the Revolution because sagging American morale was dramatically lifted, because the French consequently agreed to fight on the side of the colonists, and because the British thereafter abandoned all hope of capturing Albany.

After the battle of Saratoga, life was less turbulent. In 1779 colonists fought against the Indians and the British to the west and in 1780-81 there were small retaliatory attacks right in the city of Albany, but thereafter little battling took place in the region.

Ironically, in those years of military tempest and political turmoil, there came a group of people whose way was of peace. In 1774 Ann Lee left England to settle in the New World with followers in the United Society of Believers in the Second Coming of Christ, the Shakers. They settled in Watervliet in 1776 and later established communal societies, the first at New Lebanon in 1787. Agriculturalists and craftsmen, they left a definite mark on the area, in spite of their small numbers and quiet ways.

So too did the other people who began to come in greater numbers. In 1710 there was a major influx of Palatine Germans. After the Revolution, the prospect of land and the lure of adventure brought about major movements of colonists, particularly from Connecticut and Massachusetts. Geography brought them through the region; some stayed. Then came the waves of European immigration in the 19th century. Notable were the Irish who came first in the 1820's to work on the Erie Canal and later—one million of them between 1847-1869 to New York City—to escape the Great Famine and its tragic aftermath. In 1907 large numbers of Sicilians came in the last major ethnic immigration to the region.

The 19th century brought the railroads and the potential for growth. Once the rail link between Albany and Schenectady was laid, the cities began to grow toward one another. The 19th century also brought industry. Troy's location near natural sources of power (the Wynantskill and the Poestenkill) and beside a major natural artery of transportation (the Hudson) made it and its neighbors, Cohoes and Watervliet, the perfect sites for plants and factories. Schenectady's situation at the Mohawk River and Erie Canal made it ideal for manufacture, and Albany's location made it a logical center for transshipment. It was, for example, a crucial link in the movement of lumber from the Adirondacks.

In 1828 a retired minister in Troy began to market collars made by local women in their homes. With the subsequent invention of the sewing machine, this "piece-work" grew into a major industry which moved from the home into the factory. At the peak of the collar and cuff trade, more than twenty collar manufacturers were based in Troy.

The same years witnessed the growth of many major industries. Factories turned out many diverse products, the most famous being those derived from the iron and textile industries. The Burden Iron Works boasted of producing fifty-one million horseshoes in one year, and the metal plates for the Civil War ship the Monitor were made in the mills of Troy.

The year 1828 was also dynamic across the river in Waterford. In that year, the King's Water Power Canal was constructed according to designs by John Fuller King. This provided for the construction of two dams across the Mohawk River and a half mile canal running parallel to the river. Factories were then built along the canal, and each industry was given its own gate and sluiceway to draw and control water power. Thus knitting mills, dye works, flour mills, paper companies, machine works, twine factories, and saw mills grew up and flourished along the canal.

In Cohoes the textile industry flourished. Mills were built beside the Falls, and factories and mill houses sprouted up all along the roads leading from the Falls. Cohoes became a community based on the textile mills.

Papermaking was also a natural. With natural sources of power and an abundance of lumber being moved through the area, paper-making plants prospered. So too did the brewing industry. The high quality of the water flowing into the area made it the ideal choice for beermaking.

In 1851 Schenectady Locomotive Works (later called American Locomotive Company) began to build engines to haul trains for railroads all over the world. Then in 1892, the General Electric Company was formed by merging the Edison General Electric Company and the Thomson-Houston Company. Schenectady became a thriving center of commerce, industry and science and was called "The City that Lights and Hauls the World." This growth continued through both world wars as the city's factories were used in the production of heavy military equipment and trains for transport. In nearby Watervliet the arsenal worked night and day to turn out artillery and anti-aircraft guns.

Time has modified the focal points in the development of all these cities. With a suddenness that matched the drama of its rise, the industrial center of Troy declined. To this day conflicting reasons are advanced to explain the withdrawal of industry from the city. Some claim that persistent labor troubles drove industry to areas where labor was cheap and docile. Others say that the monopolistic attitude of industrial magnates concentrated the power dangerously in the hands of a few, kept other industry out of the region and paved the way to disaster when "the few" left. Others claim that with the development of inexpensive fuel-driven factory equipment Troy lost its competitive edge and industries began to move closer to the raw materials they had been transporting for processing in Troy. Whatever the reasons, the results were clear. Factories closed. Jobs became scarce. Capital dried up. The city suffered a serious and sudden economic decline from which it still struggles to recover. It is anticipated that the new George M. Low Center for Industrial Innovation to be constructed at RPI, and the Rensselaer Technology Park in North Greenbush will provide the stimuli needed to promote new growth in the area.

There is no mystery about the death of the brewing industry. Prohibition dealt it a fatal blow.

The post World War II shift from canals and railroads to highways and air transport brought a major industrial crisis to Schenectady. American Locomotive Company (ALCO) fought to stay alive, but in 1970 it ceased to operate. (General Electric, however, continues major design and manufacture operations in the city.)

In Albany, the growth in government, the expanded demand for higher education, and the increased call for medical care induced a great movement away from the factory into the office. Today 28% of the population works for government, with the next highest percentages engaged in health care and education. (Albany was officially designated as state capital in 1971, though it had functioned as seat of government since 1797.)

Population trends in the Capital District are typical of trends in urban areas. The post-World War II surge (1940-1960 showed growth of 21%) began to level off in the 60's (1960-70 showed gains of 4.7%) and has reached a state of equilibrium (1970-75 showed net growth of .5%).

Some statistics compiled by the Capital District Regional Planning Commission in 1983 reveal much about the nature of the area. The Capital District, defined as Albany, Rensselaer, Saratoga, and Schenectady counties, has a population of 795,000. Growth of 2.2% is anticipated by 1995. Thirty-one percent of the population lives in cities. The region has the 10th highest number of PhDs per capita in the United States and a higher general level of educational achievement than New York State or the United States.

Traces of the past can be seen everywhere in the area. Museums of course display treasures of former times or attempt to recreate life as it once was. But more palpable and real are the roads which follow Indian trails, the Republican System of orderly living, in part inspired by the Iroquois confederation, the clustering of the commercial heart of the cities at the site of original Dutch trading posts — Fort Orange, Fort Frederick and the stockade — the heterogeneity of ethnic groups among the population, the Dutch architecture of older buildings, the Indian and Dutch names on streets, buildings and clubs, and the continued preeminence of descendants of early settlers in the political, business and social life of the cities. Of inestimable value are the handsome homes constructed by those in positions of political or economic power at one time or another and the beautiful churches built throughout the area — often in homage to the lands from which the settlers had come.

This history is of necessity brief and general. It is intended to give an overview of the region in the almost four centuries of recorded history. It cannot portray the fascinating individuals or the events — incredible, horrifying, or hilarious — that make records of the past such lively reading and such important reminders of the continuity of the human life line.

Former Ticket Office of Hudson River Day Line
Michael Fredericks, Jr.

What follows, however, is a list of books, pamphlets, and papers which do tell the stories of heros and villains, triumphs and tragedies, and, of course, ordinary moments of life in this area since such things were recorded.

The libraries of the area have carefully preserved much of the printed record of the past, and the librarians, particularly at the principal branches, can help people unearth ancestry, track down elusive historical figures, or pinpoint an event. They have on record city directories, birth, death, and marriage announcements, church and cemetery records. They also have local newspapers on microfilm.

The following is an annotated bibliography of sources compiled with the help of area librarians.

General Interest

Federation Roundtable. Federation of Historical Services, Old Chatham 12136. Quarterly newsletter for students of the history of the Upper Hudson Valley.

Bergen, Judge Francis. *The History of the New York Court of Appeals, 1847-1932.* Columbia U.P., 1985. A history of the court by a retired justice.

Capital District Regional Planning Commission. *A Profile of the Capital District.* 1983. Filled with charts and data about the present and the future.

The Junior League of Albany. *Going Places: A Family Guide to the Capital District and Beyond.* 1983. A very helpful listing of sources of information.

Kenney, Alice. *Albany: Crossroads of Liberty.* Albany, 1976.

_____. *The Ganesvoorts of Albany: Dutch Patricians in the Upper Hudson Valley,* Syracuse, 1969.

_____. *Stubborn for Liberty: The Dutch in New York.* Syracuse, 1975.
    Dr. Kenney was editing the copious writings of Huibertje Pruyn Hamlin when she died in 1985. The Albany Institute is continuing with the work.

Albany County

Beebe, Richard T. *Albany Medical College and Albany Hospital—A History: 1839-1982.* 1983. A solid book by a doctor who has practiced in Albany for 50 years.

Bennett, Allison. *The People's Choice.* Albany Co. Hist. Soc., 1980. Handsomely illustrated, carefully documented, well-written history of Albany County from 1630 to the turn of the century.

_____. *Times Remembered.* 1984. Compilation of articles about the towns of Bethlehem and New Scotland originally published in *The Spotlight.*

Guide to Historical Resources in Albany County, New York Repositories. Cornell University, 1984. List of unpublished sources of information.

Hislop, Codman. *Albany—Dutch, English and American.* Angus Press, 1936. A comprehensive history.

Howell, George Roger and Jonathan Tenney. *Bicentennial History of Albany.* 1886.

Jones, Louis C. *Murder at Cherry Hill.* Historic Cherry Hill, 1982. Interesting tale of love, intrigue, and murder.

Kennedy, William. *O Albany! Improbable City of Political Wizards, Fearless Ethnics, Spectacular Aristocrats, Splendid Nobodies, and Underrated Scoundrels.* Viking and Washington Park Press, 1983. Warm, witty, informative impressions of the city's distant and recent past.

McEneny, John. *Albany: Capital City on the Hudson.* 1981. Excellent chronology, brief sketches of major commercial firms, beautiful photographs.

Old Albany. 4 Vols. Compiled by Morris Gerber from photographs taken by Stephen Schreiber. Handsome and interesting scenes of the city in the 19th and 20th century. Although these volumes have no formal text, they contain reprints of newspaper columns by Edgar Van Olinda and the full bicentennial history by Howell and Tenney. (Mr. Gerber has a sizeable collection of other photographs gathered from many sources over the years.)

Reynolds, Cuyler. *Albany Chronicles.* Albany, 1909. Abundant details on the daily life of the city from the landing of the Half Moon to 1909.

Roseberry, Cecil. *Capitol Story.* Albany, 1982. A clearly written, handsomely illustrated portrait of the Capitol building.

_____. *Albany, Three Centuries A County.* Albany County Tricentennial Commission, 1983. Brief histories of each of the towns, villages, and cities in Albany County.

Weise, Arthur James. *The History of the City of Albany.* Albany, 1884. Comprehensive scholarly history.

Wilcoxen, Charlotte. *Seventeenth Century Albany: A Dutch Profile.* Albany Institute of History and Art, 1981. A study of life in the city's first century.

Rensselaer County

These are the major histories of Troy and Rensselaer County—each with its particular emphasis.

Anderson, George Baker. *Landmarks of Rensselaer County, New York.* Syracuse: D. Mason and Company, Publishers, 1897. Detailed account of the county's early history, its towns and leading citizens.

Guide to Historical Resources in Rensselaer County, New York Repositories. Cornell University, 1983. Helpful in finding manuscripts, archival material and miscellaneous unpublished records throughout the county.

Hayner, Rutherford. *Troy and Rensselaer County New York: A History.* New York: Lewis Historical Publishing Company, Inc., 1925. The social, fraternal and cultural history of the city.

Parker, Joseph A. *Looking Back: A History of Troy and Rensselaer County, 1925-1980.* Joseph A. Parker, 1982. A chronology of recent events.

Sylvester, Nathaniel Bartlett. *History of Rensselaer County New York.* Philadelphia: Everts and Peck, 1880. Rensselaer County town histories, church histories, and biographies of pioneer citizens.

Weise, Arthur James. *The City of Troy and Its Vicinity.* Troy: Edward Green, 1886. Classified history of Troy's businesses and industries.

_____. *History of the City of Troy*. Troy: William H. Young, 1876.
Early history and growth of Troy.

_____. *Troy's One Hundred Years, 1789-1889*. Troy: William H.
Young, 1891. Industrial history of Troy.

Schenectady County

The General Electric Story: A Photo History. The Elfun Society—Hall of
History, 1976-1980. Vol. 1: *The Edison Era, 1876-1892* (1976).
Vol. 2: *The Steinmetz Era, 1892-1923* (1977). Vol. 3: *On the Shoulders
of Giants, 1924-1946* (1979). Vol. 4: *Pathways of Progress, 1947-
1978* (1980).

Guide to Historical Resources in Schenectady, New York Repositories.
Cornell University, 1983. Helpful in finding unpublished information.

Hanson, Willis T., Jr. *A History of Schenectady During the Revolution*.
1916, reprinted 1974. An invaluable account of Schenectady during
the Revolution, including a list of individual war records of
many Schenectadians.

Hart, Larry. *Schenectady, A Pictorial History: Schenectady's First Complete
Story—Presettlement to Present*. Old Dorp Books, 1984. Hart's most
recent contribution to the appreciation of Schenectady.

_____. *Schenectady's Golden Era (Between 1880 and 1930)*. Old
Dorp Books, 1974. Required reading for anyone interested in Schenectady's history; a chronology of historic events in Schenectady is appended.

_____. *Tales of Old Schenectady*. Old Dorp Books, 1975-. Vol. I:
The Formative Years (1975). Vol. II: *The Changing Scene* (1977).
The first two parts of an ongoing compilation on Schenectady's history
by the historian for Schenectady City and County who writes the "Tales
of Old Dorp" column for the *Schenectady Gazette*.

Hislop, Codman. *The Mohawk*. 1948. A wealth of historical information
on Schenectady, written by a retired Union College professor.

Maston, Bruce. *Enclave of Elegance: The General Electric Realty Plot*.
1984. A pictorial presentation of the houses and people of this
unique neighborhood.

The Schenectady Scene. Compiled by the Newcomers and Wives Club.
G.E. Corporate Research and Development, 1981. A pamphlet designed
to acquaint newcomers to Schenectady with community facilities
and activities.

Veeder, Millicent W. *Door to the Mohawk Valley: A History of Schenectady for Young People*. 1947. A general history aimed at a youthful
audience, but highly useful to adults for its factual information.

Yates, Austin A. *Schenectady County, New York: Its History to the
Close of the 19th Century*. 1902. Includes over 240 pages of
biographical sketches.

Community Development

How It Came To Be

The faces of Albany, Schenectady, and Troy have become more beautiful, their interiors have become more habitable, and the grandeur of their past has become more recognizable in recent years. All of this is the result of the financial investment and hard work of many individuals, the advocacy of community-based organizations, and the infusion of government funding.

The history of community development in the region is interesting but complex. Urban Renewal programs of the 1960's typically meant extensive demolition of commercial areas and older residential neighborhoods, often planned and supervised directly by a local government agency under federal direction. During the 1970's, reaction to these large-scale projects resulted in the Community Development Block Grant program, which encouraged partnerships between public and private sectors and changed the focus to rehabilitation and neighborhood preservation. Community Development projects often included code improvement and facade restoration of privately owned buildings.

Community Development funds came to the cities to be used for a variety of projects, large or small, short-term or long range, depending on the specific needs of each city, needs to be defined by its citizens. This was the beginning of a major trend in the United States which had a powerful impact on the Capital District. Regional residents banded together into private non-profit groups according to government guidelines and offered assistance to all those who wanted to play a part in the preservation of the cities. In many instances they fought to retain the mix of people of all socio-economic levels.

Through a complex interweaving of federal, state, county, city and private funds, the people of the three cities have drawn millions of dollars to salvage buildings on the point of collapse, restore irreplaceable interiors, and build compatible modern structures so the centers of the cities— the residential and commercial cores of the original settlements—have come back to life. In some instances, through adaptive use, they have come back in a new way. As the physical cities have resurfaced, so too has an urban sense of community in each of them.

Congress Street, Troy
Michael Fredericks, Jr.

Because of the flexibility of the system, the uses of the grants have varied from year to year and from city to city. What follows is an overview of community development in each of the cities and a description of some of the many agencies which have emerged to deal with problems along the way.

AGENCIES WITH STATE WIDE INFLUENCE

THE PRESERVATION LEAGUE OF NEW YORK STATE, located at 307 Hamilton St. in Albany, was founded in 1974 to assist citizens concerned about retaining the architectural heritage of the state. The League provides technical assistance to local preservation groups and individuals, serves as a resource center, issues publications, sponsors conferences, maintains a legislative network, produces and distributes films, provides training and information on historic district and landmark commissions, and works to arouse public awareness of the importance of preservation. Information about the specific activities of this agency is available at 462-5658.

AGENCIES WITH REGIONAL INFLUENCE

HISTORIC ALBANY FOUNDATION, 44 Central Ave Albany, 463-0622, is a non-profit organization of area residents committed to the preservation and revitalization of the historic neighborhoods and commercial districts in

Albany. The foundation (originally limited to Albany but now encompassing the other areas as well) has a diverse program of activities. It protects endangered buildings and acts as a catalyst for neighborhood revitalization. Technical preservation assistance is offered on rehabilitating and maintaining older buildings. Consultation ranges from paint color selection to brownstone and wood repair to the use of federal tax investment credits for rehabilitation work. Educational programs such as tours, historical marker plaques, and slide presentations are offered. The Foundation also works on local issues such as demolition, new construction in historic areas, and designation of new historic districts. A project of recent concern has been application for Albany to become an Urban Cultural Park. Maintaining a year-round calendar of special events—such as the holiday house tour and the Moveable Feast—rounds out the Foundation's program.

HUDSON-MOHAWK INDUSTRIAL GATEWAY, 457 Broadway Troy, 274-5267, is a non-profit cultural-educational organization established to discover and make known information about the 19th century industrial era in the Troy-Cohoes-Watervliet-Green Island region. It is perhaps best explained in the excerpt from THE BURDEN REPORT, the Gateway's monthly newsletter: "The Gateway attempts to identify community assets for economic development through researching their industrial history and protecting the visible remains. We feel that the fullest future for this area rests in large measure on successful utilization of these historic resources in a revitalized urban setting.

Our goals are: (1) continued operation of 19th century industries, and preservation of industrial and industrially-related buildings and sites through adaptive reuse; (2) development of tourism centered on these industries, buildings and sites—an educational process communicating the significance of this industrial heritage and its relation to people and communities today; (3) study of industrial and social development in America during the 19th century (focusing on the Hudson Mohawk area) to provide the educational catalyst to create an appreciation and awareness of the region's unique history."

The group works on restoration projects and runs tours of the waterways, watermills, railroads and towns along the rivers. Bus tours as well as walking and biking excursions are conducted throughout spring, summer, and fall. Sites include canal locks, water gorges, a mill complex, a cemetery, an arsenal, and beautiful homes and churches. All the tours are worthwhile—penetrating, entertaining glimpses into that interesting era. Membership information and schedules are available at the office.

HUDSON-MOHAWK URBAN CULTURAL PARK. An urban cultural park is a New York State designated area in which a visible and distinct element of the past stands immersed in a vital contemporary setting. The historic focal point must represent the heritage of the place. The purpose of designating an urban cultural park is to use private and public funds to preserve irreplaceable historic resources, reinvigorate unused resources, and serve as a fulcrum in urban revitalization.

13 Northern Blvd, Albany
Michael Fredericks, Jr.

Hudson Mohawk Urban Cultural Park is such a preserve. It consists of canals, locks, plants, factories, foundries, houses, churches, colleges, libraries, parks and railway stations along the waterways in Waterford, Cohoes, Watervliet, Troy, Green Island, and Lansingburgh. A handsome map and brochure is available through the Park Commission, 97 Mohawk St Cohoes, 237-7999.

AGENCIES AND ACTIVITIES IN ALBANY

THE URBAN RENEWAL AGENCY, 155 Washington Ave Albany, 462-8520, supervises five offices: Property Management, Rehabilitation Assistance, Emergency Rehabilitation Assistance, Economic Development, and Albany Local Development.

A considerable portion of the money Albany received through federal programs has gone into the residential areas of downtown in the form of improved streets and sidewalks as well as in direct assistance to individuals. The two most visible projects of this office are these:

THE PASTURES, a mixed residential-commercial area in the South End of the city, which is being rehabilitated through a combination of individual owners, who receive financial assistance, and developers, who may purchase the buildings and develop them with the stipulation that they will turn them into low-to-moderate income-assisted rental units.

TEN BROECK TRIANGLE, a region in the Arbor Hill section of the city, which is being developed by owners to whom the government offers assistance.

The Rehabilitation Assistance Program of the Urban Renewal Agency has been designed to preserve and improve older neighborhoods by providing incentives (in the form of financial aid and technical advice) for rehabilitation to present or prospective property owners. Under this program, four non-profit neighborhood corporations contract with the Urban Renewal Agency to process the applications for rehabilitation assistance from the neighborhoods they represent. These corporations are:

     Arbor Hill Development Corp 463-9993
     Capitol Hill Improvement Corp 462-9696
     South End Improvement Corp 436-8777
     West Hill Improvement Corp 462-6460

The city, usually in cooperation with the county, undertakes major commitments to the improvement of the quality of urban life. One recent example is **STEAMBOAT SQUARE** in the South End. This plan involves three phases—the construction of new townhouses, the restoration of 19th

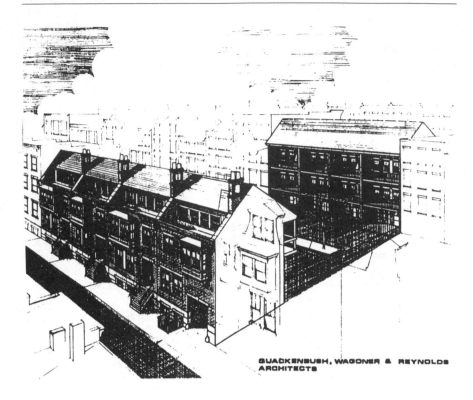

QUACKENBUSH, WAGONER & REYNOLDS
ARCHITECTS

Century rowhouses, and the rehabilitation of five troublesome low-income towers. Centered in one of the oldest sections of the city, this daring effort, if successful, will draw commercial interests back downtown and provide comfortable housing to low and middle income citizens, senior citizens, and handicapped persons.

Citizens who live within the boundaries of the city have organized into neighborhood associations, some of which, over the years, have become strong political and social forces. Recently the groups formed a coalition, the **NEIGHBORHOOD RESOURCE CENTER,** to stimulate neighborhood cooperation and to help new groups succeed. Information is available at the Center office, 340 First St Albany, 462-5636.

One of the results of the Center's formation is the subsequent creation of the **COUNCIL OF ALBANY NEIGHBORHOOD ASSOCIATIONS (CANA),** a volunteer committee drawn from representatives of active neighborhood associations. Three delegates from each member organization discuss issues, strategies, positions, and other matters of mutual concern. The Council then serves as advocate on city-wide issues of neighborhood interest. Information is available through the Center, 462-5636.

UNITED TENANTS OF ALBANY, part of the New York State Tenant and Neighborhood Coalition, is an advocacy group working to protect the rights of landlords and tenants. It staffs a hotline to respond to complaints, attempts to educate people about their rights, and works to improve the quality of code enforcement. Information is available at the office at 65 Columbia St Albany, 436-8997.

The Future

The pace of commercial development in downtown Albany quickened in 1984, with plans for the adaptive reuse of two major landmarks—Union Station and the Kenmore Hotel, with talk of a new arts center between Capital Rep and the Palace Theater, and with continuing plans for a Civic Center with related support facilities. Interestingly enough, this resurgence of interest in commercial possibilities was born in much the same way as development in the residential areas—with a few individuals who, taking one building at a time, demonstrated clearly that revitalization is not a dream of a handful of sentimental idealists but rather a workable, profitable alternative to urban decay.

AGENCIES AND ACTIVITIES IN SCHENECTADY

In Schenectady the problem of the inner city was quite straightforward. The downtown area had always been primarily commercial. In the Sixties, shopping centers with expansive parking lots lured the daytime shopper, increasingly dependent on the automobile, away from downtown. Well-established local businesses, long accustomed to serving all their customers effectively in spite of crowds, suddenly looked out onto empty sidewalks. Their very survival was in question. Some owners solved the dilemma by moving, others by banding together to do something to reverse the trend.

The city created a Department of Planning and Economic Development (Room 207 of City Hall, 382-5147) to administer grants for Community Development. The office defined five categories of concern:

Physical improvements, streets and recreation
Housing improvements
Human services
Program delivery
Economic development

Results of these efforts are now visible: an attractive pedestrian arcade has been created on Jay Street; State Street has been widened and new sidewalks have been installed; about sixty residential units have been created in rehabilitated department stores and commercial buildings; Mill Lane, the cobblestone street along the first mill in downtown Schenectady, has been revitalized; Iroquois Lake in Central Park has been restored; and the area has been officially designated an Urban Cultural Park, one of only thirteen such areas in the state.

Canal Square, Schenectady
Michael Fredericks, Jr.

On the neighborhood level, Schenectady residents work together in **BETTER NEIGHBORHOODS, INC.,** 975 Albany St Schenectady, 372-6469. Established in 1967 as a non-profit organization, Better Neighborhoods uses state and federal funds to buy and rehabilitate houses for resale to low and middle income residents. The members offer home-buyer counseling, financial planning, and rehabilitation assistance.

Schenectady has also been active in encouraging private investors to participate idependently in urban development. Canal Square (described at length in the points of interest chapter) is one product of their efforts.

AGENCIES AND ACTIVITIES IN TROY

In Troy there are several pressing needs—to preserve the beautiful structures built during the years of great prosperity, to help low and moderate income families solve serious housing problems, and to assist merchants in their attempt to restore vigor to the beleaguered downtown commercial community. Active, concerned citizens sought government funding, encouraged independent investment, and solicited contributions in an effort to meet all these needs.

THE DEPARTMENT OF PLANNING AND COMMUNITY DEVELOPMENT, located in City Hall, 270-4476, administers programs using government funds. The programs include rental rehabilitation for investment, spot rehabilitation for homeowners and tenants, commercial and residential facade and sidewalk improvement, reclamation of vacant buildings, and the definition of focus blocks for residential use. One of the larger projects currently being conducted by Planning and Development is the rehabilitation of warehouses along Lower River Street for apartments.

TAP, 406 Fulton St Troy, 274-3050, is a non-profit corporation involved with community development in low income areas. It is supported by fees and by grants solicited for specific services. Licensed architects help low income owners with their house maintenance needs—design or preservation of roofs and porches, for example. They also advise other non-profit groups. Examples of some of the larger projects of this organization are the buildings of the Rensselaer County Junior Museum, the Rensselaer County Council on the Arts, and the Legal Aid Society.

The Troy Liveability Campaign—**YOURS TROY**—was founded in October 1983 as a partnership of business, civic, cultural, and community leaders to improve the image of Troy as a place to live and work. It invites current and prospective residents to notice and appreciate the many assets of their city.

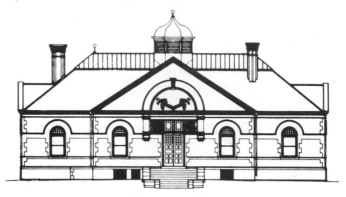

Burden Building, Troy

TRIP (Troy Rehabilitation and Improvement Program), 5 Broadway Troy, 272-8289, is a private non-profit corporation founded in 1968 to provide housing rehabilitation, with an emphasis on home ownership for families. It helps people with low and middle incomes find housing suitable for purchase and also provides help in finding acceptable low income rental housing.

THE NEIGHBORHOOD ACTION COUNCIL OF TROY, 1643 5th Ave Troy, 272-8155, is a governmentally and privately funded agency which serves in an advisory capacity to neighborhood organizations. It also acts as a liaison between the city and the neighborhoods and as mediator in landlord-tenant problems.

The Gateway

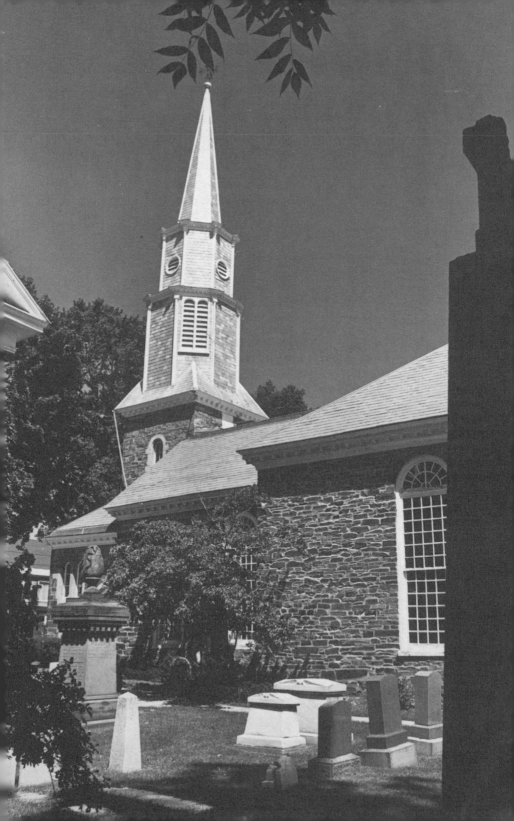

Points of Interest

THE CAPITAL DISTRICT

TOURS: HUDSON-MOHAWK TOURS, P.O. Box 842, Albany 12201, 489-3990 or (518) 668-2643. Offers customized coach and walking tours for preformed groups. Open year round.

GUIDEBOOKS: *Where to go With Kids in the Capital District,* by Dahl, Pat, Francille Ruckdeschel, and Laura Degenhart. With Kids: West Sand Lake, 12196, is a jaunty little book written to encourage family outings.

Exploring New York's Past, compiled by the New York State Office of Parks and Recreation, Agency Building 1, Empire State Plaza, Albany 12238, 474-0456, describes sites of historic significance in New York State.

ALBANY

TOURS: TOURS OF ALBANY are arranged for groups by Historic Albany Foundation, 463-0622, which emphasizes revitalization efforts around the city. Neighborhood groups in the downtown area sponsor a house tour each spring. Information regarding these tours is published in the newspaper but is also available through Historic Albany Foundation. The tours are described more fully in the chapter Other Things to Do.

TOURS OF THE CAPITOL AND THE EMPIRE STATE PLAZA are run seven days a week every hour on the hour from 9 to 4.

GUIDEBOOKS: *Albany Architects: The Present Looks at the Past,* a booklet prepared by Historic Albany Foundation, 44 Central Ave Albany 12206, describes and comments on interesting buildings in the city. It is available through Historic Albany Foundation.

St. George's Cemetery, Schenectady Stockade
Michael Fredericks, Jr.

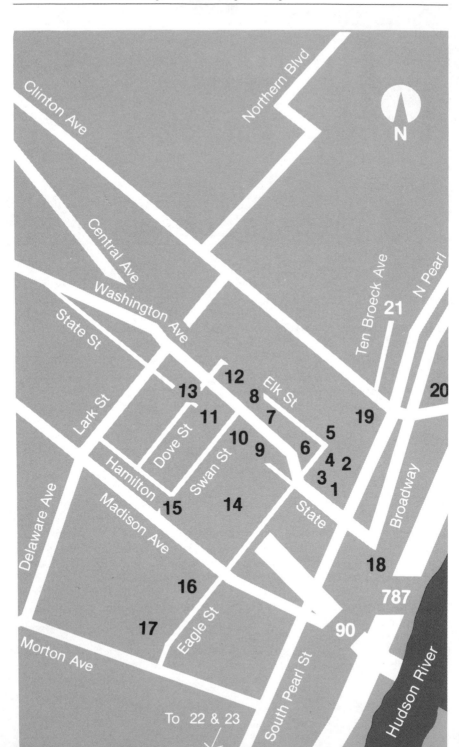

ALBANY MAP KEY

1	St. Peter's Church
2	St. Mary's on Capitol Hill
3	City Hall
4	The Court of Appeals
5	The New York State Bar Center
6	The Joseph Henry Memorial
7	State Education Building
8	Cathedral of All Saints
9	The Capitol Building
10	Capitol Park
11	The Alfred E. Smith Building
12	Albany Institute of History & Art
13	Museum of Early American Decoration
14	The Nelson A. Rockefeller Empire State Plaza
15	Robinson Square
16	Cathedral of the Immaculate Conception
17	The Executive Mansion
18	State University Plaza
19	First Church in Albany
20	Quackenbush Square
21	Ten Broeck Mansion
22	Schuyler Mansion
23	Cherry Hill

Albany Visitor Services Guide is available from the Albany County Convention and Visitor's Bureau, 600 Broadway Albany 12207, 434-1217.

DOWNTOWN RESTORATION ACTIVITIES are described in the chapter on Community Development.

Downtown Albany

The following points of interest are described in order according to the map.

ST. PETER'S CHURCH, State St., was established soon after the English took over the settlement from the Dutch because England's monarch at that time, Queen Anne, was particularly interested in sponsoring missions among the Indians. Relics of the early days of the church remain. The bell, struck in 1751, is still used. The silver communion set, on display at the rear of the church, was a gift from Queen Anne to Thomas Barclay, founder of St. Peter's parish in Albany in 1712.

ST. MARY'S ON CAPITOL HILL, built in 1798, occupies the site on which Isaac Jogues hid from the Indians who later executed him. The church is of interest too for the angel which graces its top, a departure from the cross traditional to a Roman Catholic Church. The recently refurbished church serves one of the most active congregations in the city.

Empire State Plaza
Michael Fredericks, Jr.

CITY HALL, Eagle St. between Pine and Lodge, a fine example of the unique architectural style of H.H. Richardson, was erected in 1882. The building houses the offices of the mayor and other city officials, three courtrooms, and the Common Council Chamber. Documents and paintings line corridor walls. A special feature of City Hall is the sixty bell carillon which sounds over the city each week day at noon. Visitors may tour the building guided by a fine self-tour booklet. Free. It is also interesting to sit in on the public sessions of the various courts; there are three in this building—city courts I and II and traffic court.

THE COURT OF APPEALS, Eagle Street at Pine, a beautiful structure both inside and out, is the oldest state office building in the city. The highest court in the state convenes here in a handsome oak courtroom lined with portraits of robed justices. Visitors are welcome to sit in on the hearings each afternoon or simply walk around the handsome rotunda and halls.

THE NEW YORK STATE BAR CENTER, 1 Elk St., stands opposite Academy Park and the Joseph Henry Memorial. In the late 60's the New York State Bar Association purchased the three 19th century townhouses on the corner of Elk Street opposite the Supreme Court and the Court of Appeals. The Association's announced plans to demolish the buildings and construct a modern complex on the site roused the local citizenry to furious protest. The Bar Association responded, and the two groups reached a compromise that attracted national attention and has served ever since as a model of what can be done to retain the old while adding the new.

THE JOSEPH HENRY MEMORIAL opposite City Hall was designed by Philip Hooker in 1815 as The Albany Academy, a private school for boys. When the academy outgrew this building, it was renamed the Joseph Henry Memorial in honor of Joseph Henry, who in 1830 discovered the properties of magnetic induction within its walls. The building today belongs to the city and houses the offices of the Board of Education. While the building is not open to the public for tours, groups make use of the auditorium upstairs on occasion.

STATE EDUCATION BUILDING is the colossal structure on Washington Avenue to the north of the Capitol modeled on the Greek temple, the Parthenon. It repays close study, for many little touches of sculpture—such as the teacher and child on the lamps at the entry—should not be overlooked, though they are overwhelmed by the building's massiveness. The building houses many of the offices of the State Education Department.

CATHEDRAL OF ALL SAINTS, Elk and Swan Sts., is the seat of the Episcopal Diocese of Albany. The exterior, though unfinished, is impressive in its intent. The style of the interior, with its stonework and banners, lends grace and grandeur to religious ceremonies. Also worthy of note is the Gothic front of the episcopal offices opposite the Cathedral's entrance. The Cathedral serves an active congregation and contributes to cultural life in the city by sponsoring concerts and events throughout the year.

THE CAPITOL BUILDING, an ornate structure composed of many different architectural styles, took over thirty years to complete. Within its walls many major decisions were made and many careers were forged. The chambers of the legislature, the offices of the executive, the lobbies and the hallways—all of which are open to the public—serve as the forum for lawmaking in New York State. Visitors may see these rooms as well as the million dollar staircase or watch the legislature in session (usually January-May). The handsome Senate Chamber and Gallery were restored with meticulous attention to authenticity and beauty in 1979. Six years later the Executive Chamber was restored and reopened, now as a ceremonial room designated for public bill signings and other grand occasions. The history, artistry and current function of these chambers are interestingly presented by Capitol Guides. Also of interest is the Military Museum in the Capitol Building. It includes flags, weapons and uniforms of N.Y. State militia and memorabilia of Abraham Lincoln. Tours leave from Capitol Guide Center in the building, seven days a week on the hour from 9 to 4. Further information is available at 474-2418. Free.

Executive Mansion
Rich Kraham/Design Unit

CAPITOL PARK, located at the front and back of the Capitol, is a favorite spot for people who work downtown. During the lunch hour street venders sell their wares while workers and local residents enjoy the formal gardens, the fountains, and the handsome statue of General Philip Sheridan.

THE ALFRED E. SMITH BUILDING, Swan St. between State and Washington, is a state office building named after the man who served as governor of the state until his fateful run for the Presidency in 1928. On the facade of the building are inscribed the names of the counties of New York State. The 31st floor houses an observation tower open to the public during work hours; beneath the building runs a tunnel joining the building to the Capitol.

ALBANY INSTITUTE OF HISTORY AND ART, 125 Washington Ave, is described in the chapter on museums.

MUSEUM OF EARLY AMERICAN DECORATION, 19 Dove St., is described in the chapter on museums.

THE NELSON A. ROCKEFELLER EMPIRE STATE PLAZA, generally referred to as The Mall, dominates the southeast center of downtown Albany. This modern complex for state government houses state office buildings (with

11,000 employees), the Convention Center, "The Egg" and the Cultural Education Center.

The idea for the marble complex decorated by major works of contemporary artists was conceived by Nelson A. Rockefeller in 1962 during his term as governor. Designed by Harrison and Abramowitz (architects of Rockefeller Center in New York City) to be completed in the late 60's at an estimated cost of $350 million, the structure was caught in labor disputes (inevitable perhaps when 2500 workers are under dozens of contracts at one time) and, as a result, the project was in fact completed in 1978 at an actual cost in excess of $2 billion.

The Mall is not a static location to be toured once and then forgotten; rather it is a vital center of activity. The Office of General Services coordinates a year-round schedule of activities which use all parts of the plaza. They range from car shows to fireworks displays, from ethnic celebrations to salutes to the handicapped. Also, the plaza offers a natural playground for unorganized activities—picnics, strolls, rollerskating, shopping. The visitor can do some things all year:

a. Visit the museum and library
b. Inspect the architecture
c. Tour the plaza level and enjoy the sculptured pieces
d. View the contemporary art on the concourse level
e. Observe the city and surroundings from Corning Tower
f. Shop in various stores
g. Enjoy restaurants

PARKING: It is advisable to use one of the three visitor parking lots connected to The Mall because finding a place to park on the street is very difficult, especially on weekdays.

One of the three lots is outside; it is located on Madison Avenue between the Cathedral of the Immaculate Conception and Cultural Education Building. The other two lots are located inside The Mall. The entrances are off Swan Street for those driving toward the river and off the arterials for those driving away from the river. Access to both of these lots is clearly marked.

Private parking lots are scattered about the area just below The Mall.

TOURS: Tours are conducted seven days a week at 11, 1 and 3. They take one hour. Information is available at information booths along the concourse and at Room 106 on the Concourse, the Office of Visitors' Assistance, 474-2418.

INFORMATION: Information is available from four sources:

1. Information Booths at two positions on the concourse level of The Mall.

2. *Events at the Empire State Plaza*, a biweekly calendar of events, distributed free at information booths in the complex. Call 474-5986 to be placed on the mailing list.

The Capitol, Albany
Michael Fredericks, Jr.

3. *Up and Coming at the New York State Museum*, a newssheet, published periodically and sent to a mailing list. For information call 474-5877 or write:

> The State Education Department
> New York State Museum
> Cultural Education Center
> Albany, New York 12230

4. Telephone numbers for information or assistance as listed below.

> Promotions & Public Affairs 474-4712
> *Empire State Plaza & Capitol Tours. 474-2418
> Information on use of Convention Center 474-4759
> "Egg" Box Office 473-3750

Community Box Office—Plaza Branch 473-8122
New York State Museum 474-5877
Ice Skating. 474-6647
*Assistance to Handicapped Provided

THE PLATFORM: All of the buildings except the Cultural Education Center sit on or at the edge of the main building of The Mall, the Platform. It is difficult to think of this structure as a building because only its roof (the plaza) is visible from street level. In fact, however, the building descends six floors below the ground and has a square footage of 3,807,000—nearly twice the floor space of the Empire State Building. Four of the levels provide for parking, special laboratories, delivery facilities, and service areas (mailroom, duplicating machine rooms, maintenance equipment storage for example). Above these are the concourse and the plaza.

THE CONCOURSE LEVEL: Just below the plaza level, accessible by elevators or stairways inside any of the buildings, runs a mammoth hallway called The Concourse. Leading to and from this Concourse is a network of underground passages connecting all parts of the complex and the State Capitol on the other side of State Street. The visitor will be interested in the following features:

THE NELSON A. ROCKEFELLER EMPIRE STATE PLAZA ART COLLECTION, displayed throughout the complex, is owned by the citizens of New York. The pamphlet *The Empire State Plaza Art Collection* identifies each of the pieces on clearly marked maps. It is available free of charge at the information booths or the Office of Visitors' Assistance. Tours of the collection are given each Wednesday at 10:30 and 2:30 from the Visitors Service Center. Groups must make reservations at 474-7521.

THE CONVENTION HALL is a tiered room with a stage and dance floor. It is capable of functioning as a theater, a ballroom, an exhibition hall, an auditorium or a large forum. The room, the only one of its kind in the area, may be reserved for use through the Office of General Services, 474-4759.

GENERAL FACILITIES: The Concourse also contains cafeterias, rest rooms, locker rooms for ice skaters, a post office, information booths, shops, banks, ticket offices and other services for the 11,000 persons who work in the complex and the thousands who visit. The information service posts up-to-date notices on the many bulletin boards on the concourse level. A recent addition, *Health Works*, is an educational "computer game room" designed to increase public knowledge of health and fitness.

The width of The Concourse makes it an appropriate scene for major commercial displays like the ski show, the boat show, the car show and regional craft shows. Such events are advertised in advance in the local newspapers.

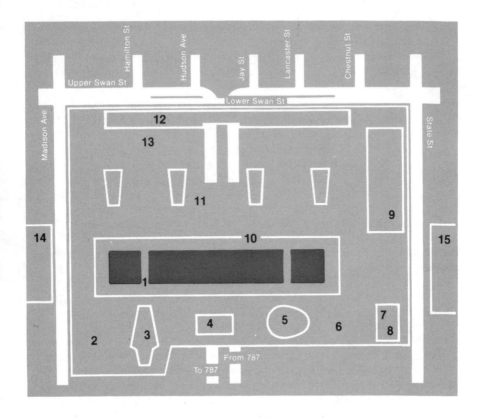

EMPIRE STATE MAP KEY

1	Reflection Pool/Calder Sculpture
2	Labyrinth
3	Corning Tower Building
4	Plaza Restaurant
5	Meeting Center/The Egg
6	Sculpture Garden
7	Justice Building
8	Vietnam Memorial
9	Legislative Building
10	"Two Line Oblique"
11	Agency Buildings
12	Swan Street Building
13	Playground
14	Cultural Education Center
15	Capitol

THE PLAZA LEVEL: The description which follows will proceed along a path defined on the maps below. The starting point is on Madison Ave., the south end of The Mall. (The visitor should be aware of the fact that the length of The Mall from one end to the other is ¼ mile. A complete tour will therefore demand a walk of more than ½ mile. At all points on the complex provision has been made for the handicapped visitor).

A REFLECTING POOL, with steel sculpture by Alexander Calder entitled "Triangles and Arches," extends from the Cultural Education Center.

LABYRINTH, a teakwood sculpture by Francoise Stahly, incorporates visual design with areas for play and sitting.

THE CORNING TOWER BUILDING, a forty-four story structure of Vermont pearl marble, houses the State Health Department as well as other government agencies. Visitors are invited to view the city from the observation deck on the top floor of this building from 9 to 4. On weekends the visitor must enter the tower from the concourse level. Also of interest are the various artworks at the entrances.

THE PLAZA RESTAURANT, The Sign of the Tree, offers a splendid view of the complex and some of the older residential streets of the city. For further description see the chapter on restaurants.

THE MEETING CENTER, also known as "The Egg," houses two handsome auditoriums, one seating 950, the other seating 450.

SCULPTURE GARDEN is an area in which the work of David Smith, a sculptor who lived nearby in Bolton Landing, is displayed.

THE JUSTICE BUILDING is a beautifully simple building which contains many of the offices and courtrooms for the State system of courts. The Vietnam Memorial on the first floor displays changing exhibits by New York State veterans of that conflict.

THE LEGISLATIVE BUILDING houses the offices of 210 members of the State Legislature.

THE AGENCY BUILDINGS, four identical pillar-like buildings of Vermont pearl marble, as their names suggest, provide office space for various government agencies.

THE SWAN STREET BUILDING, the low-rise, Georgian Cherokee white marble structure which extends the entire length of the west side of The Mall, houses the Department of Motor Vehicles.

THE SMALLER POOL serves as a reflecting pool in the spring and summer and a skating rink in the winter.

Empire State Plaza
Michael Fredericks, Jr.

"TWO LINES OBLIQUE," a stainless steel kinetic sculpture by George Rickey, moves its 54 foot needles gracefully and elegantly, propelled by changes in the wind.

THE PLAYGROUND near the Swan St entrance at Hamilton St is challenging and amusing for children of various ages. Comfortable seating for adults makes it a pleasant place for families.

CULTURAL EDUCATION CENTER houses the New York State Library, The New York State Archives, The New York State Museum, and part of the State Education Department. The museum is described in the chapter on Museums, the library and archives in the chapter on Libraries.

ROBINSON SQUARE, 325 Hamilton St between Swan and Dove, is a row of brownstones of the 1850's rescued from demolition and converted into shops and apartments in the urban restoration efforts of the 1970's. Many of the original shops have moved on, and the venture is currently in transition.

CATHEDRAL OF THE IMMACULATE CONCEPTION, Eagle St. at Madison Ave., is the seat of the Roman Catholic Diocese of Albany. Made of dark brownstone in the mid 1800's, it now sits in rather somber splendor beside its neighbors, the ornate Governor's Mansion and the ultramodern Nelson A. Rockefeller Empire State Plaza. This setting obscures the fact that it is Albany's largest church.

THE EXECUTIVE MANSION, 138 Eagle St., is the official residence of the governor of the State of New York. It was built by the Olcotts in 1850 as a private home and was subsequently rented and then purchased by the State. In 1961 the Mansion was severely damaged by fire but has since been completely restored and fireproofed. The art collection in the house represents many periods, from the Revolution to the present. For many years the house has been open to the public on New Year's Day, but whether or not it is open for public events is up to each governor. For information call 463-2295.

STATE UNIVERSITY PLAZA is the elegant grey Gothic structure at the foot of State St. on Broadway. Designed in 1918 by the prominent Albany architect Marcus T. Reynolds, it reflects the style of the Belgian Guild Hall. The six foot weathervane atop the building represents the Half Moon, the ship in which Henry Hudson sailed up the Hudson River in 1609. Formerly the offices of the Delaware and Hudson Railroad (hence its nickname among long time residents—"The D & H") and the *Albany Evening Journal*, the building has been renovated in recent years to house the central offices of the State University of New York and the apartments of the Chancellor of the University. Extensive preservation has restored the facade.

The public is welcome to stroll through the arcade, which runs the length of the building, and browse in the park in front. Scattered throughout are plaques marking historical events, such as the landing of the Half Moon, the drafting of the Articles of Confederation and the launch of the Clermont, all of which occurred near that spot.

FIRST CHURCH IN ALBANY, North Pearl St at Clinton Ave, established in 1642, is the oldest "religious community" in upstate New York. It was originally housed in the "block church" often represented in old prints of the city. Although the handsome church building itself is of more recent vintage, the pulpit dates from 1656 and the weathervane is a reproduction of the original which is on display at the Albany Institute. The church retains an active community of worship and works to meet the social needs of the people who live in its sphere.

QUACKENBUSH SQUARE, corner of Clinton Ave and Broadway, is a restored area nestled inconspicuously amidst the waterfront aterial, the Federal office building and the Palace Theater. The city undertook this project in 1976 as part of the bicentennial effort. The focal point, Quackenbush House, built in 1730, is one of the oldest houses in the city. Brick side-walks and carefully planted trees and gardens of the Dutch Colonial Period join the venerable house to the neighboring turn of the century buildings. These structures house the offices of the city's Department of Water and Water Supply. Quackenbush House itself serves as a restaurant.

Other Points of Interest Around Albany

ALBANY RURAL CEMETERY, Menands, holds some interesting individual graves—those of President Chester A. Arthur and the Schuyler family, for example. There is also some fine sculpture such as statues by Erastus Dow Palmer. One corner of the cemetery contains original stones moved from

STATE UNIVERSITY PLAZA

the early cemetery which was on State Street in what is now Washington Park. Also within its walls are graves of servicemen killed in every war fought by America.

FIRST LUTHERAN CHURCH, 181 Western Ave., though housed in a new building, is an historic congregation. Founded in 1649 in Albany, it is the oldest congregation of the Lutheran Church in America. *Swan of Albany,* a book length history of the congregation, is available at the church office or at the public library.

HISTORIC CHERRY HILL is described in the chapter on Museums.

PRUYN HOUSE CULTURAL CENTER, Old Niskayuna Rd Loudonville, was the country home of Casparus Pruyn, land and business agent to Stephen Van Rensselaer III. The house, now owned by the Town of Colonie, was opened in 1985 for public tours and for use as meeting space. The Colonie Town Historian and the Colonie Historical Society will use the home for office space, and the Colonie Art Guild will oversee a permanent display of paintings. Information is available through Charles Flanagan, 474-8831 or 785-4434.

SCHUYLER MANSION is described in the chapter on Museums.

THE SHAKER SETTLEMENT, adjacent to Albany Airport, is the first site in the United States where the Shakers owned property. It was here that they began to define their ideas about community living. The meeting house stands on the Northeast Corner of Albany Shaker Rd and Rte 155. The cemetery, a major Shaker burial ground, lies on the Northwest side. Those interested in preservation of Shaker heritage hope to establish an orientation center in the meeting house to provide visitors with an introduction to the Shaker world. For tours by reservation or information, call or write Shaker Heritage Society, Shaker Meeting House, Albany-Shaker Rd. Loudonville, 456-7890.

STATE UNIVERSITY OF NEW YORK AT ALBANY, 1400 Washington Ave., although described in the chapter on education, requires comment as an architectural entity.

The buildings rest on a flat surface carved from the once-rolling hills of the Albany Country Club golf course. Totally geometric in design, the campus has a rectangle of academic buildings at its center. At each corner, a short distance from the rectangle, is a square of residential buildings from which rises a square twenty-two story tower, also for housing. In the middle of the academic complex is a perfectly proportioned rectangular pool with a splendid fountain and a tall, slender carillon tower. Also on the campus are an observatory, a weather station, a greenhouse, a gallery, a gymnasium, an infirmary, a commissary and a meeting hall with solar heating. All the buildings except the last were designed by Edward Durrell Stone in 1964 to blend into a single pattern and theme and provide a homogeneous setting for the rapidly expanding University. Visitors are welcome to roam the grounds of the campus.

The buildings of the old campus, the red brick structures between Washington and Western Avenues, Partridge and Robin Streets, continue to serve as classrooms and dormitories. The University provides shuttle service between the two.

TEN BROECK MANSION is described in the chapter on Museums.

THE PORT OF ALBANY receives over 10 million tons of cargo each year, molasses, bananas, cars and gypsum being the principal shipments. A grain elevator with a 13,500,000 bushel capacity stores wheat to be exported to England, India and Russia. A continuing program for development and improvement insures a healthy future for the port.

The port occasionally hosts a visiting mercantile vessel, sailing ship or military craft, open for inspection by the public.

WASHINGTON PARK, see chapter on Sports and Recreation.

WILLIAM S. NEWMAN BREWING CO., 32 Learned St., is a small brewery which specializes in producing fine ales. It is open for public tours and tasting each Saturday at 12. For groups, arrangements should be made in advance, 465-8501.

Angel atop St. Mary's Church, Albany
Michael Fredericks, Jr.

SCHENECTADY

Downtown

CANAL SQUARE is a triumph of civic pride, optimism and planning. This commercial shopping and office area situated in the center of the city rose up from the shell of abandoned or neglected buildings typical of downtown areas in small cities across the country in the 1960s. Residents of Schenectady determined to infuse renewed vigor into this area and set about doing it with a combination of private and government funds. What has come into being incorporates restoration with contemporary construction. The tin ceilings, brass, handsome woodwork and brick work remain to give a sense of the past; modern additions of bright colors, open spaces and practical amenities add comfort and convenience.

Another unique feature of this shopping plaza is the canal system, in which paddle boats float in warm weather and on which skaters glide in winter. Parking for 1200 cars is to be available.

CENTER CITY, 433 State St., was completed in 1979. Government funding was used to restore the Wallace building and to add new construction. The building provides office space, stores and an indoor skating rink.

CITY HALL, 105 Jay St, is a handsome Georgian Revival structure constructed in 1930 according to the designs of McKim, Mead and White. During restoration efforts in 1983, the clock tower was accidentally set aflame and destroyed. Reconstruction has been conducted with care for the overall authenticity of the building, which is listed on the National Register of Historic Places. City Hall houses the offices of Schenectady City government.

DOWNTOWN RESTORATION ACTIVITIES are described in the chapter on Community Development.

GENERAL ELECTRIC was born in Schenectady in 1892 when the Edison General Electric Company merged with the Thomson-Houston Company. Today the weathered plant occupies many city blocks and operates the world's largest turbine and generator facility. As the principal employer in the city, GE infuses the commercial lifeblood of Schenectady. The importance of this industrial giant to the community cannot be over-estimated.

General Electric Company

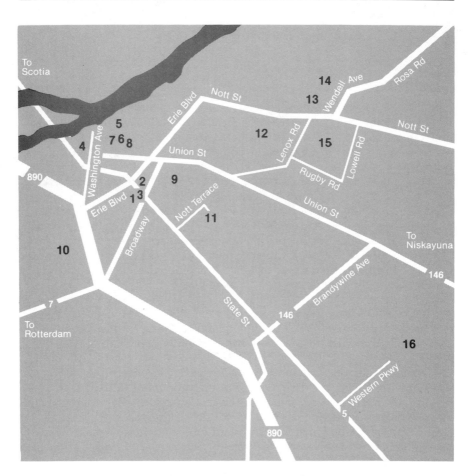

SCHENECTADY MAP KEY

1	Canal Square	12	Union College
2	Center City	13	First Unitarian Church
3	Proctor's Theatre	14	Steinmetz Memorial
4	Schenectady County	15	GE Realty Plot
	Historical Society	16	Central Park
5	The Stockade		
6	St. George's Church		
7	The First Presbyterian Church		
8	The First Reformed Church		
9	City Hall		
10	General Electric		
11	Schenectady Museum		

PROCTOR'S THEATRE, 432 State St, is located in the center of Canal Square. This elegantly restored former Vaudeville House features the best in Broadway, dance, music, "name" entertainers and classic films on a regular basis. Built in 1926, this 2,700 seat theater is now a nationally recognized non-profit performing arts center.

Proctor's Gift Centre with items of theater memorabilia is located in Proctor's Arcade, a 1926 precursor of the present-day shopping mall. For information on shows and free public tours, call 382-1083. To purchase tickets, call the box office at 346-6204.

SCHENECTADY COUNTY HISTORICAL SOCIETY, 32 Washington Ave., is described in the chapter on Museums.

THE STOCKADE, a residential district of several hundred homes in the downtown area of the city, stands on the site of the original Dutch settlement. Although the original homes were all destroyed by the French and Indian attack in 1690 and many of their replacements were demolished by a catastrophic fire in 1819, more than a dozen homes there predate the Revolution, and scores of homes have stood since the early 1800's. Because of this and because building in the area continued well into the 19th century, the Stockade harbors an interesting blend of architectural styles. Moreover, all of the houses function today as private homes and thus exhibit signs of life, individuality and sense of purpose often missing in "monuments" or areas designated as Historic Sites.

M. Kenyon '85

Schenectady City Hall
M. Kenyon/Preservation League of New York

There are three historical churches within this area. **ST. GEORGE'S,** North Ferry St., was founded in 1735 and **THE FIRST PRESBYTERIAN CHURCH,** Union St., was founded in 1809. These two churches are right beside each other and both have old cemeteries within their church yards. **THE FIRST REFORMED CHURCH,** at the corner of Union and Church Streets, was organized some time before 1674 and was the first church in the Mohawk Valley. From its Church Academy of 1785 grew Union College in 1795.

A well-written, helpfully illustrated map of the area is available at the **SCHENECTADY COUNTY HISTORICAL SOCIETY,** 32 Washington Ave., 374-0263. Open: daily 1-5.

The Historical Society cooperates with the Stockade Association to sponsor a walkabout every September. This is described in the chapter on Other Things to Do.

Other Points of Interest Around Schenectady

CENTRAL PARK is a lovely area of rolling hills and little lakes. A well-maintained, adventurously planned playground, shelters for ducks, swans and more exotic fowl, and a train ride make this park particularly attractive to families. Also, the gentle slopes are perfect for tobagganing and cross-country skiing when snow covers the grass. In June the rose gardens (entrance off Central Parkway) burst into a dizzy array of color. In summer, highly competitive tennis tournaments are arranged. For information about any of the programs, call 382-5152.

Directions: Take Fehr Ave. off State St. by Boardman Ltd.

THE FIRST UNITARIAN SOCIETY, 1221 Wendell Ave., 374-4446, was built in 1961 according to designs of Edward Durrell Stone, the architect responsible for the SUNYA campus. The exterior is constructed of customized cement blocks which form interlocking circles. The walls and fountains are lighted at night to dramatic effect. Inside, the Great Hall is an amphitheater with 300 seats on circular benches beneath a 60 foot wide dome. This gives "a sense of enclosure without constraint, unity without construction." The Hall serves as religious center, dramatic stage, recital hall, dance platform, and lecture rostrum.

Also of interest are the gardens and sculpture.

GENERAL ELECTRIC REALTY PLOT, bounded by Lowell Rd., Nott St., Lenox Rd., and Rugby Rd., was developed in 1899 for scientists and executives of the company. The book, *Enclave of Elegance*, chronicles the evolution of this area, describes its homes, and narrates the fascinating lives that were lived within its boundaries.

GLEN-SANDERS MANSION, 1 Glen Ave Scotia, 377-8839, is a colonial home built in 1658 along the north bank of the Mohawk River. It remained as the family home for 303 years. Soon after it was sold, the original furnishings, silver, and artwork were acquired for Colonial Williamsburg restoration. In 1974, the house was purchased and restored for Eblings Associates, who use part of the building as a computer center. Open: June-Oct T-Sat 10-4; Jan-May groups only and by appointment. There are special holiday events in December. Directions: Thruway to Exit 26; Rte 890 to Washington Ave Exit. Alternate directions: Rte 5 over Mohawk River Bridge; first building on left.

Yates House, Schenectady Stockade
Michael Fredericks, Jr.

JACKSON'S GARDENS, on the Union College Campus, are beautifully planned, well-maintained formal gardens. The plantings, begun in the early 1800's by Isaac Jackson, professor of Mathematics, have been continued since then by the college gardeners.

THE KNOLLS ATOMIC POWER LAB, River Road in Niskayuna, is a branch of General Electric devoted to theoretical and laboratory research into uses of atomic energy. It is located next to the **RESEARCH AND DEVELOPMENT CENTER,** another branch of General Electric. Both of these centers attract major figures in the scientific community and both have won worldwide recognition for their contributions to the pure and applied sciences. The Knolls Lab is often the site of protest by opponents of Atomic Energy.

SCHENECTADY MUSEUM, Nott Terrace Heights, is described in the chapter on museums.

STEINMETZ MEMORIAL, Wendell Ave, marks the site where Charles Proteus Steinmetz, a pioneer in electrical engineering, lived from 1903 to 1923 while he worked for the General Electric Company and served as Professor of Engineering at Union College.

UNION COLLEGE CAMPUS, between Union and Nott Streets, presents an interesting assemblage of architectural styles. It was planned in 1813 as a wheel design with a 16 sided domed structure (now the home of a bookstore and theater) at its center. Expansion of the facilities to meet the needs of a growing student body have noticeably altered the original plan, violating its symmetry, but the campus has nevertheless retained a handsome sense of continuity and integrity. The curriculum and student body are described in the chapter on Education.

TROY

TOURS: The Rensselaer County Historical Society, 57-59 Second St., 272-7232, sponsors Walking Theme Tours of Troy by appointment.

GUIDE BOOKLET: *Historic Troy: A Downtown Tour* is the title of a brochure produced by Rensselaer County Historical Society, Hudson-Mohawk Industrial Gateway, and Russell Sage College. It provides a map and information about Russell Sage College, historic churches and homes, civic buildings, and the parks and squares in the downtown area. The booklet is available at the Rensselaer County Historical Society, 57-59 Second St., 272-7232.

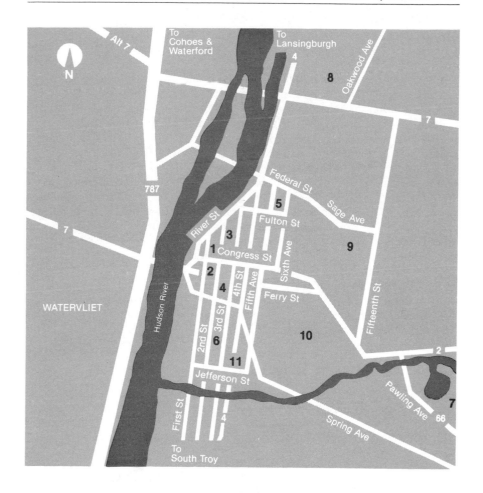

TROY MAP KEY

1	Hart-Cluett Mansion
2	Russell Sage College
3	Troy Music Hall
4	Troy Public Library
5	Teledyne Gurley Company
6	Washington Park
7	Emma Willard School
8	Oakwood Cemetery
9	Rensselaer Polytechnic Institute
10	Prospect Park
11	Gasholder House

DOWNTOWN RESTORATION ACTIVITIES are described in the chapter on Community Development.

THE STORY OF UNCLE SAM is well told in the book *"Uncle Sam: The Man and the Legend"* by Alton Ketchum, available at area libraries.

It is a fascinating tale of a legend seeded by chance and fertilized by the human imagination in quest of a symbol. Sam Wilson, a meat packer whose business was centered in Troy, was congenially dubbed Uncle Sam by the men who worked for him. When the War of 1812 broke out, the firm was contracted to send meat to the troops. The barrels for shipment to the military were marked U.S. for United States, but dockworkers joked that it meant Uncle Sam. When they were subsequently inducted into the army, they told the joke to soldiers from other parts of the country. Soon the words Uncle Sam and United States became synonymous. The cartoon figure, another concoction of many minds, appeared first in 1830, was dressed in stars and stripes at mid-century and given a beard at the time of the Civil War.

Sam Wilson, the "source" of the legend, meanwhile lived simply, peacefully in Troy for 88 years. His obituary in 1854 described him as a "promient businessman, involved in slooping, brickmaking, farming, slaughtering and distilling, and very active in local politics."

Near the River in Troy

BURDEN BUILDING, at the foot of Polk St. in South Troy, was the office for the Burden Iron Company. It is now owned by the Hudson Mohawk Industrial Gateway which spearheaded the restoration of this building. **THE INDUSTRIAL GATEWAY** is described in the chapter on Community Development.

HART-CLUETT MANSION, 59 Second St. Troy, is described in the section on Historic House Museums in the chapter on Museums. Open T-Sat 10-4.

RUSSELL SAGE COLLEGE, between First and Second Streets and Congress and Ferry Streets, is housed in a variety of buildings, many of which face onto Sage Park, a lovely square maintained by the college. The college has also acquired many of the handsome buildings around the square. Once private homes or offices, they now serve as classrooms, academic offices and residence halls. Vail House, an 1818 Federal style townhouse, is used by the president for entertaining. Julia Howard Bush Memorial Center, formerly the First Presbyterian Church, is a lecture and concert hall (available for community use). Sage Hall, Vanderheyden, Wool House, Gurley Hall, and Anna Plum Memorial are also buildings of note. Some of them formed the original nucleus of Emma Willard School prior to its move to Pawling Avenue in the early 1900's.

THE TROY GAS LIGHT COMPANY GASHOLDER HOUSE, Jefferson St. and 5th Ave., is an unusual landmark. In 1872 this "eight-sided" circular building

provide opportunities for continuing education for industry. The building should be completed in 1986. It will house three centers: the center for interactive computer graphics; the center for manufacturing, productivity, and technology transfer; and the center for integrated electronics.

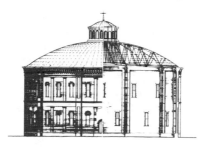

Gasholder House
The Gateway

TROY MUSIC HALL, 32 Second St. over the Troy Savings Bank, is renowned for its superior acoustics and its magnificent nineteenth century concert organ. Fine musicians from far and near readily accept an invitation to perform in this center, and the Music Hall hosts excellent concert series throughout the year. Information is available at 273-0038.

THE TROY PUBLIC LIBRARY, on the corner of South Ferry and Second Sts., is a beautiful building. Erected in 1897 as a gift to the city by Mary E. Hart, the building is constructed of white Vermont marble in the Italian Renaissance style. The exterior is decorated with carved arched windows, a rich modillion and denticulated cornice, and a full balustrade. The interior features marble walls, gold leaf highlights, wainscoting, a coffered ceiling, and many other handsome touches. Of particular note is the Tiffany glass window in which is written, "Study as if you were to live forever and live as if you were to die tomorrow." Information about the library and the window are available at the library.

TELEDYNE GURLEY CO., Fulton St. and 5th Ave., Troy 272-6300, contains a museum of surveying instruments as well as other engineering tools made by Gurley Company and other firms in the 19th century. The building itself is handsome and has recently been designated a National Historic Landmark.

WASHINGTON PARK, beginning at 189 Second St., is a lovely little ornamental green surrounded by beautiful row houses dating to the 19th century. Occasionally tours of the homes are arranged through cultural or historical groups. The residents maintain the park through a monthly tax, a system still in service in London, England.

Historic Churches
CHURCHES in Troy have interesting pasts. Some were erected as splendid houses of worship for the affluent families who directed the industry. Others were to serve the laborers who came to the city to work in the

factories. Because many of these laborers came to Troy as first or second generation immigrants, their churches often assumed an ethnic identity which shaped design and decoration. Because the times were marked by such prosperity, many of the churches were embellished by beautiful works of art.

ST. JOSEPH'S CHURCH, 416 Third St., is said to have the largest number of Tiffany windows of any parish in America. Tiffany windows may also be seen in **ST. PAUL'S CHURCH,** 58 Third St., in **ST. JOHN'S CHURCH,** 146 First St., and in **THE FIRST PRESBYTERIAN CHURCH,** which is now the Julia Howard Bush Center at Russell Sage College.

Up the Hill in Troy

EMMA WILLARD SCHOOL, 285 Pawling Ave., occupies a 55 acre campus on the East Side of Troy. The grey Gothic style buildings were designed to look very much like an English college. They house classrooms, offices, and dormitories. A modern library, arts, and music building echoes the colors and architectural lines of the original buildings. Most of the students are boarders, and many of the faculty and administrators reside on the campus of this school known throughout the nation for its versatility and rigor.

OAKWOOD CEMETERY, Oakwood Ave., is a lovely cemetery with attractive landscaping, impressive monuments, and a fine view of the Hudson Mohawk area. It is the site of Uncle Sam's grave.

THE RENSSELAER POLYTECHNIC INSTITUTE CAMPUS, perched atop the slope rising from the river, is recognizable to those approaching Troy from the south by the predominance of three-story brick buildings topped by copper roofs. In addition, the campus holds some noteworthy buildings of contemporary architecture—a student union, a library and a center of engineering—as well as some lovely conventional homes which serve as fraternity houses. The college is particularly proud of its **VOORHEES COMPUTER CENTER.** The building is an interesting modern adaption of architecture. Using a Gothic church located on campus, architects erected a building within a building, thus conserving energy and providing handsome vistas and commodius, varied work space. Visitors are welcome to tour the building.

    THE CAMPUS INFORMATION CENTER is an experiment in design for energy conservation. It features a passive solar collector, configurative placement of the building to make maximum use of the sun, an earth berme and a sunspace for insulation, and mirroring of light to minimize need for artifically generated power. The building uses about 1/3 the energy required by a conventional building, even though it is open 24 hours a day.

    New to the RPI campus is the **GEORGE M. LOW CENTER FOR INDUSTRIAL INNOVATION.** Housed in a $30,000,000 building constructed by New York

Troy Public Library
Michael Fredericks, Jr.

State funds, the center will be used by industries and academic institutions throughout the country to solve problems in American industry and to can industry and to provide opportunities for continuing education for industry. The building should be completed in 1986. It will house three centers: the center for interactive computer graphics; the center for manufacturing, productivity, and technology transfer; and the center for integrated electronics.

RENSSELAER TECHNOLOGY PARK is both a place and a concept. In 1981, RPI announced that it would commit $3 million for the development of a 1,200 acre site in North Greenbush as a base for high technology enterprises. The college and the community would offer expertise and service to the industries that responded, and the industries would offer opportunities for experience and employment. RPI has established guidelines and restrictions so that the development will "insure an environment of the highest quality."

SLAVIN HOUSE, RENSSELAER NEWMAN CHAPEL AND CULTURAL CENTER, Burdett Ave. at Sherry Rd, 274-7793, is a multipurpose building supervised by the Rensselaer Newman Foundation. It provides a center for worship and meditation, a focus for cultural activities, and a meeting place for campus and townspeople, especially for educational and social events.

COHOES, WATERFORD & WATERVLIET

Cohoes
COHOES was a major center for the manufacture of woven and knit cotton in the mid 19th century. The Mohawk River and the Cohoes Falls produced the water power necessary to run the textile mills. The complex of mills and housing built by the dominant Harmony Manufacturing Company are still in existence. The city is part of the Hudson-Mohawk Urban Cultural Park described in the chapter on community development.

Waterford
WATERFORD is the oldest incorporated village in the United States. It sits like a pen dipped into a well made by the Mohawk River on one side and the Hudson on the other. It is of interest to the visitor because of the unique style of some of the older residential buildings, the visible remains of its formidable industrial past, the operational system of canals, and the collection of materials in the village museum.

PEEBLES ISLAND, an undeveloped state park in the Hudson River near Waterford, holds the building which once functioned as the bleachery for Cluett Peabody, the Troy-based manufacturer of fine men's shirts. Here the process of sanforization of cotton (named for Sanford Cluett) was devel-

oped. The building, which now serves as the administrative headquarters of the Bureau of Historic Sites, is open once a year in May during National Preservation Week. Information is available through the Department of Parks, Recreation and Historic Preservation, Bureau of Historic Sites, Peebles Island, Waterford, 12188, 237-8090.

THE WATERFORD FLIGHT is a set of "lift locks" that raises boats from the Hudson River to the Mohawk River above the Cohoes Falls. Each of the five locks lifts the craft 33 to 34.5 feet. Each boat is thereby raised a total of 168.8 feet. The trail is well marked, and facilities are provided for visitors by the Department of Parks and Recreation. A brochure with more information is available through the Waterford Historical Museum (open Saturday and Sunday afternoons) or the New York State Department of Transportation, 457-4420.

Watervliet

WATERVLIET ARSENAL, Broadway, Watervliet, 266-5111, is a major U.S. Army Defense Plant which has been engaged in the manufacture of heavy artillery since the War of 1812. On the grounds are points of interest—the museum, the cast-iron storehouse and old residences including the home of poet Stephen Vincent Benet. Tours of the facility are arranged throughout the year by the Hudson-Mohawk Industrial Gateway.

Sources of Information

Newspapers

Five major daily papers and two score weekly papers cover the area.

Dailies

KNICKERBOCKER NEWS, Box 15,000 Albany 12212, 454-5694, is an evening paper published Mon-Sat. by Capital Newspapers, part of the Gannett chain. It carries international, national, and local news, has syndicated columns and features as well as local features. The Friday paper carries *The Entertainer*, a thorough survey of the arts and entertainment in the week to come.

THE SARATOGIAN, 20 Lake Ave. Saratoga Springs 12866, 584-4242, is published daily except Saturday.

SCHENECTADY GAZETTE, 332 State St. Schenectady 12301, 374-4141, a family-owned local newspaper now in its second generation, is published each morning Monday-Saturday. Its staff writes news, features, and editorials, and the paper carries nationally syndicated columns and features. The magazine section on Saturday has book, movie, art, music and restaurant reviews as well as the TV guide for the week.

THE TIMES RECORD, 501 Broadway, Troy 12181, 272-2000, is published in Troy each evening. It covers major international and national news and stresses local news. The Sunday paper has multiple sections; the Friday issue contains *Stepping Out*, an arts and leisure section; the Saturday issue contains a TV guide section.

TIMES UNION, Box 15,000, Albany 12212, 454-5694 is the daily with the largest circulation in the area. It appears each morning— including Sunday when it has many sections including the comics. The *T.U.*, as it is called, is a publication of Capital Newspapers, a link in the Gannett chain.

Troy Public Library
Michael Fredericks, Jr.

It contains nationally syndicated columns and features as well as local news, editorials, features, and arts. The real estate and classified sections are very thorough.

Suburban Papers

Name	Address	Area Served	Schedule
Altamont Enterprise	123 Maple Ave. Altamont 12009 861-6641	Albany County	Weekly
Ballston Journal	72 West High St. Ballston Spa 12020 885-4341	Ballston Spa	Weekly
Chatham Courier	P.O. Box 355 Chatham, N.Y. 12037 392-4141	Columbia and Rensselaer Co.	Weekly
Colonian	20 S. Ferry Albany, N.Y. 12202	Albany	Weekly
Commercial News	Northway 9 Plaza Clifton Park, NY 12065	Saratoga Co.	Weekly
East Glenville Weekly	443 Saratoga Road Scotia, NY 12302 399-9133	East Glenville, Burnt Hills, Ballston Spa, Ballston Lake, Clifton Park Saratoga	Weekly
Greenbush Area News	P.O. Box 31 East Greenbush 12061 286-6600	S. Rens. Co.	Weekly
The Spotlight	125 Adams St. Delmar 12054 439-4949	Delmar	Weekly

Special Interest Papers and Magazines and Journals

THE ALBANY EAGLE, 20 S. Ferry Albany 12202, 462-2640, offers local features and in-depth coverage of events and organizations in the city and county of Albany.

CAPITAL DISTRICT BUSINESS REVIEW, 76 Exchange St, Colonie 12205, 458-7000, provides news and information about business and the business community in northeastern New York.

THE EVANGELIST, 39 Philip St. Albany 12207, 434-0107, carries news and features concerning the Roman Catholic Diocese of Albany which includes Albany and 14 surrounding counties.

GROUNDSWELL is a triannual review published by the Hudson Valley Writers Guild to serve as a forum for the many excellent writers in the area. Each issue focuses on the work of a regional author with a biographical sketch, an interview, a critique, and previously unpublished work. Also included in each issue are works by area poets, essayists, and fiction writers. Information is available through the Guild Press, P.O. Box 3 Chatham 12037.

JEWISH WORLD, 1104 Central Ave. Albany, 12205, 459-8455, covers news and features of interest to the Jewish Community of the region.

METROLAND, 12 Vatrano Ave. Albany 12205, 459-5371, carries in-depth coverage of the arts, media and entertainment in the Capital District.

PLAZA MAGAZINE, P.O. Box 322, Chatham 12037, 392-9686, appears monthly. It describes activities and ventures in the tri-city area.

SOUTH END SCENE, 15-17 Trinity Place Albany 12202, 449-5155, carries news and information of interest to residents of Arbor Hill, the South End, North and West Albany. It carries detailed explanations of programs, services, and events available to residents of this area of the city.

Regional Magazines

ADIRONDACK LIFE is a stunning magazine about the natural beauty, the arts, crafts, recreation, history and conservation of the area.

THE CONSERVATIONIST is a beautiful and interesting magazine published bimonthly by the New York State Department of Environmental Conservation. It treats topics of interest to those concerned wtih wildlife, waterways, land and buildings. For information or subscription forms, write The Conservationist, P.O. Box 1500, Latham, NY 12110.

NEW YORK ALIVE, 152 Washington Ave. Albany, 465-7511, is a bimonthly magazine sponsored by the Business Council of New York State. It is a general interest periodical with articles on business, education, recreation, sports, and rural, urban, and suburban life in New York State. It also features pieces on personalities, history, travel, and restaurants.

The Media

Television

Six local stations are available to all homes:

       Channel 6, WRGB, an affiliate of CBS.
       Channel 10, WTEN, an affiliate of ABC.

Channel 13, WNYT, an affiliate of NBC.
Channel 17, WMHT, public television.
Channel 23, WXXA, an alternative broadcasting station.
Channel 45, WUSV, an alternative broadcasting station.

Programming is announced in the local papers. Members of WMHT receive monthly schedules. For membership in WMHT call 356-1700.

CAPITOL CABLEVISION brings additional stations as well as 24 hour teletype of Reuters News Service, Wall Street prices, weather, off track betting and T.V. programming for a monthly fee. For an additional fee the subscriber may add Home Box Office which runs recent feature length films—uncut and uninterrupted, and MTV which presents popular music videos. There is an installation charge. For information call 869-5500.

Radio

This region has access to excellent radio programming. The stations are many in number and varied in their offerings. Schedules are not published in the newspapers, but Capital Newspapers periodically publishes a list with a brief description of principal focus of programming of each station.

WMHT and WAMC, both listener-supported stations, send monthly programs to subscribers. These are described in the music section of the chapter on the Arts.

Maps

A good map of the tri-city area is available at Albany-Colonie Regional Chamber of Commerce, 14 Corporate Woods Blvd Albany, 434-1214.

A good touring map of Rensselaer County is available at Greater Troy Chamber of Commerce, 251 River St. Troy, 274-7020.

JIMAPCO, 15 Lawmar Lane Burnt Hills, 399-8632, produces clear complete maps of the fifteen county area and distributes maps made by other concerns. A catalogue is available.

BOOK HOUSE, Stuyvesant Plaza, Albany, 489-4761, has a wide selection of maps—national and regional.

Calendars of Events

THE ALBANY LEAGUE OF THE ARTS CALENDAR, a monthly listing of cultural events for the Capital District, is available through membership or at 19 Clinton Ave., Albany, 449-5380. Those scheduling a public event may call the above number to avoid conflict with other groups.

TROY LIVEABILITY CAMPAIGN CALENDAR is a bi-monthly calendar of events produced and distributed by the Rensselaer County Council on the Arts. It is available at 189 Second Street Troy 12180 or by calling 273-0552.

Mailing Lists

Mailing lists are used by many area groups to keep their supporters informed of upcoming events. Colleges, museums, galleries, theater companies, dance troups, professional societies, neighborhood groups, libraries, musical societies and area night spots periodically send out notices to those they know are interested. Addresses of such groups appear throughout the book.

Telephone Numbers for General Information

Federal Tax Assistance . . . . (800) 424-1040
State Income Tax Assistance 457-1133
Weather, Time, and Temperature 476-1122

Agencies

ALBANY COUNTY CONVENTION AND VISITORS BUREAU, 600 Broadway Albany, 434-1217, has as its main objective the promotion of the area. It serves to assist in the smooth functioning of events scheduled in the city, performing such services as providing typewriters, brochures and badges, and coordinating the needs of groups with facilities at meeting sites and hotels.

ALBANY COLONIE REGIONAL CHAMBER OF COMMERCE, 14 Corporate Woods Blvd. Albany 12211, 434-1214.

ALBANY COUNTY HISTORICAL ASSOCIATION, 9 TenBroeck Place Albany, 436-9826, will answer questions about Albany's past.

GREATER TROY CHAMBER OF COMMERCE, 1831 5th Ave Troy, 274-7020.

I LOVE N.Y., a Commerce Department venture designed to promote the products and tourist attractions of New York State, has an information office at 99 Washington Ave Albany, 474-4116 (or at dial I Love N.Y.). Excellent maps and interesting brochures are available upon request.

THE INTERNATIONAL CENTER, INC., Wellington Hotel, Room 202, 136 State St Albany, 436-9741, provides service and advice for the foreign visitor and temporary resident. It also gives members of the community the opportunity to offer hospitality to visitors. In recent years it has concentrated its efforts in the resettlement of refugees from Viet Nam and Cambodia.

NEW YORK STATE LEGISLATIVE FORUM is a non-partisan, non-profit group designed to stimulate active interest in New York State legislation by providing information on current issues. The Forum meets for twelve consecutive Tuesdays during the legislative session to report on bills before the Legislature and to discuss current issues with state leaders. A weekly "Clipsheet" reports on bills discussed. Meetings, held from 10-12 AM in Chancellor's Hall (in the State Education Building), start the first Tuesday in February.

RENSSELAER COUNTY HISTORICAL SOCIETY, 59 2nd St, Troy, 272-7232, works to preserve the heritage of Troy and to pass along information about the region's past. Membership is open to all. Trips, lectures, and programs are planned for members and friends throughout the year. Office open: M-F 9-5.

SCHENECTADY CHAMBER OF COMMERCE, 240 Canal Sq., 372-5656.

SCHENECTADY COUNTY HISTORICAL SOCIETY, 32 Washington Ave., 374-0263, is described in the section on museums.

Regional Writers

Several area writers have used Albany as the setting of their imaginative work. (An annotated bibliography of non-fiction works is listed at the end of the chapter on The Past.)

Kennedy, William. *Billy Phelan's Greatest Game.* Penguin, 1983. A novel set on Broadway at the time of the kidnapping of Dan O'Connell's nephew.

_____. *Ink Truck.* Viking, 1984. A novel set in Albany during a newspaper strike in the mid 1960's.

_____. *Ironweed.* Penguin, 1985. A novel set in the North and South ends of Albany in 1933.

_____. *Legs.* Penguin, 1983. A novel based on the exploits of Jack 'Legs' Diamond.

_____. *O Albany! Improbable City of Political Wizards, Fearless Ethnics, Spectacular Aristocrats, Splendid Nobodies,* and *Underrated Scoundrels.* Viking-Washington Park Press, 1983. A book of essays about life in Albany.

McPheeters, Sam and Mark MacGregor Stease. *Traveler's Tales: Rumors and Legends of the Albany Saratoga Region.* Independently published at 50 Elm St. Witty, lively description of ghosts, mysteries, comic occurrences.

Rosen, Hy. The collected work of a cartoonist for *Times Union.*

Writings From the Beaver Trail. Albany Public Library, 1981. Memoirs, poems, essays, and short fiction by senior adults of Albany and Rensselaer Counties.

Transportation

Airlines

ALBANY COUNTY AIRPORT, located off the Northway at Exit 5, is served by **AMERICAN** (463-5551), **BAR HARBOR** (800-343-3210), **COMMAND** (465-3596), **EASTERN** (436-4721), **MALL** (785-3383), **PEOPLE'S EXPRESS** (465-4422), **US AIR** (462-5881), **REPUBLIC** (800-441-1414), and **UNITED** (462-4494). Most other major airlines have offices in the area or have toll-free numbers listed in the telephone directory.

Limousine Service

AIRPORT LIMOUSINE SERVICE, 869-2258, offers transportation between Albany County Airport and downtown Albany.

HUDSON VALLEY AIRPORTER, 465-1523, provides direct transportation to Kennedy and LaGuardia Airports and connections to Newark Airport. The service runs every day from the Turf Inn, Wolf Road, Albany on a reservation basis only. The fee is reasonable. Because these cars fill up quickly, it is wise to reserve early.

Returning passengers with reservations notify the service of their actual arrival by dialing 757-5325 for JFK and LaGuardia; 1-201-623-0069 for Newark.

Trains

AMTRAK has two passenger stations; one serves Albany and Troy and is located in Rensselaer at East and Herrick Sts, 462-5763. The other serves Schenectady and is located at Liberty and Erie Blvd, 346-8651. Local bus service is available from the stations. Schedules are posted.

Hudson River
Michael Fredericks, Jr.

Buses

Local Buses

THE CAPITAL DISTRICT TRANSPORTATION AUTHORITY (CDTA) runs buses frequently and on schedule. Routes follow the main arteries and make special concessions to major residential complexes. Exact fare is required, with free transfers provided for those who must travel on more than one route. Commuter passes and tokens are available at local banks. Senior citizens and the disabled ride for ½ fare with appropriate CDTA identification. Children under 5 ride for free if accompanied by a fare-paying adult. (Limit of 3 children to an adult.) Bus passes and tokens are available to school children for use to and from school.

During July and August CDTA runs buses from Albany to John Boyd Thatcher State Park, and from Troy to Grafton Lakes State Park. Most city parks are on the CDTA bus routes.

Schedules are available at banks, office buildings, and visitor information centers throughout the tri-city area. CDTA information numbers are 482-8822 for Albany, Saratoga and Troy area, 393-2101 for the Schenectady area. Information on other CDTA services is available at 482-3371.

CHARTER BUSES—For events within Albany, Schenectady, Rensselaer or Saratoga County, CDTA offers charter service at very reasonable rates. For information and reservations, write CDTA Charter Sales, 110 Watervliet Ave Albany 12206 or call 489-9191 (8:30-4 weekdays).

For events outside this area reliable charter service is offered by Yankee Trails, 286-2400, Mountain View, 756-2176, or Wade Tours, 355-4500.

SUNYA runs a shuttle service between the new campus, the old campus and the Wellington Hotel. The silver-green buses, intended for use of students, faculty and staff only, keep a tight schedule.

Inter-City and Inter-State Buses

ADIRONDACK TRAILWAYS, 360 Broadway Albany, 436-9651, and 22 State St, Schenectady, 346-3415, services many small localities in New York State and offers connecting routes to many major cities from New York City. The line has commuter services to Albany from as far west as Gloversville and in summer runs routes north to popular vacation sites. Schedules are available at the terminals.

GREYHOUND BUS LINES, which has terminals at 34 Hamilton Street (near Madison and Broadway) in Albany, 434-0121, 22 State St Schenectady, 346-6113, and 84 Ferry St Troy, 274-4351, provides direct service to major American cities. Into its terminal come buses of other lines to provide connections to other states. Local bus service is available from bus terminals. Schedules are posted in the terminals.

Both Adirondack Trailways and Greyhound offer excellent package express service to regions they serve.

Peripheral Parking with Bus Service

Peripheral parking with charter bus service to downtown Albany is available for state employees at two locations: the Washington Avenue lot, opposite the SUNYA campus, and the McCarty Avenue lot, adjacent to Exit 23 of the New York State Thruway. Buses run every five minutes at peak commuting hours and make six stops downtown. Between peak hours a shuttle service operates from each of these lots every 45 minutes, weaving among other state office buildings. Schedules for this service are available from the Bureau of Parking Services, 474-8118. This service is also put into effect on weekends when there are special events at the Empire State Plaza.

Special Transportation for Handicapped Senior Citizens

Capital District

STAR, Special Transit Available by Request, is a CDTA service for Capital District Residents who are disabled. Transportation for shopping, visiting, appointments or work is provided for a reasonable cost. CDTA requests that reservations be made 48 hours in advance, at 482-2022.

Albany

TRANSPORTATION SERVICE, 25 Delaware Ave Albany, will transport any resident over 60 years old to any of the Senior Service Centers or to a physician's office with 24 hour notice. Transportation for the handicapped is also available. Small fee. 434-4219.

SHOPPING ASSISTANCE AND/OR TRANSPORTATION is available to the handicapped and to the homebound handicapped on Tuesday, Wednesday and Thursday, 465-3322.

Schenectady

AMERICAN RED CROSS provides free transportation to anyone in need. (The majority of its clients are over 60.) Reservations are required in advance at 374-9180.

Troy

THE RENSSELAER COUNTY DEPARTMENT FOR THE AGING, 270-2734, provides transportation for senior citizens to Senior Citizen Centers, to health and social service appointments, and for shopping. They require 48 hour advance notice, which may be made at the above number from 9-12 a.m. daily. Suggested contribution.

Taxis

Taxis can be found at stands at the railroad station, at the airport and at the bus terminals, or may be called. A full listing of city and suburban taxis is found in the yellow pages of the telephone directory. They operate on a fee schedule determined by zones and are shared by passengers headed in a common direction, all of whom pay the set fee.

Car Pools

Car pools are not coordinated by any central office. Bulletin boards in office buildings sometimes display requests for rides or riders. City and business leaders are cooperating to make these arrangements more attractive.

Road Names and Numbers

Sometimes the interchange of names and numbers of routes confuses the newcomer. The following is a list of various names for the same roads.

Adirondack Northway	I-87
Thomas E. Dewey New York State Thruway	
Albany to Buffalo	I-90
Albany to New York City	I-87
Western Avenue	Rte. 20
Central Avenue (Albany)—State Street (Schenectady)	Rte. 5
Slingerlands By-pass	Rte. 85
Riverfront Arterial	Rte. 787
Troy-Schenectady Road	Rte. 7
East-West Arterial joining the Northway, Exit 24 of the Thruway and the Massachusetts Turnpike	I-90
Delaware Avenue and Loudonville Road	Rte. 9

Lodging

A great number of factors have combined in recent years to make the Capital District, particularly Albany, a convention center drawing thousands of visitors daily. One result has been a burgeoning of hostelries. Because it would serve little purpose for this book to describe all possible places to stay, we have chosen to give an overview, presenting detailed information on the most distinctive and the most economical, and appending a list directing readers to information about others, particularly local franchises of national chains.

Most Distinctive

ALBANY HILTON HOTEL, State and Lodge Streets Albany, 462-6611, is a full service hotel run by the international Hilton chain. It features adaptable space for meetings, celebrations, and gatherings, and offers various levels of food catering; thus the Hilton frequently hosts conventions, weddings, proms, and large private parties. The hotel's location in the downtown area, its recreational facilities and its choice of restaurants also make it attractive to independent visitors. A courtesy bus provides transportation to area sites and to the airport. Rates are moderate to expensive.

ALBANY MARRIOTT HOTEL, 189 Wolf Road Colonie, 458-8444, is a full service contemporary hotel located near Albany Airport and several major shopping centers. All the public rooms—the restaurants, shops, health facilities (pools, saunas, exercise club), meeting rooms and ballrooms—are tastefully decorated in pleasant but lively combinations of forest green, mauve, and cream, accented by brass accessories. The facilities are open to the general public as well as to registered guests. Rates are moderate to expensive, with special packages (the ESCAPE Weekend being one of the most dramatic) available upon request.

THE AMERICANA INN, Albany Shaker Road (Northway (87) Exit 4) Colonie, 869-9271, was designed with an interesting layout—a series of three-story

Courtyard at Americana Hotel
Michael Fredericks, Jr.

quadrangles arranged to give the illusion of smallness (thus concealing the fact that the facility houses hundreds of guests). The inn, which is relatively new, has avoided predictable contemporary motel accessories, furnishing the rooms with Colonial pieces instead. The inn maintains recreational facilities—pools, sauna, workout room, jacuzzi—and a billiard parlor off the lobby. The rates are moderate to expensive.

COOPER INN, Cooperstown, (607) 547-9931, is a handsome colonial house near the base of Lake Otsego in the lovely planned village of Cooperstown. Although the services here are limited to lodging and breakfast, all the facilities of the Otesaga Hotel (described hereafter) are available to Cooper Inn guests. The Inn is open May 1-October 20. The rate, which includes breadfast, is moderate.

FEDERAL HOUSE INN, South Lee MA, (413) 243-1824, an early nineteenth century home, offers seven rooms for guests, each with private bath. Another attraction is the restaurant downstairs—one of the best in the Berkshires. Breakfast is included in the room rate, which is moderate off season and expensive in season.

GIDEON PUTNAM, Saratoga Spa State Park, Saratoga Springs, 584-3000, is a full service, year-round resort hotel complete with tennis courts, golf course, swimming pool, gift shop, restaurants, and beautiful walks. Summertime guests have the convenience of being located beside SPAC, and wintertime guests can ice skate or cross country ski in the adjoining Saratoga State Park. All rooms are offered on either a Full American Plan or the European Plan. In August the hotel is booked solid with racing fans who pay double the usual rate. Attractive weekend packages are available throughout the off-season, with excellent winter specials.

GREGORY HOUSE, Rte 43 Averill Park, 674-3774, a country farmhouse which serves as a continental restaurant, has added twelve guest rooms. Breakfast is included in the moderate rate.

L'HOSTELLERIE BRESSANE, Hillsdale, NY, 325-3412, welcomes travelers in its cozy upstairs rooms. The restaurant which occupies the lower floor is superb. Room rate, which is moderate, includes a French breakfast.

MOHONK MOUNTAIN HOUSE, Lake Mohonk/New Paltz 12561, (914) 255-1000, is a full service, year-round resort hotel, complete with lake, golf course, riding stable, and courts for handball, racquetball, and tennis. The imaginative optional activities program includes such things as bird-watching excursions and treasure hunts. The House is an eccentric Victorian building which dominates the beautiful landscape surrounding it. The tone of the hotel matches its architecture, with attention paid to gracious service and traditional amenities. The staff requires similar behavior from guests, who must, for example, dress for meals. The rates, which include American Plan, are expensive.

Mohonk Mountain House

OTESAGA HOTEL, Lake Road Cooperstown, (607) 547-9931, is a commodious summer resort hotel presiding at the base of Lake Otsego. Guests visit the nearby Baseball Hall of Fame, Farmer's Museum, and Fennimore House and return for a meal on the pool patio, which overlooks a beautiful expanse of grass, lake, hills, and sky. Weekday lunches and Sunday brunch are particularly popular, both for guests and visitors. The hotel is open from May 1 to October 20. The rates, which include dinner and breakfast, are expensive.

RAMADA RENAISSANCE HOTEL, 543 Broadway at City Center, Saratoga Springs, 584-4000, has been newly built as a flagship in the Ramada chain. Located beside Saratoga's new convention center — City Center — the Renaissance is a luxury hotel equipped to meet the needs of large groups. The hotel offers dramatically reduced off-season weekend specials. Room rates are moderate to expensive.

RED LION INN, Stockbridge MA, (413) 298-5545, has functioned as an inn since 1773. It is a charming place, a comfortable combination of traditional grace and contemporary efficiency. With 100 rooms and a variety of common rooms—all furnished in 18th century decor—the Inn can function as a convention center as well as a temporary retreat for travelers. It's the perfect spot for music lovers in summer, for leaf-lookers in fall, for skiers in winter and for meanderers in spring. The food and dining facilities are excellent. The rates are moderate.

THE SAGAMORE, Green Island (literally an island off Bolton Landing on Lake George), 644-9400, is a year-round luxury resort hotel built in 1882 and restored to lavish splendor in 1985. Through its many years of service, the hotel maintained a distinguished reputation for comfort and style. The accoutrements—eight dining areas, a championship golf course, a commissioned yacht, riding stables, a veranda and promenade, "loofa and herbal wrap" rooms, and the like—are designed with royalty in mind. Guests have full access to the facility, and visitors are welcome to some extent. (Golf memberships and athletic club memberships are available, for example, and individuals or groups are invited to use the facilities for meetings or celebrations. Guided tours are scheduled 9 am to 2 pm throughout the summer.) There is great flexibility in accommodations, meal plans, and tariffs, with off-season rates being less than half peak season rates. No matter what the time of year, the rate remains expensive.

Best Buy

THE TOM SAWYER, 1444 Western Ave Albany, 438-3594, is a simple, homey motel. The buildings are well-kept, and the service is congenial. It is located across from the excellent shopping center, Stuyvesant Plaza, and is within easy walking distance of six restaurants and two fast-food emporiums. The rates are inexpensive.

Appendix

The greatest concentration of rooms is located in Albany along Wolf Road between Central Avenue and Albany Shaker Road. Many of these motels, as franchises of national chains, offer service as prescribed by a central office. The following chart indicates how to make reservations or seek further information.

Name	Location	Telephone	Price Range
Comfort Inn	866 Alb Shak Rd Latham	783-1900	inexpensive
Days Inn	16 Wolf Rd Alb	459-3600	inexpensive
Holiday Inn	1614 Central Clne	869-0281	moderate
	946 New Loudon Rd	783-6161	moderate
	575 Broadway Mends	463-1121	moderate
	100 Nott Terr Schdy	393-4141	moderate

Name	Location	Telephone	Price Range
Quality Inn	I-90 & Everett Rd Alb	438-8431	moderate
Ramada Inn	1228 Western Ave Alb	489-2981	moderate
	450 Nott Terr Schdy	370-7151	moderate
Red Roof Inn	188 Wolf Rd Alb	459-1971	inexpensive
Sheraton-Airport	200 Wolf Rd Alb	458-1000	moderate
Susse Chalet	44 Wolf Rd Alb	459-5670	inexpensive
Travelodge	1230 Western Ave Alb	489-4423	moderate
	759 State St Schdy	393-6692	moderate
Turf Inn	205 Wolf Rd Alb	458-7250	mod-exp

Restaurants

One goal of this book is to enable residents and visitors to take full advantage of the assets of the Capital District. A factor which sometimes limits this full appreciation is the perception of boundaries between the smaller units of the community. Because food, perhaps more than anything else, entices people to forget provincial preconceptions, we have approached this chapter with a total disregard for geography. Following the example of Arthur Frommer, author of excellent guidebooks to great cities, we have arranged this chapter by level of cost:

> THE MOST EXPENSIVE
> THE MODERATELY PRICED
> THE LESS EXPENSIVE
> SPECIAL POCKET PLEASERS.

Within the four levels, wherein restaurants are arranged in alphabetical order, we describe a wide range of cuisines. What the restaurants described do have in common is that they all offer good value; that is, no matter what the price, we perceive it to be a fair compensation for the food, the service, and the general atmosphere that each offers. At the end of the chapter we have included two lists—the restaurants by type of cuisine, and the restaurants by location. We hope that these lists, plus the fact that each restaurant is cited in the index, will help readers find information quickly.

N.B. It is, of course, impossible to describe everyone's favorite restaurant in a book this size. In no way do we imply that restaurants not included in this survey are inferior.

SARATOGA SCRATCH: The ever-changing restaurant scene in Saratoga is much like its racing scene—as filled with incomparable aristocrats as with ne'r-do-wells. Dozens of restaurants flourish in and around that city, some of them "summertime things," others steady, sturdy year-round goers. In "Saratoga Style," a special supplement to the July 29, 1984 SUNDAY TIMES UNION, area restaurant critics Fred LeBrun and Vinod Chhabra reviewed thirty-six restaurants in Saratoga. Some of these are included in this chapter, but readers wanting a thorough survey of Saratoga restaurants should look up that supplement in the local library.

Troy restaurant and tavern owners
Photographers & Co/Troy Liveability Campaign

THE MOST EXPENSIVE

These restaurants offer superior cuisine, excellent service, and pleasant surroundings. They are the perfect place to celebrate a grand occasion, recognize an outstanding accomplishment, or entertain the palate on an evening to be remembered. (Visitors from larger cities are amused that denizens of this area call these restaurants—where the tab may run 20-30 dollars per person—expensive.)

ALGONQUIN BAR AND RESTAURANT, Bolton Landing, 644-9442, overlooking the handsome shoreline of Lake George, has been a favorite dining spot in northeastern New York for many years. Patrons travel miles to sample the American cuisine and enjoy the stunning natural surroundings. Open: June-Sept daily, noon-10; Sept-June weekdays, noon-8:30 or 9:30, and weekends, noon-9:30 or 10:30. Closed March and November. Dinner and sandwich menu throughout the day. Directions: Northway (I-87) to Exit 22; Rte 9 North. Restaurant is on right, beside the lake.

CAFE CAPRICCIO, 49 Grand St Albany, 465-0439, is an intimate Italian restaurant, opened in 1983 by Chef Jim Rua, who pleased cognoscenti for many years while working in other area kitchens. His changing menu always includes a selection of delicious seafood dishes (the paella for two or more is terrific), lamb, veal, and chicken. The pasta presentations are also interesting. The cheesecake, delicately flavored with a touch of orange peel, may be the best in the Capital District. Open: M-Sat 6-10.

NOTE: When this restaurant closed for vacation in summer 1985, rumors circulated that it might not reopen. If this is the case, watch for it to re-surface or for Jimmy Rua to re-appear elsewhere.

CHEZ RENE FRENCH RESTAURANT, Rte. 9 Glenmont (3 miles south of Thruway Exit 23), 463-5130, offers traditional French cuisine in the informal setting of a charming colonial home. It is open for dinner only. Reservations are suggested. Open: T-Sat, 5-10.

CHEZ SOPHIE, 69 Caroline St Saratoga, 587-0440, presents exceptional French cuisine to patrons who have made reservations at least one day in advance. This is the restaurant to which lovers of the thoroughbreds flock in such great numbers that it is difficult to secure reservations during the racing season. Gourmands of the Capital District knowingly allow August visitors first call to the tables, at which they themselves can enjoy the same menu (at a lower price) when the horses head south. Open: Hours vary, so diners should call in advance.

CULINARY INSTITUTE OF AMERICA, Hyde Park, (914) 452-9600, is both a "point of interest" and a restaurant. It is, in fact, a vocational college where sixteen hundred full-time students study the arts of preparation and presentation of fine foods under a faculty of executive chefs. In two dining rooms the public may sample the end products of instruction. In the Escoffier Room, decorated in classical French motif, students present French cuisine; and in the lush red American Bounty Room, they serve regional American cooking. All menus are fixed price. Reservations are required, and it is advisable to make them as early as possible, especially when travel is easy, for people journey far to this renowned institution. The reservation line (914) 471-6608 operates M-F 9-5. Open: Escoffier Room T-Sat 12-1 for lunch, 6:30-8 for dinner; American Bounty Room T-Sat 11:30-1 for lunch, 6:30-8 for dinner. Directions: Thruway to Exit 18; east on Rte 299 to Rte 9W South; follow signs to Mid-Hudson Bridge; cross river and go north on Rte 9; Institute will be on the left.

DePUYS CANAL HOUSE, High Falls, (914) 687-7700, is charmingly situated in a stone house on a lock of the Delaware and Hudson Canal. The setting is outdone by the food, which can best be described as creative international cuisine. One may choose between an 8 course dinner or a 4 course dinner. Reservations are suggested for this popular little gem. Open: Winter F-Sat 5:30-10; Sun 11:30-1:30 for lunch and 3-8 for dinner; Summer same as winter plus Th 5:30-10. Directions: Thruway to Exit 19; Rte 209 South to Rte 213 to Highland Falls. Restaurant, a stone house with shutters, is marked by a small sign.

FEDERAL HOUSE INN, South Lee MA, (413) 243-1824, is considered to be one of the best restaurants in the Berkshires, a distinct honor considering the number of fine eating places which punctuate the area. The restaurant, set in a home built in 1824, specializes in European cuisine. Although three of the downstairs rooms serve as the dining area, it is advisable to make reservations in advance to avoid being disappointed. This inn offers seven rooms upstairs for visitors who will spend the night. Open: (Because hours change with the seasons, it is best to call before going.) Closed Tuesdays year round and Mondays January-April or May. Directions: I-90 East to Mass Pike; take Exit 2; go left and then right onto 102 East; proceed three miles; restaurant will be on right.

GIDEON PUTNAM HOTEL, Saratoga Spa State Park, 584-3000, has a handsome formal room for year round dining and a contemporary porch for summer service. This hotel offers a wide variety of foods. The restaurant proper presents a traditional menu. (Open: daily 12-2 for lunch; Sun-Th 6-9 and F-Sat 6-10 for dinner.) In July and August, the outside cafe offers light dining (Open: 11-11). The full facility is used for a popular Sunday brunch (Open: For reserved seating on the half hour from 11-2, with the last seating at 1:30). Directions: Northway (87) to Exit 13N; north on Rte 9; left into Saratoga State Park at sign.

L'AUBERGE, 351 Broadway Albany, 465-1111, housed in the former ticket office of the Hudson River Day Line, has long been a favorite classical French restaurant. As is often the case with this level of restaurant, the luncheon menu includes "plat du jour" specials at lower than dinner prices.

Reservations recommended. Open: M-F 12-2:30 for lunch; M-Sat 6:00-10 for dinner.

L'HOSTELLERIE BRESSANE, Hillsdale, 325-3412, is often pronounced the best French restaurant within a fifty mile radius of the Capital. Located in a charming 18th Century house in the center of the village, this "Country" French restaurant offers a sophisticated and extensive menu. The food is superb. Reservations are advised. No credit cards accepted. Open: April-May and Sept-Jan, W-F 6:30-9; Sat 5:30-9:30; Sun 4-8:30; June-Aug, T-Sat 5:30-9:30; Sun 4-8:30. Those wishing to stay over after their fine meal may take advantage of the fact that the name of this restaurant is literal; it is in fact an inn and offers lovely little rooms upstairs, complete with French breakfast. Of special note is that a cooking school is available four days a week except July and August. Directions: I-90 East to Thruway to Taconic Parkway; exit at Hillsdale; go south on Rte 23; restaurant will be on left.

LA GRIGLIA, Windham, 734-4499, was opened in 1976 by a family who had owned a restaurant for many years on Long Island. The chef, who comes from Trieste Italy, specializes in Northern Italian Renaissance dishes (dinner only). The atmosphere in the three dining rooms is best described as casually elegant. Open: Jan, Feb, July and August, daily 5-10:30; other months, W-Sun 5-10:30. Directions: Thruway to Exit 21; Rte 23 West to 296; left onto Rte 296; restaurant is 2/10 mile on right.

LA RIVE, Old King's Road, Catskill, 943-4888, is a French country restaurant that can best be described as comfortable, interesting, and well worth the effort of finding it. The menu varies from day to day, to take advantage of the freshest meats and fish available—and probably to respond to the whims of the owner-chef. Everything here, from the appetizers to the desserts, is prepared on the premises and presented with pride in the little rooms which form this restaurant. Open: Mother's Day through October, Tu-Sat 6-10; Sun 2-8:30. Directions: Thruway to Exit 21; follow signs for 9W South to 23A West; follow 23W over the Thruway; first left onto Old King's Road; go 1½ miles to sign on right for restaurant.

MOUNTAIN VILLA, Rte 7 outside Duanesburg, 895-8907, opened in 1981 and quietly became known in the area through word-of-mouth promotion. The cuisine is traditional French, with rich, smooth sauces accented with just the right amount of wine or brandy. The thoughtful, highly original presentations and the warm, tasteful decor have made this unpretentious restaurant a success. Reservations only. No credit cards. Open: W-Sat 6-closing; Sun 4-7. Directions: Rte 20 to Duanesburg; Rte 7 West six miles to Mountain Villa.

RED LION INN, Stockbridge MA, (413) 298-5545, offers several levels of dining—a formal dining room (in which a jacket and tie are required), a tavern, and an outside courtyard. All of them serve food which is quintessentially American. Situated in a large, rambling, meticulously cared for old inn on the square of this picturesque New England town, The Red Lion attracts people from far and near. For this reason, reservations are strongly recommended throughout the year. Open: M-Sat 12-2:15 for lunch; M-F 6-9 and Sat 5-10 for dinner; Sun 12-4 for brunch and 4-9 for dinner. In summer, a light menu is available from 2:15-4 and 10-11 pm. Directions: I-90 East to Mass Pike to Exit 2; Rte 102 South to Stockbridge.

SAM'S PLACE, Rte 9 in Malta, 587-5943, is a diner-with-a-difference. Delicious Italian food is served to the accompaniment of lucious Italian sounds—the voices of Luciano Pavarotti and Frank Sinatra. Waiters clad in black pants, suspenders, and bow ties carry house specialties to patrons seated in booths (or at tables in the "back room"). The menu varies considerably, and many regulars suggest just going with what the chef recommends. Apparently that act of trust will make the meal—always fresh and zesty—even better. An amusing touch in summer is the availability of valet parking. Open: Hours vary so it's best to call. **Note:** A fire in August 1985 temporarily closed this restaurant.

VAN DYCK RESTAURANT, 237 Union St Schenectady, 374-2406, has a long-standing reputation for fine food served with a background of superior music—first rate live jazz played Friday and Saturday evenings. This restaurant is also excellent value for lunch, with many of the dinner specials offered at a reduced price. Open: M-Sat 11:30-4 for lunch; M 5-11, Tu-Th 5-12, F-Sat 5-12:30 for dinner; Sun 11-3 for brunch, 12-9 for dinner.

THE MODERATELY PRICED

ADELPHI HOTEL, 365 Broadway, Saratoga, 587-4688, is a fascinating place—a vintage Saratoga garden cafe housed in the original building, an old Saratoga Hotel. The furnishings are laden with tassels, and willowy palms decorate the lobby, the overall effect being that one has stepped back decades. It sometimes seems that the guests have entered the spirit of the place, their costumes, their posture, and even their gestures appearing Edwardian. It is very popular as a stop for soup, sandwiches and dessert in summer after an evening at SPAC. Open: July and August W-Sun 11 am-2 am.

BALSAM HOUSE, Friends Lake, 494-2828 or 494-4431, is an elegant old white frame country inn offering country French cuisine. It is a popular spot, especially in summer, so reservations are recommended. Open: M-Sat 6-9; Sun 11-3 for brunch, 5-8:30 for dinner. In summer, a lunch is presented 11-3. Directions: Northway (87) to Exit 23 (Warrensburg); Rte 9N four miles to Rte 28 (on the left); Rte 28 for three miles to Potterbrook Rd (on the right); four miles on Potterbrook; Balsam House will be on the left, with parking on the right.

BARNSIDER, Colonie Center, 459-6161, is all that a steak house should be: the decor is ruggedly honest, and the beef is the best there is. The lunch, served in the bar, features huge, juicy charcoal broiled hamburgers, hearty soups, and salads. The dinner menu offers various steaks and chops, all cooked to the specifications of the diner. No reservations are accepted. Open: M-Sat 11:30-2 for lunch; M-F 5-10; Sat 5-11; Sun 4-9 for dinner.

THE BEAR'S, Rte 7 outside of Duanesburg, 895-2509, is not even listed in the phone book. Those who love food—especialy beef—have ferreted it out, however, and that seems to be what owner Robert Payne wants, customers who love food enough to seek it out. Prime beef is served in enormous portions, accompanied by delicious homemade soups and desserts. Directions: Rte 20 to Rte 7 West in Duanesburg. Restaurant is not far along Rte 7 in colonial house on right hand side. Open: T-Sat 5-8.

BEEKMAN ARMS, Rhinebeck, (914) 876-7077, is a charming old hotel which has proffered rooms and fine food to travelers since 1700. The owners have succeeded in retaining the colonial ambiance of this coach house in the decor and the service. With some advance notice, the restaurant happily accommodates small groups, so this is a pleasant place to rendezvous with friends coming up from New York or over from New England. Because this is a full service hotel, the dining room is open much of the day. The specific hours are these: Daily 8-10 for breakfast, 11:30-3 for lunch; M-F 3-5 for light meals; M-Sat 5-10, Sun 3-9 for dinner; Sun 10-2 for brunch. Directions: Rte 9 to Rhinebeck; hotel is at junction of Rtes 9 and 308.

BEVERWYCK, 275 Lark St. Albany, 472-9043, offers a wide variety of luncheon dishes and full continental dining in tastefully decorated rooms in a renovated 1885 commercial building. Here, in the heart of the restoration area in Albany, customers can huddle beside a warm fireplace on wintry evenings or eat on an outdoor patio when the weather turns fine. Reservations are requested. Open: M-F 11:30-2:30 for lunch: M-Th 6-10:30, F-Sat 6-11 for dinner; Sun 11-3 for brunch, 5-9:30 for dinner.

BOAT SLIP, 258 Lark St Albany, 436-7704, is a fresh fish restaurant also featuring prime ribs and steak. Situated in the former Carp's Tavern, the Boat Slip has retained that restaurant's loyal clientele and developed a strongly enthusiastic following of its own. Live music also makes the bar a local attraction. Open: Restaurant, M-Th 11:30-11; F-Sat 11:30-12; Sun 12-10; Bar till 4 am, with late night dining till 1 am.

BUTCHER BLOCK, 1632A Central Ave Colonie (¾ mile west of Northway), 456-1653, is a steak and seafood house with a traditional menu augmented by a soup and salad bar and a good selection of sandwiches. In addition to the principal rooms decorated in rustic brick and barnsiding, there is a solarium filled with plants. Open: M-F 11:30-2:30 for lunch; M-Th 5-10:30, F-Sat 5-11, Sun 5-9 for dinner.

CAFFE ITALIA RISTORANTE, 662 Central Ave Albany, 482-9433, is a perennial nominee in the perpetual debate about "Best Italian Restaurant." It has become such a favorite among itinerant legislators during lawmaking sessions that many menu items claim legislative "sponsors." It truly merits their attention. The selection blends traditional with original fare, and selections are well-spiced and tasty. Because all entrees are made to order, this restaurant is best when there is no need to rush. Open: M-Sat 5-11.

CASINO, 453 Washington Ave Albany, 463-9369, is a small Italian-American restaurant which serves excellent food (dinner only) from a sophisticated menu. It is busy on weekends and patrons often must wait. Open: W-Sun 5:30-1. Vacation in the summer months.

CAPE HOUSE, 254 Broadway Troy, 274-0168 or 274-0167, is a new seafood restaurant in the recently rehabilitated Keenan Building in downtown Troy. The menu includes a clam and oyster bar as well as choice seafood items. Open: M-F 11:30-3 for lunch; M-Th 5-10, F-Sat 5-11 for dinner. Raw Bar open M-Th 11:30-midnight, F 11:30-1; Sat 5-1.

CENTURY HOUSE, Rte 9 Latham (One mile north of Latham Circle), 785-0834, is the architypical American family restaurant. Dinner is preceded by relish trays and warm rolls, the menu offers foods similar to those prepared at home, and the portions are substantial. The restaurant has expanded recently to accommodate hundreds of diners. It is a popular spot, especially on those holidays when families traditionally dine out. Open: M-F 11-3 for lunch; M-Th 4-9:45, F-Sat 4-10:45, Sun 1-9 for dinner.

CHEZ NICOLE, 1 Mill Lane Schenectady, 382-9784, is an excellent French restaurant in an historic area of Schenectady's downtown. The menu is extensive, imaginative, and varied, and the prices are reasonable—especially considering the quality of food presented. It is wise to call for specific directions to this restaurant. Open: T-Sat 5-10, Sun 4-9.

COCO'S RESTAURANT, 1470 Western Ave Albany, 456-0297, is as much a place of entertainment as a restaurant, and most of its patrons go as much to have fun as to eat. Drinks come in unusual glasses, balloons sprout from plates of food, waiters burst into song, and the clientele—men, women, and children—chatter and laugh. The sprightly decorations seem to put people in a jovial mood. The menu is varied, with a dramatic salad bar (offering enough to make a meal for even the most hearty eater) open to all. Open: M-F 11-3 for lunch, 4:30-1 for dinner; Sat-Sun 12-1 am.

THE CRANBERRY BOG, 56 Wolf Rd Colonie, 459-5110, has become a lively point of convergence for a variety of folk. It is really almost two places—a restaurant and a tavern/lounge. The restaurant, with seafood, veal, steaks, prime ribs and lighter foods, appeals to families and business persons; the greenhouse and patio lounge, with light food and exotic drinks, attracts young couples and singles. On summer evenings in particular, the patio

Cranberry Bog, Colonie
Michael Fredericks, Jr.

fills as offices empty. Restaurant open: M-Sat 11:30-2:30 for lunch; M-F 5-10, Sat 5-11 for dinner; Sun 11:30-3 for brunch and 4-9 for dinner. Lounge and patio open: Sun-Tu 11:30-2 am, W-Sat 11:30-4 am.

FANNIES, 472 Troy Schenectady Rd Latham, 785-5404, presents depth and breadth in its menu of Italian specialties. This restaurant is probably best described as mellow and confident, an eminently comfortable place to dine. Open: M-Th 11:30-2 for lunch; M-Sat 5-11, Sun 5-9 for dinner.

GREGORY HOUSE COUNTRY INN AND RESTAURANT, Averill Park, 674-3774, sits inconspicuously beside the road in a red colonial home. The menu features continental cuisine. There are twelve rooms available for guests. Open: Tu-Sat 5-10; Sun 1-8. Directions: I-90 East to Exit 7; left at end of ramp onto Washington Ave; cross Rte 4 to Rte 43 to Averill Park (about 10 miles). Restaurant is on left just past blinking light.

HIRO'S JAPANESE RESTAURANT, 1933 Central Ave Colonie, 456-1180, specializes in two types of Japanese cooking—tabletop, in which pre-sliced meat, vegetables and fish are tossed quickly on a hot surface set in the table, and tempura, in which food dipped in batter is deep fried. Watching Hiro's experienced tableside chefs slice, mince, stir with consummate dexterity and astounding speed provides unexpected entertainment. The tables at Hiro's seat eight, and the management tries to fill the tables before the chef begins preparation, so those who do not like taking their luck with strangers should try to make up a party of seven or eight. Open: Tu-F 12-1 for lunch, 5-10 for dinner; Sat 3-10:30; Sun 3-10.

HORSE BARN RESTAURANT, Beresford Farms, Chadwick Rd Delanson, 895-2346, operates in the upper floor of the old barn which also serves as the lodge of this small four season resort. It is the perfect place for a hearty country dinner after a day of working the trails. Open: F 5-9; Sat 5-10; Sun 10-8. (When cross country skiing is good, open every day 10-8.)

HUNAN, 1094 Madison Ave Albany, 489-6966, as the name suggests, serves firey Hunan food. For the less daring, the menu includes Szechuan, Mandarin, and Cantonese selections. This relatively new restaurant, decorated in a low key contemporary style, has quickly become one of the busiest and most popular Chinese restaurants in the region. Take out orders are welcome. Open: Sun-Th 11-11; F-Sat 11-midnight.

ITALIAN AMERICAN COMMUNITY CENTER, Washington Avenue Ext. Albany, 456-0292, has become a very popular place to eat because of quality, service, and price. Set in a building designed as a meeting and recreational facility for members only, various rooms are open to the public both as dining rooms and banquet centers. The restaurant is open to the public for both lunch and dinner. Open: M-F 11:30-2:30 for lunch; M-Sat 5-10, Sun 2-9:30 for dinner.

JACK'S OYSTER HOUSE, 42 State St Albany, 465-8854, the oldest restaurant in downtown Albany, has been pleasing residents, travelers, legislators, and visiting dignitaries for over 70 years. Clients sitting in booths or at small tables can study photographs and drawings depicting the 300 years of the life of the city. The extensive menu features seafood, steak, and chops. Excellent service by attentive waiters (all of whom are particularly good with children) has been a characteristic of this restaurant since its founding. Open: Daily 11:30-10:00.

JOE'S RESTAURANT, 851 Madison Ave Albany, 489-4062, is an old Albany standby recently re-opened with new management but the old menu. Most Albany residents hope the attempted reincarnation is a success, for this American Kosher Deli and restaurant always made the best sandwiches, cheesecake, and chocolate cream pie in town. (The dinner specials were also excellent.) Open: T-Th 11-10, F-Sat 11-11; Sun 11-10.

LA SERRE, 14 Green St Albany, 463-6056, serves French-Continental cuisine in a building which formerly housed Green's Stationery Store. The main room, with its many potted plants, is intentionally decorated to resemble a flourishing greenhouse. A pleasant outdoor terrace is open for cocktails in summer. Open: M-F 11:30-2:30 for lunch; M-Th 6-10 and F-Sat 6-10:30 for dinner.

LILLIAN'S, 408 Broadway Saratoga, 587-7766, is a charming, beloved old-timer. The interior is warm and inviting, and the food, traditional American fare (seafood, steak sandwiches and the like) is very good. This restaurant is owned by the same family that operates Thacher's in Albany. Open: M-Sat 11-4 for lunch; M-Th 5-10, F-Sat 5-11 for dinner. Late night menu 10-12 weekdays, 11-1 weekends.

LOBSTER POUND, Rte 9 Latham, 785-0061, serves delicious meals. As the name implies, lobster and seafood, all very well prepared, dominate the menu, but the steaks, chops, and other items are also available. Many area residents who are not confined to an office during the day order luncheon specials and consider that the main meal for the day. Open: M-Th 11:30-9; F-Sat 11:30-10; Sun 12:30-9. (In summer the restaurant is open one half hour later and offers lighter meals—omelets, salads, and sandwiches.)

LOMBARDO'S, 121 Madison Ave Albany, 462-9180, established in 1916, has, as the saying goes, "seen it all." The restaurant, built in the midst of the Italian neighborhood, barely survived the massive demolition which preceded construction of the Empire State Plaza, and now finds itself sitting beside the Pastures, one of the most exciting urban restoration efforts attempted in this region. This port-in-a-storm has persisted, offering a solid, traditional Italian menu throughout, the rich sauce seeming never to vary from day to day no matter what is going up or coming down in the immediate vicinity. Open: W-Sun 11-9.

MERRILL MAGEE HOUSE, Warrensburg, 623-2449, was, until recently, a private estate. Now, in this Greek Revival home surrounded by extensive lawns and picket fences, the proprietors serve freshly prepared, carefully cooked food with an emphasis on American selections. Open: T-Sun 11-2:30 for lunch, 5:30-9 for dinner; Sunday Brunch 10:30-2. (In July and August the restaurant is open seven days a week.) Bed and breakfast accommodations are available within the house. Directions: Northway (87) to Exit 23; follow signs to Warrensburg. House is on town's main thoroughfare.

MICHELE DA VERONA, 1192 Western Ave Albany, 482-0345, is a welcome addition to the Capital District. Opened in early 1984 in a converted two-family home opposite SUNYA, the pleasant, simple decor and delicately spiced Italian foods have made it popular at lunch and dinner. The glassed-in porch on the main floor, which gives a view of the University and the activities of McKownville, is complemented in summer by a pleasant upper deck. Open: M-F 11:30-3 for lunch; M-Th 5-10:30, F-Sat 5-11 for dinner.

MRS. LONDON'S, 33 Phila St Saratoga, 584-6633, opened in 1979 as a patisserie featuring exquisite, rich French baked goods. It subsequently added a small dining area offering a few choice items for breakfast, lunch and dinner. Because the restaurant responds somewhat to seasonal demand, it is best to inquire about what meals they will serve on a particular day.

OGDEN'S, Howard St at Lodge, Albany, 463-6605, opened in 1977 as an experiment in innovative re-use of an architecturally interesting building, has been a great success from the beginning. The decor, with wood, brass, potted plants, and dramatic wall hangings, underscores the restaurant's urbane, sophisticated atmosphere. In pleasant weather, a spacious outside deck accommodates additional diners. The menu is interesting, the food excellent. Especially of interest is the chocolate velvet pie, renowned in the Capital District for its richness. Open: M-F 11:30-3:00 for lunch, 3:30-5:30 for cafe menu; M-Sat 5:30-10 for dinner.

OLDE BRYAN INN, 123 Maple Ave Saratoga, 587-9741, serves "starters," light foods, sandwiches, and entrees all day. The restaurant is housed on a site which first served as an inn in 1773. Present owners are working to restore the building. Open: Daily 11:30-midnight.

OLD DALEY INN, 499 Second Ave North Troy, 235-2656, is a family run restaurant noted for prime ribs and crab legs served in generous portions. The building, dating to 1771, has been, for most of those years, an inn, a tavern, and a restaurant. The lunch menu includes salads and sandwiches as well as full meals. Open: Tu-F 11-2:30 for lunch; Tu-Th 5-9, F-Sat 5-11, Sun 2-9 for dinner.

OLD JOURNEY'S END, Rte 43 West Sand Lake, 674-2701, is convenient to many corners of the Capital District. Fifteen minutes from Exit 7 of I-90, the restaurant draws its patrons from all directions. The dining rooms, situated on the first floor of an old colonial home, are best described as sprightly, with bright green accessories and countless plants creating an impression of an arboretum in mid summer. The cuisine is continental, and the servings are substantial. Open: M-Th 5-9; F-Sat 5-9:30; Sun 11-2 for brunch, 2-8 for dinner.

P.D. LADD'S, 32 Dove St Albany, 463-9382, has stood for many years at the corner of State Street, its distinctive awning serving to unite—at least symbolically—the residential and business communities in the downtown area. The offerings for lunch and dinner are international, with ever-changing daily specials. A cafe menu is available into the wee hours. The outdoor cafe, one of the first in the area, remains one of the most handsome and the one best situated for interesting viewing. Open: M-Sat 12-10 for full meals, with light menu available until closing.

PEKING RESTAURANT, 1100 Madison Ave Albany, 489-0606, is owned and operated by Tony Pak, a chef with 45 years of experience. This was the first restaurant to introduce northern spicey Chinese cuisine into Albany. The menu includes Hunan, Szechuan, Mandarin and Cantonese cooking as well as house specialties. (Take out option available.) Open: Sun-Th 11:30-10; F-Sat 11:30-11.

PLUM BLOSSON, 685 Hoosick St Troy, 272-0036, presents an extraordinarily comprehensive menu of Szechuan, Hunan, Cantonese, and Mandarin cuisine, including some of the hot and spicy dishes which have been becoming more popular in the Capital District in recent years. Open: M-Th 11-11; F-Sat 11-11:30; Sun noon to 10:30.

PUMPKIN PATCH, 901 McClellan St Schenectady, 393-2186, is one of the most popular restaurants in the Electric City. The menu features creole cooking, steaks and seafood. The atmosphere is lively. Open: M-Th 5-10; F-Sat 5-11; Sun 4-9.

QUACKENBUSH HOUSE RESTAURANT, Quackenbush Square and Broadway Albany, 465-0909, is located in one of the oldest houses in the city. The restoration, which has been simply and tastefully done, allows clients to sit in small, quiet rooms. For this reason, it appears to be an excellent spot for the serious business lunch or for the intimate dinner with friends. The menu, presenting traditional continental fare, is varied, and service is pleasant. Open: M-F 11:30-3 for lunch; M-Sat 5-10 for dinner; Sun 4-9.

QUALTERS' PINE HILLS RESTAURANT, 1108 Madison Ave Albany, 489-8859, is a wonderful place. It is run by a man who, after years of high school teaching, decided to pursue a long-standing dream. He started a modest neighborhood coffee shop open for breakfast and lunch only. He soon gained a city-wide reputation for excellent omelets, fair prices, and friendly service. As lines literally began to form on the sidewalk, he remodeled,

adding a few tables and a few items to the menu but retaining the quality
and friendliness. Recently he and his wife, who supervises the front rooms,
have added dinner hours. Now the daily menu includes the same omelets
and sandwiches (served on homemade breads), but there is also a fish of
the day for lunch, and the dinner menu includes delicately seasoned pasta,
veal, steak and chicken. Open: M-F 7-3, Sat 7:30-2, Sun 8 am-10 am for
light meals; W-Sat 5:30-10 for dinner.

SARATOGA FLAT TRACK invites patrons to breakfast in the clubhouse area
during morning workout. Breakfast is served 7-9 (except Tuesday) during
the racing season.

SASSY SWEDE, 5 Bridge Ave Cohoes, 235-9829, an attractive restaurant
with Scandanavian decor and international menu, provides refuge for
spent shoppers, weary after an intense quest for bargains among Cohoes
specialty outlets. In fact, to counteract withdrawal symptoms, Sassy Swede
has incorporated its own little gift shop into the restaurant. Open:
T-F 11:30-2 for lunch; Th-Sat 5-9 for dinner.

THE SCRIMSHAW, Americana Inn, 660 Albany Shaker Road Colonie,
869-8100, offers a setting unusual in this area—Colonial Williamsburg

decor with a homelike atmosphere. It specializes in seafood, steak, and veal. The food is excellent. A pianist plays background music nightly in this comfortable, low-key, first rate restaurant. Jackets and suitable attire are required in the evening. Reservations are recommended. Open: M-F 11:30-2 for lunch; M-Sun 5:30-10 for dinner.

THE SHIPYARD, 1171 Troy Schenectady Rd Latham, 785-1711, has become an area favorite, especially at lunch. The restaurant is set in the warm, inviting interior of an old Shaker house. The menu is varied: lunch includes seafood, fresh cheese and fruit platters, and sandwiches; dinner includes a full range of Continental cuisine. Open: M-F 11:30-12; Sat 6 pm-1 am.

SIGN OF THE TREE, Empire State Plaza Albany, 436-1022, commands the most wonderful view of the city and the plaza of any restaurant in town. In good weather patrons may dine on the outside terrace overlooking the riverfront. The decor is simple but elegant, and the food is very good. Because the restaurant functions primarily during the week, it is available for private parties on nights and weekends. Open: M-F 11:30-2:30 for lunch, 11:30-6:30 for cocktails.

SITAR INDIAN RESTAURANT, 1929 Central Ave Colonie, 456-6670, has an open Tandoor, a deep stone furnace at which a skilled chef prepares different foods, from breads to kabobs. At this restaurant, patrons may watch the agile chef at work. The foods are prepared for those who prefer mild spicing, but patrons are encouraged to request more spices if they prefer Indian food hot. Open: Tu-F 11:30-2 for lunch; Tu-Sun 5-10 for dinner; Sun 12-3 for brunch.

SMITHS RESTAURANT, 171 Remsen St Cohoes, 237-9809, consists of two parts—a long, wide barroom and a dark-paneled dining room. What makes this place appealing (in addition to good food) is that it seems as much like a movie set as a real place. It so represents the times in which it flourished as premier meeting spot for politicians and other wielders of power that one can easily summon images of the past. Open: M-Sat 11:30-2:30 for lunch; M-Th 5-9, F-Sat 5-10 for dinner.

SUGI, 1579 State St Schenectady, 374-4858, once a small diner, now functions as an authentic Japanese restaurant featuring sukiyaki, tempura, teriyaki and a sushi bar. Open: Tu-F noon-2:00 for lunch; Sun-Th 5-10, F-Sat 5-11 for dinner.

THACHERS, 272 Delaware Ave Albany, 465-0115, is a cozy, casual restaurant serving American food. Steak, seafood, and sandwiches are specialties at this thoughtful restaurant whose waitresses respond to customer needs— speeding orders for those pressed for time, respecting the privacy of those who wish to dally. Open: M-F 11:30-3 for lunch; M-F 5-10; Sat 5-11 for dinner.

TRUFFLES SUPPER CLUB in Albany Hilton, 462-6611,is an elegant spot for dinner and dancing. The atmosphere is formal (jackets are required of men), and service is abundant. Cuisine is "continental with an accent on the French." Reservations recommended. Open M-Sat 6-10 for dinner; Sun 11-3 for brunch.

UNLIMITED FEAST, 340 Hamilton St Albany, 463-6223, began, like **THE FINISHING TOUCH** in Troy, primarily as a catering and gourmet take-out shop. It has subsequently added a dining area and acquired an enthusiastic following. (In warm weather the outdoor patio increases the in-house capacity.) The menu features unusual selections—inventive uses of spices and herbs, and unique combinations of foods. Everything, including the breads and desserts, is made by the restaurant chefs. Open: M-Sat 11:30-3 for lunch; Th-Sat 5-9 for dinner. (The shop, which is described in greater length elsewhere in this book, is open M-F 10:30-6:30; Sat 10:30-5.)

VERDILE'S, 572 2nd Ave Lansingburgh, 235-8879, has long been one of North Troy's treasures. The menu at this family-run Italian restaurant includes all the traditional favorites. The pleasantness of the dining room and the consistency with which the kitchen presents fine meals make Verdile's the first choice of many area families. Open: M-Th 11:30-10; F-Sat 11:30-11; Sun noon-9.

YATES STREET, 492 Yates St Albany, 438-2012, is located in an older building—complete with pressed tin ceilings and a handsome paneled bar—which has functioned as both neighborhood tavern and steadfast restaurant since 1923. Under new owners, this restaurant (formerly Hilary's) presents delicately spiced, carefully prepared selections, many of them cooked over mesquite. Open: M-Th 6-10:30; F-Sat 6-11:30.

THE LESS EXPENSIVE

CAVALERI RESTAURANT, 334 2nd St Albany, 463-9047, is indisputably the most popular neighborhood Italian restaurant in the region. On any day, cars line the curbs for blocks around, and patrons patiently await seating. The secret of this success is twofold—well-seasoned Italian fare and abundant servings. (Everyone leaves Cavaleri with "doggie bags" filled.) Open: W-Sun 4-12.

CHINA GARDEN, 1028 State St Schenectady, 370-0160, has served Mandarin, Szechuan, Cantonese, and Hunan specialties in the Capital District for over ten years. Included on the menu are area exclusives—sizzling rice soup and fresh sea bass, for example. Open: M-W-Th-Sun 11:30-10; F-Sat 11:30-11.

CLAY'S, Sand Creek Road just off Wolf Rd in Colonie, 459-2696, is a small, clean, cafeteria-style restaurant which specializes in fish and seafood. Its casual atmosphere and solid fare make it a favorite with families. Take-out orders are prepared, and uncooked fresh fish is for sale. Open: M-Sat 11-10; Sun 12-9.

THE DELI WORKS, 855 Central Ave Albany, 489-7953, is a deli-restaurant situated in the space once occupied by The Shanghai. Its menu ranges from standard delicatessen fare to steaks and ribs. Prices at this efficient, cordial, all-purpose restaurant are very reasonable. Open: M-F 6:30 am to 11; Sat 10 am-11 pm; Sun noon-10.

EL LOCO MEXICAN CAFE, 465 Madison Ave Albany, 436-1855, offers interesting presentations of Tex-Mex and traditional Mexican food: hearty chili is served in a bowl fashioned from a tortilla, for example. Mexican and other imported beers and wines are available. The restaurant proper, small and cozy, expands onto a pleasant patio. On Sunday evenings, musicians of the international folk tradition perform. Open: W-F 11:25-4 for lunch; T-Th 4-10, F-Sun 4-11 for dinner.

GERSHORN'S DELICATESSEN, 1600 Union St Schenectady, 393-0617, is proclaimed by displaced New Yorkers (deli connoisseurs par excellence) to be the premier delicatessen in the area. Its salads, sandwiches, spreads and such are the choice for many gatherings. Seating is very limited, and much of the food is made to be carried out or to be catered. Open: M-F 7-7; Sat 7-5; Sun 7-1 (counter only).

THE GINGER MAN, 234 Western Ave Albany, 463-9253, serves from a menu of light meals—quiches, omelets, soups, hot sandwiches, and daily entree specials—served to accompany a beverage chosen from a list of 55 wines and 37 beers. One particularly popular item is a cheese board—a selection of well aged, appropriately chilled cheeses and fresh fruits. The interior, a pleasant combination of urban and rustic touches, is very welcoming. Mike Byron, who runs the successful Washington Tavern not many doors away, oversees this cafe. Open: M-F 11:30-2:30 for lunch; M-Th 4:30-11:30, F-Sat 4:30-12:30 for dinner; between and after meals and M-Th till 1 and F-Sat till 2 for cocktails.

H.P. MULLIGAN'S, 112 Wolf Rd Colonie, 458-7300, has a menu which includes unusual finger foods (fried mozarella sticks, potato skins, and the like) interesting sandwiches, and unique combinations of cuisines. It caters to a mixed clientele, with families and young couples equally comfortable. Open: M-Th 11:30 am to midnight; F-Sat 11:30-1 am; Sun 12-11.

HATTIES CHICKEN SHACK AND RESTAURANT, 45 Phila St Saratoga, 584-4790, is famous among its devotees for simple food, the specialty being Southern Fried Chicken. The interior of this restaurant is basic, so when scores of patient fans line the sidewalks in August, one knows that surely something special must be coming their way from inside. Open: Daily 11-3; 4-9. (In August, 8 am to 1 am.)

Siena College.

FOR A CAPITAL EDUCATION.

We share in the stimulating environment of the Capital Region, and bring to it an exciting dimension of our own. We're Siena College, 2600 students and 150 professors strong, and committed to quality Undergraduate education.

Siena offers a wide variety of academic programs in the arts, sciences and business, emphasizing the critical thinking and problem-solving abilities so vital to success in today's world.

With tuition, room and board charges of well under $10,000, Siena is among the select group of colleges in 'The Best Buys in College Education,' by Edward B. Fiske, Education Editor of The New York Times.

We also offer outstanding opportunities in Continuing Education, including several evening degree programs.

Financial aid is available from a variety of sources.

Siena College has plans for your future! For a campus visit and personal interview, phone (518) 783-2423.

Loudonville, New York

HOLMES AND WATSON, 450 Broadway Troy, 272-8526, is a great pub. It offers patrons a choice of 54 kinds of beer as well as a good selection of soups, sandwiches, salads, and desserts. In terms of both atmosphere and nourishment, this is probably the closest approximation to a traditional English pub one can find in the area. Open: Daily 11 am-2 am; Sunday brunch 11:30-3.

HUDSON RIVER TRADING CO., 388 Broadway Albany, 465-8782, serves good American food from an all-day menu to which specials are added at dinner time. The interior of the old building blends brick and wood in a casual decor. The clientele is mixed in age and style. Open: M-Th 11-11; F-Sat 11 am-1 am.

ITALIA, 24 4th St Troy, 273-8773, is a bar, a restaurant, and a top-rated jazz club. Located in a newly restored building in downtown, with an interior decorated with etched glass and the work of local artists, Italia is a friendly, casual place. This family business, which began as a pizza parlor on Congress St, offers very good service and a solid menu of traditional Italian fare and house specialties. Open: M-Th 11-10; F-Sat 11-12; Sun 2-10. (It is best to call in advance for information about live music.)

JACK'S CHINESE AND AMERICAN RESTAURANT, 1881 Central Ave Colonie, 456-5588, usually takes its first time customers by surprise. The idea of a Chinese restaurant attached to a motel along Rte 5 does not hold much promise. Jack's comes through, however. The menu is extensive (including the column A, column B, column C routine which stand-up comics have made famous), and the food is good. In fact, many people form a group to go to Jacks and make their own smorgasbord of Cantonese entrees. Take out orders are available. Open: Daily 11-11.

LUNCHEON GALLERY, Albany Institute of History and Art, 125 Washington Ave Albany, 463-4478, is run by volunteers as a service to the Institute. It features soups, light lunches, and select desserts made by members. Open: Mid-Sept to end of May, Tu-F 11:30-1:30.

McGEARY'S, 4 Clinton Square Albany, 463-1455, is a warmly welcoming neighborhood tavern with good pub food. See McGeary's Eldorado below for specific information about menu and opening hours.

McGEARY'S ELDORADO, 121 4th St Troy, 272-4403, is a recently redecorated restaurant in an old Troy hotel, owned and run by the people who run McGeary's Restaurant in Albany. Both of these homey pubs have loyal patrons who return repeatedly for the comfortable atmosphere and simple food. The chicken wings are a particular favorite. The menu and the hours of opening are the same for both. Open: M-Th 11:30-midnight; F-Sat 11:30-1.

PARC V CAFE CABARET, 661 Albany Shaker Rd Colonie, 869-9976, is a lively, "upscale" eating spot popular at all times. The extensive menu of light foods (soups, salads, sandwiches, omelets, and snacks) is available through-out the day and evening. The bar draws a young professional crowd. Open: M-Th 11-1; F-Sat 11-2; Sun 12-12.

ROMA APPIAN WAY, 1839 Van Vranken Ave Schenectady, 370-4030, is run by a family whose members say about themselves, "We care about people and we love to cook." This explains why the restaurant is so successful. The menu, service, and atmosphere show thoughtful concern for the comfort and pleasure of the patron. Open: W-M 11:30-2 for lunch, 5-10 for dinner.

SOUTH END TAVERN, 757 Burden Ave Troy, 272-9661, (sometimes called Patty Burke's) is a Troy institution. This family-run business has served family fare in a friendly, no frills atmosphere for over 50 years. Third generations of area residents come to take advantage of the immutable daily specials—the Thursday corned beef and the Friday fish dinner being among the most popular. Open: 11 am-midnight.

YIP'S, 117 Columbia Turnpike, (Rtes 9 & 20) Rensselaer, 449-2030, special-izes in Cantonese food in the finest tradition of oriental style cooking. Open: M-F 11-11; Sat 11:30-11; Sun 12-11.

YORKSTONE PUB, 78 North Pearl St Albany, 462-9033, offers pub food—burgers, soups, sandwiches, salads. Accustomed to the whimsy or impa-tience or weight-consciousness of its downtown crowd, Yorkstone was one of the first area restaurants to offer a meal of a cup of soup and half a sandwich. Kitchen open: M 11:30-10; T-Sat 11:30-1.

SPECIAL POCKET PLEASERS

A FRAME, 1135 Central Ave Albany, 459-9038, makes great sandwiches. Specialities are burgers, and regular or triple-decker sandwiches. Open: M-Sat 11-1 am.

BAR-B-Q BILLY'S, 202-204 Northern Blvd Albany, 463-3457, prepares take-out foods from a menu including ribs and chicken smoked on the prem-ises, chopped barbeque sandwiches, fried chicken, shrimp, fish, and chicken nuggets. Open: M-W 11-10; Th-Sat 11-12.

BRUEGGERS BAGEL BAKERY, 55 Congress St Troy and Stuyvesant Plaza Albany, serves hearty fresh soups and imaginative bagel sandwiches. Open: in Troy, M-Sat 7-7, Sun 7-3; in Albany, M-F 7-9, Sat 7-6, Sun 7-5.

CAPITAL PARK AT NOON, Albany, abounds in vendors who sell a wide variety of food, from hot dogs to quiche.

DUNCAN'S DAIRY BAR, 890 Hoosick St (Rte 7) Troy, 279-9985, has been a family business since 1939 when Mr. Duncan began selling ice cream cones and milk shakes. After the war, the family expanded the menu to include full meals. Also on the menu are homemade buns, muffins, pies, and breads. As the open hours show, Duncan's caters to everyone—from night shift workers returning home and farm laborers getting a jump on the day to school children, travelers and professionals. Open: March-Jan 1, 3 am to 9 pm.

THE FINISHING TOUCH BY PITTS AND PITTS, 461 Broadway Troy, 271-1555, is really a gourmet-to-go shop with a few tables for those who wish to eat at the store (or at the outside cafe during the warm weather). The menu changes daily, but pasta salads, tasty soups, croissant sandwiches, quiche, and interesting desserts are constants. Catering menus are available. These are described more fully in the food section of the shopping chapter. Open: M-Sat 9-6.

OZZIE'S, 423 Madison Ave Albany, 465-6525, is a zany place: its ornamentation includes such things as neon lights, porcelain-topped tables, and a functioning jukebox. It is best known for its specialty omelets, deli sandwiches, and fish steak burgers. Open: M-Th 7 am-midnight; F-Sat 7 am-2 am; Sun 7 am-11 pm.

PASTA EXPRESS, 304 Lark St Albany, 449-8973, offers gourmet Italian fast food to take out or eat in. The chefs make their own pasta and sauces, gladly putting up special orders for large parties. Open: M-Th 11:30-10; F-Sat 11:30-11.

PIZZA RESTAURANTS
Recommending pizza is almost impossible, for people are passionate about such issues as the appropriate degree of spiciness and quantity of sauce, the proportion of cheese to sauce, and the texture of the crust. Below is a list of what a heterogeneous "committee" of pizza lovers considers the best pizza in the Capital District.

> **CITONE'S**
> 457 Elk St Albany 462-9116
> **FANNIES PIZZA AND CLAM BAR**
> 187 Old Loudon Rd Latham 785-1232
> **FIRESIDE PIZZERIA**
> 1631 Eastern Parkway Schenectady . . . 382-1616
> **JG'S PIZZA**
> 195 Lark St Albany 465-1922
> **KNOTTY PINE TAVERN**
> 2301 15th St Troy . . . . . . 272-4557 or 272-9383
> **MADISON GRILL**
> 331 Madison Ave Albany 434-1938
> **PURPLE PUB**
> 50 Cohoes Rd Watervliet 273-9646

RED FRONT RESTAURANT AND TAVERN
71 Division St Troy 272-9241
RIVER ROAD CAFE
2850 River Rd Schenectady 374-8357
SAM'S
125 Southern Blvd Albany 463-3433

QUALTER'S PINE HILLS RESTAURANT, described in full with the moderately expensive restaurants, also has wonderful inexpensive offerings.

QUINTESSENCE, 11 New Scotland Ave Albany, 434-8186, offers simple food from a limited menu in the entertaining surroundings of a converted Art Deco diner. The offerings are soups, salads, and charbroil specialties. Open: M-Sat 11:30-2 am; Sun 12-2 am. Bar closes at 4 am.

SCUBBER'S INC, 465 River St Troy, 271-0368, calls itself "Capitaland's Home of Buffalo Style Wings," and that may in fact be accurate. Although several pubs serve excellent wings, no one else seems to offer so many varieties—from mild to "atomic." Take out orders are made up from 10 to 80 pieces, all with celery and blue cheese dressing. Open: 11-9 daily.

SPIAK'S, Archibald St and Rte 32 Watervliet, 273-9796, is a wonderful neighborhood Italian restaurant serving good, inexpensive food—Italian specialties, seafood, chops, and daily specials. A children's menu is available. Open: M-Sat 11:30-12:30.

STRAWBERRY LANE, Mill Lane (off State St) Schenectady, 346-8345, is an intimate luncheon spot literally tucked into Schenectady's downtown area. Lunch (from a menu of light foods) is served from 11:30-2:30. At 2:30 the diminutive restaurant switches briefly to a tea room serving wine, tea, and beer until three. Saturday dinner is available by reservation (which must be made by Friday).

THE TAP ROOM in the Trojan Hotel, 43 3rd St Troy, 272-8200, is a simple grill which offers good food—soups, salads, sandwiches and specials—at a low price. There is nothing fancy about this spot, a favorite of those who work in the neighborhood. Open: M-Th 11-8; F 11-10; Sat lunch only.

THIRSTY'S, 605 New Scotland Ave Albany, 482-5347 or 482-5349, is a gem of a pub which will deliver its pub food anywhere in uptown Albany well into the night. The menu is extensive, with chicken wings being among the favorites. Open: Daily 5 pm-1 am.

CUISINE

AMERICAN
Algonquin Bar and Restaurant
Beekman Arms
Century House
Coco's
Cranberry Bog
Culinary Institute of America
Duncan's Dairy Bar
Hattie's Chicken Shack
The Horse Barn
Hudson River Trading Co
Joe's Restaurant
Lillian's
Merrill Magee House
Old Daley Inn
Red Lion Inn
Scrimshaw
Smith's
South End Tavern
Thacher's
Van Dyck

CONTINENTAL
Beverwyck
DePuys Canal House
Federal House Inn
Gideon Putnam
Gregory House
LaSerre
Mrs. London's
Ogden's
Old Journey's End
P.D. Ladd's
Quackenbush House
Qualters' Pine Hills Restaurant
Sassy Swede
The Shipyard
Truffles
Unlimited Feast
Yates Street

FRENCH
Balsam House
Chez Nicole
Chez Rene

Chez Sophie
Culinary Institute of America
L'Auberge
L'Hostellerie Bressane
La Rive
Mountain Villa

INDIAN
Sitar

ITALIAN
Cafe Capriccio
Caffe Italia Ristorante
Casino
Cavaleri Restaurant
Citone's
Fannie's Pizza and Clam Bar
Fannie's Restaurant
Fireside
Italia
Italian American Community Center
J.G.'s
Knotty Pine
LaGriglia
Lombardo's
Madison Grill
Michele Da Verona
Pasta Express
Purple Pub
Red Front
River Road Cafe
Roma Appian Way
Sam's (Albany)
Sam's Place (Malta)
Spiak's
Verdile's

MEXICAN
El Loco

ORIENTAL
China Garden
Hiro's
Hunan
Jack's Chinese American Restaurant

Peking
Plum Blossom
Sugi
Yip's

SEA FOOD
Boat Slip
Cape House
Clay's
Jack's Oyster House
Lobster Pound
Scrimshaw

STEAK AND CHOPS
Barnsider
The Bear's
Butcher Block
Jack's Oyster House
Pumpkin Patch

OCCASIONAL FOODS

LIGHT FOODS
A-Frame
Adelphi Hotel
Bar-B-Q Billy's
Bruegger's Bagel Bakery
Deli Works
Duncan's Dairy Bar
Finishing Touch by Pitts and Pitts
Gershorn's
Ginger Man
H.P. Mulligan's

Holmes and Watson
Luncheon Gallery at the Institute
McGeary's
McGeary's Eldorado
Olde Bryan Inn
Ozzie's
Parc V Cafe
Qualters' Pine Hills Restaurant
Quintessence
Saratoga Flat Track
Scrubber's Inc
Sign of the Tree
Strawberry Lane
The Tap Room
Thirsty's
Unlimited Feast
Yorkstone Pub

SUNDAY BRUNCH
Balsam House
Beekman Arms
Beverwyck
Cranberry Bog
Gideon Putnam
Holmes and Watson
Merrill Magee House
Old Journey's End
Red Lion Inn
Sitar
Truffles
Van Dyck

LOCATION INDEX

ALBANY
A Frame
Bar-B-Q Billy's
Beverwyck
Boat Slip
Bruegger's Bagel Bakery
Cafe Capriccio
Caffe Italia Ristorante
Casino
Cavaleri
Citone's
Coco's

Deli Works
El Loco
Ginger Man
Hudson River Trading Company
Hunan
Italian American Community Center
J.G.'s
Jack's Oyster House
Joe's
La Serre
L'Auberge
Lombardo's

Luncheon Gallery at the Institute
Madison Grill
McGeary's
Michele Da Verona
Ogden's
Ozzie's
P.D. Ladd's
Pasta Express
Peking
Quackenbush House
Qualters' Pine Hills Restaurant
Quintessence
Sam's
Sign of the Tree
Thacher's
Thirsty's
Truffles
Unlimited Feast
Yates Street
Yorkstone Pub

AVERILL PARK
Gregory House

BOLTON LANDING (ON LAKE GEORGE)
Algonquin Bar and Restaurant

CATSKILL
La Rive

COHOES
Sassy Swede
Smith's

COLONIE
Barnsider
Butcher Block
Clay's
Cranberry Bog
H.P. Mulligan's
Hiro's
Jack's Chinese American Restaurant
Parc V Cafe
Scrimshaw
Sitar

DELANSON
The Horse Barn

DUANESBURG
The Bear's
Mountain Villa

FRIENDS LAKE
Balsam House

GLENMONT
Chez Rene

HIGH FALLS
DePuys Canal House

HILLSDALE
L'Hostellerie Bressane

HYDE PARK
Culinary Institute of America

LATHAM
Century House
Fannie's Pizza and Clam Bar
Fannie's Restaurant
Lobster Pound
The Shipyard

MALTA
Sam's Place

RENSSELAER
Yip's

RHINEBECK
Beekman Arms

SARATOGA
Adelphi Hotel
Chez Sophie
Gideon Putnam
Hatties Chicken Shack
Lillian's
Mrs London's
Old Bryan Inn
Saratoga Flat Track

SCHENECTADY
Chez Nicole
China Garden

Fireside
Gershorn's
Pumpkin Patch
River Road
Roma Appian Way
Strawberry Lane
Sugi
Van Dyck

SOUTH LEE, MA
Federal House Inn

STOCKBRIDGE
Red Lion Inn

TROY
Bruegger's Bagel Bakery
Cape House
Duncan's Dairy Bar
Finishing Touch by Pitts and Pitts
Holmes and Watson
Italia

Knotty Pine
McGeary's Eldorado
Old Daley Inn
Plum Blosson
Red Front
Scubber's Inc
South End Tavern
The Tap Room
Verdile's

WARRENSBURG
Merrill Magee House

WATERVLIET
Purple Pub
Spiak's

WEST SAND LAKE
Old Journey's End

WINDHAM
La Griglia

Night Life

Although the entire Capital District has, at various times, supported a vibrant public nightlife, both licit (swank night spots with sensuous music, dancers, and comedians) and illicit (widespread gambling, prostitution, and embibing), presently most after-hours entertainment takes the form of gala fund-raisers for the many non-profit organizations in the region or private entertaining at home. There are several major exceptions to this: most dramatic is the rock concert circuit, its top cards drawing thousands of devotees for one-night revels; most enduring is the pub scene, the weekend late evening gathering of adults and young adults at select watering holes—many of them adjacent to the area's 14 colleges; most glittering is the trendy discotheque realm, the world of sophisticated late night dance halls with pop culture motifs and planned opportunities for "singles" to meet. (N.B. What impact the raising of the drinking age in New York will have on all this has yet to be seen.) What follows is a description of these three levels of entertainment within the Capital District.

Concerts

WQBK (104) maintains a 24-hour concert line (465-1104) with information about upcoming appearances within the region (the region reaching as far in this case as New York City, The Meadowlands, Springfield, Hartford, Worcester, Boston, and Syracuse). QBK also broadcasts a rock concert calendar each day at 5:35, 7:35, and 10:35.

METROLAND, the weekly lively arts newspaper, reviews current shows and posts a calendar of coming events. It is indispensible for those wanting to keep up with the after-hours scene.

DUCK SOUP, 1416 4th St Rensselaer, hosts predominantly area bands with occasional headlining national bands. New wave music.

Empire State Plaza
M. Kinney/Capital District Newspapers

eba CHAPTER HOUSE THEATRE, 351 Hudson Ave Albany, 465-9916, creates opportunities for music lovers who are dissatisfied with live shows at area night clubs and for those who are prevented from hearing live music because of age to hear local bands at inexpensive prices. Shows are scheduled every 4-6 weeks in the fall, winter and spring.

J.B.'S THEATER, Westgate, Albany, 438-2515, hosts all levels of musical performers, from the nationally renown to the up-and-coming. The site, a former roller rink, accommodates 2000 patrons, and arrangements have been made to permit 17-21-year-olds to be served soft drinks while those above 21 may purchase alcoholic beverages. J.B.'s Theater is a direct descendent of J.B. Scotts, the musical nightclub destroyed by a fire in the early 80's. Admission charges vary with the level of entertainment. Hours are as follows: Sun-Th/Doors open at 6:30, opening act at 8:00, headline act at 9:30; F-Sat/Doors open at 8:00, opening act at 9:30, headline act at 11:00.

SPAC publishes its calendar of special events (dominated in June and late August by popular music performers) in early spring. Tickets to SPAC concerts—available at ticketron offices and at the SPAC Box Office—often sell out in one day. Savvy, assertive residents snap up all the amphitheater tickets. (Members of SPAC may purchase special events tickets in advance, a strong argument in favor of membership.)

OTHER CONCERT CENTERS are described in the music section of the chapter on the Arts. Telephone numbers for area college and university box offices are also supplied.

The Pub Scene

Here, as in some other activities, the Capital District remains quite segmented, with Trojans, Albanians, Schenectadians, and suburbanites sticking close to home. This may be beginning to change. In recent years, the concept of Designated Driver, imported from Scandanavia in response to New York's "Get Tough on Drunk Drivers" policy, has liberated groups from the need to patronize the neighborhood pub exclusively. (Designated Driver means that a group of people going out for an evening on the town determine who will be behind the wheel that night, and agree that the driver will refrain from alcoholic beverages during the evening. SUNYA students and area pub owners worked together in 1984 to encourage more widespread adoption of the designated driver concept by defining a policy whereby pubs supply free soft beverages all evening to Designated Drivers.)
   The lists which follow divide pubs in each city into four categories:

1. Quiet pubs whose patrons tend to be adults and young working adults who prefer soft music and quiet conversation.
2. Lively pubs whose patrons are students wanting to play pub games, table hop, and listen to the latest in rock music.

3. Pubs featuring live music (jazz or rock) and appealing to a mixed clientele drawn by the desire to dance or to listen to music.
4. Plain pubs whose loyal clientele focus on pub talk, TV viewing and serious drinking.

ALBANY

Quiet Pubs/Adults and Young Adults

Americana Inn*
660 Albany Shaker Rd
Colonie 869-8100
Piano bar

Coco's*
1470 Western Ave
Albany 456-0297
Disc jockey

Cranberry Bog
56 Wolf Rd
Colonie 459-5110

Friday's (TGI Friday's)
Stuyvesant Plaza
Albany 489-1661

Parc V Cafe
661 Albany-Shaker Rd
Colonie 869-9976

Son's Tavern
1186 Western Ave
Albany 482-4389

Lively Pubs/College Students

Downtown Athletic Club
29 Maiden Lane
Albany 434-0485

Justin McNeils*
301 Lark St
Albany 436-7008
Live jazz in dining area

The Lamp Post
Western Ave & Quail St
Albany 436-7740

The Lark Tavern*
453 Madison Ave
Albany 463-9779
Live background music

Margarita's
286 Lark St
Albany 463-9040

McGeary's*
4 Clinton Square
Albany 463-1455
Students mix with townsfolk here.

Quintessence*
11 New Scotland Ave
Albany 434-8186
Live background music

Sutter's Mill and Mining Co.*
1200 Western Ave
Albany 489-4910
A SUNYA favorite

Washington Tavern
250 Western Ave
Albany 462-9179

Pubs with Live Music/Mixed Crowd

Bogies
297 Ontario Street
Albany 482-4368

Pauly's Hotel
337 Central Ave
Albany 463-9082

Flirtations
Albany Marriott
189 Wolf Road
Colonie 458-8444

Plain Pubs/Mixed Crowd

Harpo's
6 New Scotland Ave
Albany 465-9077

Hurley's
613 Clinton Ave
Albany 434-6854

O'Heaney's
184 Ontario St
Albany 449-9978

Thirsty's
605 New Scotland Ave
Albany 482-5347

SCHENECTADY

Quiet Pubs/Adults and Young Adults

Friar Tuck Pub
1208 Troy Schenectady Road
Latham 785-8854

Peggy's Restaurant*
426 State Street
Schenectady 382-8649
Outdoor TGIF in Canal Square May-Sept.

Shipyard Restaurant
1171 Troy Schenectady Rd
Latham 785-1711

Sunday's Restaurant*
616 Union St
Schenectady 374-0511
Popular after-theater spot

Tiffany's Restaurant*
1548 State St
Schenectady 382-9139
Hors d'oeuvres

Van Dyck Restaurant*
237 Union St
Schenectady 374-2406
Jazz Fri and Sat 9-1

Lively Pubs/College Students

Geppetto's
547 Nott Street
Schenectady 382-9066

The Rathskeller*
Union College Campus Center
Schenectady
Open during college sessions (non-students welcome)

The Press Box*
326 State St
Schenectady
Near GAZETTE office

Slapshots
501 Hattie St
Schenectady 393-0594

Pubs with Live Music/Mixed Crowd

Cardinal Puff's Pub*
1400 Altamont Avenue
Rotterdam 355-9924
Gourmet sandwiches

The Rafters*
Kaydeross Park
Saratoga Springs 584-9826
Upbeat, crowded

Plain Pubs/Mixed Crowd

Copper Keg
848 Eastern Avenue
Schenectady 382-8908

Fireside Pizzeria Inc
1631 Eastern Parkway
Schenectady 382-1616

Pressure Pub
803 Eastern Avenue
Schenectady 382-9128

TROY

Quiet Pubs/Adults and Young Adults

Capehouse
254 Broadway
Troy 274-0167

Holmes and Watson Ltd*
450 Broadway
Troy 273-8526
Around the world beer competition

It's Your Move
255 River St
Troy 274-0221

Lively Pubs/College Students

Copper Mug
2253 15th St
Troy 273-1283

Country Grove
10 North Greenbush Ave
Troy 283-9866

Dividends*
297 River St
Troy 274-5585
*Dancing/students and older adults mix here

Elda's
120 4th St
Troy 274-2544

Italia*
4th St
Troy 273-8773
*Live jazz Thurs at 9

Pubs with Live Music/Mixed Crowd

Petar's
194 River St
Troy 273-1553

Rexford's
60 Vandenburg Ave
Troy 272-4122

Rolls Touring Club Inc
87 4th St
Troy 272-5453

Plain Pubs/Mixed Crowd

McGreary's Eldorado*
121 4th St
Troy 272-4403
*Formerly all male

Knotty Pine*
2301 15th St
Troy 272-4557
*Baseball crowd/older men

Night Spots and Discotheques

There are several of these contemporary phenomena, spirited blends of two Twentieth Century traditions—the dance hall and the night club.

Patrons dance to live music or to recorded sounds selected and introduced by a disc-jockey/MC. Among the most popular and durable of such spots are these:

Cahoots Discotheque*
Hilton Hotel
Albany 462-6611
Open: M-Th 4-2; F-Sat 4-4
Recorded music with DJ/MC
  Message exchange

LP's*
Western Ave and Quail (downstairs from Lamp Post)
Albany 436-7740
Open: W-S 9-4
21 year old minimum age
  Proper attire required
  Largest dance floor in area
  Sophisticated tone
  Top 40's music with DJ commentary

Puttin' on the Ritz*
8 Central Ave
Albany
Live bands M, Tu, Wed, Fri
  Recorded music Thurs, Sat, Sun
  New wave music and crowd

288 Lark*
288 Lark St
Albany
Open: 10 pm-4 am
Recorded music upstairs
  Tu, Wed, Thurs, live bands
  New wave music and crowd

The Shelf
DeWitt Clinton Bldg
39 Eagle St
Albany 436-7707
Open: M-F 4 till closing; Sat 9 pm-4am

Shopping

What William Kennedy says in O ALBANY!—that Albany is a microcosm of the United States, a place in which the continuum of the American experience is writ small—is as true of shopping as it is of politics, religion, and immigration. In the beginning, stores and houses sat side by side in the center of town, residential and commercial life inseparable. Early pictures of Albany, Schenectady, and Troy show obvious harmony between shop and home. With the passage of time, residential areas began to develop on the periphery, leaving shops and business to dominate the geographic centers of the towns. Throughout the early years of this century, downtown was a place to go. Residents would don their better clothes and journey into the center of the city to shop, knowing that the occasion would also allow them to visit friends who were doing the same thing. Photographs of the early decades of this century show crowds of people, some walking four abreast down the sidewalks, others talking animatedly at corners. Going downtown was an entertainment, and shopping, while sometimes necessary, was also a way for people to get out of the house and to see their friends.

With the sixties, all of that changed. The building of highways and the development of suburbs drew people even further from the geographic center of town and laid the ground for the birth of the shopping center. The commercial hearts of all three cities have endured various stages of stagnation, decay, resurgence as centers of consumer activity, with only a few of the original merchants surviving into the New Downtown, a streamlined, weekday version of its former self.

Meanwhile, residents of the Capital District, like their American counterparts everywhere, have turned shopping into an extraordinary entertainment industry, second only, it seems, to television. A survey of regional shopping arenas reveals a staggering array of merchandise and an impressive assortment of sales techniques.

This chapter will first survey the major shopping areas. Next it will describe those stores which the authors believe present the best merchandise at the best prices, with particular emphasis on stores that shoppers may not otherwise know about unless they have lived in the Capital

Colonie Center
Michael Fredericks, Jr.

District for some time and to stores that residents of one town may take for granted while those outside may not know about at all. The organization is this: Food, Clothing and Goods.

N.B. This text, as the title indicates, is intended as a guide to the newcomer as well as to the long term resident, and in preparing it we have consulted with both. In our quest for accuracy and completeness, we have visited scores of establishments. Yet even as we write, we know it cannot be accurate (daily stores will open and others will close) or complete (we cannot cover every store in every city and suburb.) We apologize in advance to those we have missed and hereby affirm that we do not in any way imply that those merchants whom we have not included are in any way unworthy. The Yellow Pages gives a complete listing of all merchants.

SHOPPING AREAS

Albany

DOWNTOWN, the area between Broadway and Pearl Street to the north and south of State Street, has been coming back to life, with concerned citizens of the business community rehabilitating old buildings and restoring them to commercial use. The prospects are now very good for a revitalized commercial downtown area, particularly one serving the needs of the people who work in the offices on the streets which were always the heart of this old city.

LARK STREET—from Washington to Madison Avenues—swings. Here, more than anywhere in the Capital District, the looks, the smells, and the sounds of the trendy world are on display. With antique shops, clothing stores, restaurants, and pubs, Lark Street has become the center for those immersed in contemporary culture.

Schenectady

DOWNTOWN LOWER STATE STREET is engaged in a major effort—focused on Canal Square and Center City—to consolidate small, single owner stores into a major shopping area with Carl Company (a department store) and Proctor's Theater as primary attractions. As part of the effort, Jay Street has been converted into a pedestrian walkway lined with small shops, and many of the older buildings have been renovated to include shops and apartments.

UPPER UNION STREET resembles an ordinary city neighborhood shopping cluster, with a newsroom, a cleaners, a liquor store, a delicatessen etc.; what makes it noteworthy is the superior, though understated, quality of its merchants.

Troy

DOWNTOWN TROY, from 2nd Street to 4th Street, Fulton to Ferry, is the expansive region which was once the center of commerce in Troy. In recent years many of the buildings have been rehabilitated for use as offices, stores, and restaurants, and those durable long-time merchants who were able to hang on long enough have welcomed newcomers in a resurgence of commercial activity. This very pleasant area is one more testimony to the faith that some people have in their cities and the risk they are willing to take to back what they believe in.

UNCLE SAM ATRIUM, Fulton Street, between 3rd and 4th Streets, is a modern, architecturally interesting shopping complex—a downtown shopping mall with Carl Co. as anchor.

THE MALLS ON THE PERIPHERY

The most intensive concentration of diversified stores in the Capital District lies between Adirondack Northway Exits 1-5. Here, on land which not many years ago functioned as wilderness or farmsoil, stand five multimillion dollar shopping plazas and a fast developing commercial strip.

1. **STUYVESANT PLAZA** houses the finest selection of locally owned specialty shops in the region. At these stores (Wells and Coverly, Honigsbaum's, Pappagallo, Crabtree and Evelyn, and Pearl Grant Richman's, for example), the merchandise is well selected, the service courteous, and the atmosphere pleasant.

2. **CROSSGATES** is a Pyramid Mall, an enormous complex combining mid-price range chain stores with elegant smaller specialty shops, with Caldor and J.C. Penney as bookends and Filene's and Jordan Marsh as anchors. The Mall, which had been opposed energetically by environmentalists, got off to a disappointing start but is approaching expected levels of business. It aims ultimately to be the universal mall, with stores in every range of interest, taste, and price. The twelve screen cinema draws sizable crowds.

3. **NORTHWAY MALL/THE OFF PRICE CENTER,** originally a retail center featuring reasonably priced merchandise, redefined its role in the early 80's as the commercial field became more competitive. The Center now offers 60 shops, one half of which offer first quality, brand name merchandise discounted 20-70% below retail. The principal store on the site is Montgomery Ward.

4. **COLONIE CENTER** is one of the most stable and prosperous shopping malls in the nation and certainly the reigning queen in the Capital District. With Macy's and Sears holding up the North and South ends and comfortable mall space adaptable for shows and demonstrations, Colonie Center attracts people from a hundred miles in all directions. In fact, the devoted shopper will feel triumphant merely by finding a parking place during holiday shopping times. Most of the stores in this mall, Macy's included, feeling the competition from other malls, have begun an aggressive policy of frequent sales and dramatic discounts.

5. **WOLF ROAD,** between Northway Exits 2 and 3, is a thoroughfare along which single shops or colonies of shops have settled, enticed primarily by the success of the neighboring shopping malls.

6. **LATHAM CIRCLE MALL,** at the juncture of Routes 9 and 7, draws residents of Latham, Troy and Niskayuna to its many shops and to its anchors, The Boston Store, Caldor, and J.C. Penney.

There are various other smaller suburban malls in the Capital District, many of them collections of good stores. Although they will not be presented in detail here, some of the shops will be described in the relevant places in the text. There are, however, two other major shopping malls, each standing slightly apart from the dense cluster in the Colonie-Guilderland area.

1. **MOHAWK MALL,** Balltown Road in Schenectady, is a handsome mall, its central aisle sectioned into pleasant areas for sitting and visiting. The Mall's anchors are Boston Store and Montgomery Ward.

2. **CLIFTON COUNTRY MALL,** at Northway Exit 9 and Rte 146, features J.C. Penney and The Carl Co., as well as branches of many chain stores.

DEPARTMENT STORES

Five major department stores serve the region, drawing shoppers from over 100 miles in all directions:

1. **FILENE'S,** the Albany branch of Boston's famous store, is a dazzler. The beautiful interior highlights dramatic displays of premium merchandise. The emphasis is definitely on women—with women's clothing, cosmetics and jewelry occupying more than half the store—but there are also handsome departments for men's and children's clothing, and fine items for the home. The rumor persists that a Filene's Basement, famous for its automatic mark-down policy, will open at some point at this store. Filene's, located at Crossgates Mall, is open mall hours, M-Sat 10-9:30 and Sun 10-6.

2. **JORDAN MARSH,** also a branch of a Boston-based chain, is a traditional full range department store; that is, it stocks a wide array of merchandise—clothing, furniture, fine foods, kitchen supplies, electronic equipment, jewelry, and linens, for example—in price levels ranging from moderate to more costly. Located at Crossgates Mall, Jordan Marsh is open mall hours, M-Sat 10-9:30 and Sun 10-6.

3. **MACY'S,** the Albany branch of the world's largest department store, has been serving the region since 1966. At Macy's, clothing dominates, with well stocked, moderately priced departments for men, women, youth, and children. Other strong sections include kitchenware, furniture, carpeting, bed and bath, and gourmet foods. Respecting tradition, Macy's, the centerpiece of the fictional MIRACLE AT 34TH STREET, adds a real toy and tree trim department at Christmas. The frequent sales in all departments are hard to beat. Macy's, located at Colonie Center, is open M-Sat 10-9:30, Sun 12-5.

4. **SEAR'S,** the nation's largest catalogue and retail house, maintains one of its most comprehensive and most successful stores at Colonie Center. Known for sturdy, dependable merchandise, Sears features large departments in appliances, sporting goods, home furnishings, automotive supplies, garden equipment, and clothing. The branch maintains a service center complete with a fleet of trucks to repair all Sears appliances. A catalogue order desk is located on the lower floor. The store is open M-Sat 10-9:30, Sun 12-5.

5. **THE CARL CO.,** a local chain of department stores, is the only one of its kind to have held its own after the arrival of powerful nation-wide chains began in the 60's and inner cities started to buckle under. This hearty enterprise maintained the principal store in downtown Schenectady and opened branches in Clifton Park, Rotterdam, Scotia, and Troy. The merchandising emphasis at all locations is on moderately priced clothing and home supplies. The hours of each branch match the hours of surrounding stores. Information is available at 374-9111.

THE CATALOG HOUSES

Three catalog houses—Boardmans, Present Company, and Service Merchandise—serve the region. All three offer year-round savings and frequent sales. Applications for the catalogs are available at the distribution centers, listed in the telephone directory.

DISCOUNTS AT A DISTANCE

CHARLESTOWN in Utica lures bargain hunters from miles away. Here 40 factory outlet stores—many featuring wearing apparel, home furnishings, and gifts—are assembled under the single roof of what was once a firearms factory. A brochure describing the facility is available at (315) 724-8175. Directions: Take Thruway to Exit 31. Go over bridge into downtown Utica onto Broad St. At third light go left onto Rte 5S East, 1¾ miles to Turner Street. 1½ hours.

FOOD

This section is dedicated to culinary wizards looking for ingredients and to sybarites craving delicious food already made. In the interest of efficiency, we present the material in chart form, indicating specialties, describing the nature of the item being recommended, noting areas of particular excellence, and, where appropriate, commenting on cost.

Bakeries: All these shops carry delicious fare:

Bagel Baron	Bagels: all varieties
279 New Scotland Ave/Albany	Baked daily
	Very hearty
Bania's	Ethnic breads,
2428 4th Ave/Watervliet	pies and cookies
561 Congress St/Troy	
Old Loudon Rd South of Rte 7	Sat-Sun only, 7-2
Bruegger's	Bagels
55 Congress St/Troy	Excellent flavor
Stuyvesant Plaza/Albany	Always fresh
Brooks Doughnuts	Doughnuts
176 No. Blvd/Albany	Simple and tasty
Corcione	Italian Bread and Rolls
37 Robin St/Albany	Crisp crust/airy center
	Only in supermarkets
French Confection	Delicious Croissants
1042 Troy Schdy Rd/Latham	French bread & pastries
	Also sold at Macy's
Freihofer's	Legendary Chocolate
Sold in all fine markets	Chip Cookies
Fiorello Bakery	Italian Bread and Rolls
1180A Western Ave/Albany	Crisp crust with soft, thick center

Grandma's Restaurant
1273 Central Ave/Albany

Pies
Baked daily from sunrise to sunset

Joan's Cake Chateau
Rte 155 (600 ft west of Exit 5)
Colonie

Special Design Cakes
Baked goods to order

Leo's
28 Maple Ave/Albany

Full line of Kosher
Baked goods/Whipped cream
cakes/challah bread and desserts

Mrs. London's
Phila St/Saratoga

Fine Continental baked goods/
Rich, beautiful and expensive

Mt. Pleasant
941 Crane St/Schdy
73 Wolf Rd/Albany

Russian Rye/Barnsider
Rye/Hard Rolls

Nelligan's
32 4th St/Troy

Irish soda bread
Meltaway buns/donuts

Nino's
718 Central Avenue/Albany

Italian Bread and Rolls
Thick, rich, and tasty

Perreca's
33 North Jay St/Schdy

Italian Bread

Phil's
38 Central Ave/Albany

Cinnamon Bread
Dutch hearth bread/kuchen
Donuts

Prediger's
98 Hudson Ave/Green Island

Rye Bread
Reputedly the best there is

Rappazzo's
Crestwood Plaza/Albany

Italian Pastries
Butter Cookies

Schuyler Pastry Shop
637 3rd Ave/Watervliet

Miniature danish
Indisputably best value
Hearty donuts
Specialty cakes
Home-made look and taste

Villa Italia
3028 Hamburg St/Rotterdam
(Near Thruway Exit 25)

Italian cookies
Pastries/Cakes
Everything excellent

Beer, Liquor and Wine: The best selection and best prices on wine
and liquor on a day-to-day basis can be found at the following:

Barbara's World
197 Wolf Rd/Colonie

In-depth selection

Madison Liquor and Wine
1078 Madison Ave/Albany

Helpful advice

William S. Newman Brewing Co.
32 Learned St/Albany

Beer and ale made in Albany
Available in small kegs

Wine shop
265 New Scotland Ave/Albany

Candy: The following merchants sell candies which meet the standards of the most demanding sweet tooth:

Candy Kraft	Homemade chocolates
McCormick Corners	Fudge/Christmas
Rte 20	Easter Candy
Guilderland	Beautiful and delicious
Sweet Stuff	Godiva and specialty candies
Stuyvesant Plaza/Albany	
Verstandigs	Imported candies for
454 Delaware Ave/Delmar	Easter and Christmas

Cheese: The following merchants stock and care for a good variety of interesting and tasty cheeses. They are also able to assist customers in selecting an appropriate cheese.

**Barbara's World of Beer,
   Cheese and Gifts**
Wolf Road/Colonie

The Cheese Connection
Stuyvesant Plaza/Albany

Grand Union
Loudonville and Delmar

Hickory Farms
Colonie Center, Latham Center,
Mohawk Mall
Macy's
Colonie Center
Scullen and Meyer Fine Foods
435 Loudonville Rd/Loudonville

Coffee and Tea: The following merchants carry and care for a good selection of fresh teas and coffees:

The Daily Grind
204 Lark St/Albany
258 Broadway/Troy
Pearl Grant-Richman's
Stuyvesant Plaza/Albany
Macy's
Colonie Center

Fresh Fish: The following merchants sell a good variety of carefully refrigerated fresh fish:

A.C. Thomas 25 Central Ave/Albany	Good chowders
Fleres 534 Broadway/Schdy	
Grand Union Stores All locations	
L&B Fish and Clam Market 1241 Central Ave/Albany	Good specials
Lobster Pound Latham, Westmere, Elsmere and Burnt Hills	Lobster specials sometimes dramatic
Two Cousins Fish Market 581 Livingston Ave/Albany	Probably the widest variety on a daily basis

Fruits and Vegetables: Albany, Schenectady and Troy all host Farmers' Markets, a modern version of the traditional weekly town square day.

On designated days, farmers gather to sell their wares directly to consumers from the backs of their trucks. The times and places of these wandering fairs are published in the local newspapers. Prices vary according to locale, with farmers assessing the ability of the clientele to pay, and bargaining is sometimes allowed.

In addition to the usual commodities available at these markets, it should be noted that the region produces its own exotica, Hand Melons, lush fruit harvested and sold only during August. (The fact they mature as the flat track opens has linked them forever with thoroughbreds; predictably, they are all the rage in Saratoga.)

Community Gardens cater to those who wish to grow their own produce. Two organizations assist personal gardeners:

1. **CAPITAL DISTRICT COMMUNITY GARDENS**, 83 4th St. Troy, 274-8685, coordinates activity at 16 community garden sites in Rensselaer and North Albany counties. A modest fee is charged for each person wishing to cultivate a plot. The group deliberately keeps the fee low because the group cooperates in several projects: growing food for regional food pantries, supervising youth gardening programs, publishing an informative newsletter, placing annual seed and tree orders, and running the weekly Troy Farmers' Market (each Saturday morning 9-1 on Broadway between 3rd and 4th in Troy).

2. **COMMUNITY GARDENS OF ALBANY**, Martin Rd. in Voorheesville, 765-3635, is run by the Cooperative Extension of Albany County in cooperation with the City of Albany. This group administers 22 garden sites, each with large and small plots available for use by local residents.

What follows is a list of markets known for the freshness and variety of their produce:

MARKET	SPECIALTY
Menands Market Broadway/Menands (Just south of Menands Bridge)	Largest group of vendors Wholesale and retail Open all year, early morning to early afternoon
Engel's Farm Stand Albany Shaker Rd (Opposite Americana Inn)	Open May 1 to Thanksgiving Baked goods, jams and jellies
Fo Castle Country Store Burnt Hills	Apple picking encouraged Baked goods too
Indian Ladder Farms Altamont	Comprehensive Farm stand Apple, grape, and raspberry picking cider/baked goods
Krug's Farm Stand Everett Rd/Albany	Excellent corn Summer only
Samscott Orchards Kinderhook	Large variety of fruit for picking
Shaker Shed 945 Watervliet Shaker Rd Colonie	Farm stand
W.F. Ryan 114 Railroad Ave/Albany	Broad selection/in season and out Good prices
Yonder Farms Rte 4/Troy Rte 155/Colonie	Fresh fruit/berry picking Baked goods/cheese/cider Flowers

Herbs and Spices: Three shops sell fresh food flavorings, the first and last on the list presenting spices they have grown and prepared on their own:

Cottage Herb Farm Shop
311 State St/Albany

Scullen and Meyer
435 Loudon Road/Loudonville

Shuttle Hill Herbs
241 Delaware Ave/Elsmere

Ice Cream and Frozen Confections: Deep, thick ice cream, rich in
butterfat and naturally flavored, is prepared at two area stores, and another shop prepares its own ices. Several others distribute excellent confections made elsewhere:

Ben and Jerry's
1705 Union St/Schdy
Crossgates Mall
579 New Scotland Ave/Albany

Vermont made ice cream
Interesting concoctions

Carvel
222 Delaware Ave/Elsmere
1321 Central Ave/Albany

Good specialties and
Cakes made from soft ice cream

Cream Machine
53 Congress St/Troy

Homemade Ice Cream

Dahlia Supreme Ice Cream
858 Madison Ave/Albany

Homemade Ice Cream

Kurver Kreme
1349 Central Ave/Albany

Excellent soft ice cream
Summer only

Rappazzo's
Crestwood Plaza/Albany

Italian ice, ice cream,
frozen desserts

Imported Foods and Ethnic Specialties: Because of the rich
cultural mix represented within the population of the Capital District, foods native to other countries form a base for the regional diet and are widely available.

Italian Emphasis:

Codino's
1735 Van Vranken Ave/Schdy

DeFazio Imports
264 4th St/Troy

Also New Skeet
Monastery Cheesecakes

Pellegrino Michael Importing Co.
1117 Central Ave/Albany

Fresh filo leaves
Italian and Greek

Pellegrino Importing Co.
165 Madison Ave/Albany

Homemade pasta
Cut to order

Roma Importing Co.
9 Cobbe Rd/Latham

Oriental Emphasis:

Kim's Oriental Shoppe
1649 Central Ave/Colonie

Nien Hsuan
284 Troy Schdy Rd.
(1 Mi E of Latham Circle)

Meat: The following butcher shops offer superior meats and skilled service:

Crestwood Market 22 Picotte Drive/Albany	Butchers from former Modern Food Market
Emil Meister's Market 329 Ontario St/Albany	German style bologna and sausage
Guertze Farm Market Rte 9W/Glenmont	Fresh chickens and pigs
Helmbold's Industrial Park/Troy	Make own hot dogs and sausages Reasonable prices and excellent specials
Primo's Prime Meats 540 Clinton Ave/Albany	Friendly good service
Rolf's Pork Store 70 Lexington Ave/Albany	Skilled, amiable butchers
Troy Pork Store 158 4th St/Troy	Also carry meat low in sodium and nitrates and without coloring

Natural Foods: The best selection of legitimate natural foods is available at these three locations:

Ceres Natural Food
77 4th St/Troy

Earthly Delights
162 Jay St/Schdy

Miles Natural Foods
28 Central Ave/Albany

Nuts: Nuts—salted or unsalted, shelled or unshelled, whole, sliced or crushed—all indubitably fresh, are sold at these outlets, where you may buy whatever quantity you choose and even save a few dollars on broken or unsightly pieces:

Empire State Nut Co. 880 Broadway/Albany 1593 Central Ave/Albany Plaza 7/Latham	Wholesale and retail
Peanut Store 5 Pearl St/Albany	

Specialty Stores: These stores offer ready-to-eat fresh and frozen foods, food stuffs, party foods and catering services:

Cheese Connection
Stuyvesant Plaza/Albany

Gourmet foods
Fresh and frozen prepared foods
Catering

Gershon's Delicatessen
1600 Union St/Schdy

Salads and cold cuts
Catering

Pitts and Pitts
461 Broadway/Troy

Prepared soups, salads and desserts
Baskets for Saratoga
Catering

Platt's Place
44 Wolf Rd/Colonie

Salads and cold cuts
Catering

Scullen and Meyer Fine Foods
435 Loudon Rd.
Loudonville

Gourmet Foods
Fresh and frozen prepared foods
Full dinners
Catering/gourmet meals

SYSCO Cash and Carry
71 Fuller Rd/Albany

Wholesale foods
Frozen hors d'oeurves
Large orders specialty
New Skeet Cheesecakes
(no catering)

Unlimited Feast
340 Hamilton St/Albany

Interesting, unusual
prepared foods
Catering

Catering: In addition to the specialty shops just described, which offer catering as well as prepared foods, the following three businesses provide commendable catering service.

Geurtze
Glenmont 434-8903

Barbeques
Chicken, roast pig, roast beef

Kaye's
Albany 438-5275

Kosher and non-Kosher

Michael's
Green Island 273-9814

CLOTHING

This segment is categorized according to customer, and then subdivided according to price. It begins with a presentation of shops carrying attire for the entire family, followed by stores serving only women, then by those serving only men and finally by those specializing in children's apparel.

Clothing for Men and Women and Children

This section is subdivided into two sections according to price. The first part describes superior clothing at retail price; the second part, everyday clothing at reduced prices.

A. Superior Clothes

BENETTON, Crossgates Mall, a franchise of an international company, carries handsome Italian-made sweaters for men and women.

COHOES SPECIALTY STORES, LTD, 43 Mohawk St. Cohoes, offers designer clothes, fine apparel, and moderately-priced lines of clothing, including a handsome collection of accessories. The shoe and handbag departments are particularly noted for their wide selection. Charter buses from New York, Long Island, and Connecticut bring shoppers for full-day buying sprees at this now well-known store. So dramatic are the semi-annual sales that lines begin to form hours before the doors open. Discounted.

DALLS LTD, 1222 Troy-Schenectady Rd. Niskayna, a distinguished store in Schenectady for many years, features select clothing in a quiet, pleasant atmosphere half way between Latham and Schenectady. Discounted.

HOFFMAN'S LTD, 626 New Loudon Road Latham, carries country casual clothes (including a substantial selection of Pendleton woolens and other imported lines) with a limited selection for children.

KROLL'S LTD, One Second St Troy, 272-6621, a long-established firm in Troy, stocks fine traditional clothing for men and women.

B. Moderately Priced, Good Quality Clothing

ADIRONDACK DAN-ARMY NAVY STORE, 59 N. Pearl St Albany, **SCHAFFERS,** 640 Central Ave, Albany, and **CRAMER'S ARMORY,** Columbia and Main St Cohoes, stock reasonably priced jeans, T-shirts, workpants, fatigues, and khakis in most sizes and makes. These no-nonsense stores supply uniforms, work-clothes, and heavy duty outerwear and shoes for laborers, students, children and anyone in the Capital District seeking comfortable, durable clothes.

STANDARD MANUFACTURING OUTLET STORE, 750 2nd St. Troy, offers discounted outerwear for the family.

CB SPORTS OUTLET STORE, 168 North St. Bennington, carries seconds, discontinued styles, and manufacturers' samples of expensive sportswear at substantial discount.

PETER HARRIS CLOTHES, in four area locations, markets sportswear for all sizes at reduced prices. The end-of-season sales make these clothes hard to pass up.

CHAMPION FACTORY OUTLET STORES, Westgate Plaza in Albany and Cross-town Plaza in Schenectady, feature athletic and recreational clothing for children and adults. The clothes are stocked in bins, so shoppers must really know what they are after in order to succeed.

Clothing for Women

Small shops geared to special clientele complement the department stores' array of women's fashions. What follow are descriptions of some of the most distinctive of these shops. The word "Discounted" appears at the end of a description when by policy the shop sells all merchandise at less than retail prices.

BARBIZON FASHION SHOPS, on Wolf Road and at Westgate in Albany, carry junior and women's sizes in a wide variety of mid-range styles. Discounted.

BORELLI COLLECTION, Crossgates Mall, carries a select collection of fashionable women's separates and accessories. Knowledgeable, helpful sales personnel willingly assist in putting clothes together with flair.

CARRIAGE TRADE, 475 Albany Shaker Rd. Colonie and **THE COUNTRY MISS,** Stop 26, Troy-Schenectady Road, take pride in the attention their sales personnel devote to advising customers in the selection of appropriate and fashionable clothing. Such consultation has, over the years, won these shops dedicated, loyal customers.

CASUAL SET, Stuyvesant Plaza Albany, and **TOWN AND TWEED,** Delaware Shopping Plaza, Delmar, feature sporty clothes from superior manu-facturers at moderate prices. (Both of these stores conduct dramatic end-of-season sales.)

THE DIFFERENCE IS, 118 S. Ferry St. Schenectady, offers a wide selection of separates for women.

THE GATE POST, Mohawk Mall, a New England style boutique, carries fine quality casual clothes for teens and women. Discounted.

HONIGSBAUMS, Stuyvesant Plaza, was established years ago as a family business with an emphasis on handsome traditional women's clothing. The experienced, relaxed sales personnel are willing to help or to let customers make their own choices. Discounted.

LOEHMANN'S, Loehmann's Plaza (formerly 20 Mall) Guilderland, is part of a nationwide chain that avid shoppers call a "Bargain Hunter's Paradise." There are no frills here, and one must comb through racks overflowing with merchandise of all varieties, but the dedicated shopper can come away triumphant. (The Back Room contains the designer clothes.) Discounted.

MATERIAL GAINS, 361 Broadway, Saratoga Springs, markets an unusual line of custom-made clothing from hand-painted and handwoven fabrics. The shop also sells sweaters, jewelry, and accessories, as well as evening and casual wear.

MONKEY BUSINESS, 855 Central Ave. Albany, has pleased its loyal customers each year by offering personalized service in the selection of fine clothes. One may call ahead for an appointment at this business which is on the third floor of an office building. (Because most of the clients of Monkey Business shop in advance of the season, it is wise to visit the store early.)

PAPPAGALLO, a tiny store tucked in the central corner of Stuyvesant Plaza in Albany, carries a distinctive line of classic women's separates, shoes, and accessories.

PEGASUS, 204 Lark St. Albany, carries antique and modern clothing.

SPECTOR'S, 233 Central Ave. Albany, long known for traditional men's clothing, had added a women's section catering particularly to the clothing needs of women in business and the professions.

SPORTIQUE, Wolf Rd Colonie, markets junior and women's clothing, always discounted, sometimes dramatically. Discounted.

TALBOT'S SURPLUS STORE, Shopper's Park, Wolf Rd., opened at Christmas 1984 to market tailored traditional clothing from major manufacturers. Discounted.

URSULA OF SWITZERLAND SPECIALTY STORES is a local business: the clothing is designed in Albany and manufactured in Waterford. The line includes casual, business, and After-five styles at affordable prices. The stores themselves are located at 144 Washington Ave. Albany and 447 State St. Schenectady.

Clothing for Men

In addition to the several stores previously listed as serving the family, men may choose from several stores which cater to them alone.

THE CUSTOM SHOP, Crossgates Mall, will custom tailor shirts in a wide selection of styles and fabrics. Customers must order a minimum of four shirts. Though the prices appear high, they are in fact only a few dollars above moderately priced shirts (lower, in fact, than many designers) and the shirts last — as long as the man keeps his size.

KELLY CLOTHES, INC., 886 New Loudon Rd Latham, sells clothes made in the region. Discounted.

Arlene Croce. Outerbridge & _azard. Inc.

Ginger Rogers did everything Astaire did— except backwards and on high heels.

With the right education, your daughter can do and be anything she dreams of. Girls Academy can be the first step.

FOUNDED 1814

GirlsAcademy

ALBANY ACADEMY FOR GIRLS

Grades K-12 • 140 Academy Road • Albany, N.Y. 12208 • (518) 463-2201

RODINOS, 348 Congress St Troy, provides traditional clothing for men and boys, insuring fine fit with expert tailoring services. On a balcony overlooking the men's department is a complementary collection of women's attire.

SHERMAN'S, 92 State St. Albany, offers traditional men's styles and boasts a particularly good selection of ties.

SPECTOR'S, 233 Central Ave. Albany, carries a wide selection of fine clothing in average sizes and willingly serves the needs of the hard-to-fit youth and adult. The tailoring of clothing is excellent.

STULMAKERS, 8 James St. Albany, presents superior clothing and features excellent custom tailoring from a handsome selection of fabrics.

WELLS AND COVERLY, Stuyvesant Plaza Albany, carries well-made traditional clothing for men and boys. (A section of select clothing for women was added in 1984.)

Clothing for Children

Department stores throughout the region, particularly Macy's, stock a wide array of junior fashions, and many of the stores mentioned in the section on clothing for the entire family are wall-to-wall with sturdy wear, but several small shops are well worth trying for variety, for fashion, or price.

BABYLAND, 16 Central Ave. Albany, has for decades dressed young children (from newborn to size 6X) in charming clothing.

BEAR'S BUREAU, 200 Broadway at the corner of 2nd St. and Monument Square in Troy, has recently opened to market clothes for boys and girls size newborn to 14. Among the specialties are hand smocked and appliqued dresses, which may be purchased ready-made or specially ordered.

CRACKERS, 58 Remsen St. Cohoes, sells designer clothes from infant size to 18 or 20. Discounted.

CHRISTOPHER'S TREE HOUSE, Robinson Square, Albany, has specialty clothes and accessories for children to size 7.

GIGGLES, Stuyvesant Plaza Albany, carries playful and beautiful clothing for infants and young children and has a wide selection of accessories for the older child.

KIDS SAMPLES, 632 Central Ave. Albany, sells select children's clothing at dramatic mark-downs. (Open Thurs, Fri, Sat only.) Discounted.

US KIDS, in Clifton Country Mall, Colonie Center, Delaware Plaza, and Mohawk Mall, presents a good selection of traditional clothing for children and teens.

PERFECT PRESENT, 110 Wolf Rd. Colonie, markets a select line of clothes for children newborn to toddler four.

WELLS AND COVERLY, Stuyvesant Plaza Albany, can outfit boys from age six in fine traditional clothing.

Shoes

COHOES SPECIALTY STORES, 43 Mohawk St. Cohoes, carries shoes for both men and women, with their selection of women's shoes being the largest in the area. Discounted.

THE FRENCH BOOT SHOP, Stuyvesant Plaza Albany, has an interesting combination of traditional and trendy shoes for women. The men's line definitely emphasizes the contemporary look.

J & D DESIGNER SHOES, Loehmann's Plaza Guilderland, receives daily shipments of women's shoes which it discounts 30-50%.

MAXINE, 110 Wolf Rd. Colonie, discounts designer shoes.

PAPPAGALLO, Stuyvesant Plaza Albany, carries a good range of the handsome classic shoes made for Pappagallo.

SPECTOR'S, 233 Central Ave Albany, has recently been remodeled and expanded to include a good department for men's shoes.

GOODS

This section presents those shops known to the authors to offer excellent merchandise, expert advice, and superior service.

Antiques: Many small shops and barns on the roads leading away from the urban centers sell antiques of all varieties. In addition, many local families put estates up for auction. For information about these sources, the afficionado should watch the classified section of the newspapers in the Spring and Fall, especially on Thursdays. In addition, there are several dealers in the region with permanent shops.

Albany Collection
297 Hamilton St/Albany

Dolls, toys, quilts, jewelry, furniture, wedding gowns

Antiques at the Tollgate 1569 New Scotland Rd/ Slingerlands	Shaker, pine, and period furniture and accessories
Daybreak 199 Central Ave/Albany	Antique clothing for men and women
Parts Warehouse 206 N. Pearl St/Albany	Articles for rehabilitation: mantles, doors, hardware, architectural details
Pegasus 204 Lark St/Albany	Women's clothing from 1880 to 1950
Sign of the Coffee Mill 67 Adams Place/Delmar	Furniture, silver, glass, and china
Traditions Stuyvesant Plaza/Albany	Period antiques and Traditional decoration

Artist and Technical Drawing Supplies and Services: These shops carry a full range of equipment for the professional and give careful, competent advice to the amateur.

Arlene's Artist Materials
57 Fuller Road/Albany

Crafts Plus
Stuyvesant/Albany

Robert Hill and Co.
451 Broadway/Troy

Northco Products Inc.
1843 Central Ave/Colonie

Union Book
131 State St/Schdy
Clifton Country Mall

Books: As in other parts of the United States, the Capital District marketplace for books is dominated by chains with branches in shopping plazas. (**WALDENBOOKS** is in Colonie Center, Crossgates, Mohawk Mall, Latham Circle, and Clifton Country Mall; and **B. DALTON BOOKSELLER** is at Crossgates, Clifton Country Mall and Latham Circle Mall. All these branches carry great quantities of recent titles in the full range of popular interest.) In spite of the power of these outlets, small stores maintained by rugged individuals persist, offering readers additional variety, quality, and service.

The largest of the independent stores is **BOOK HOUSE** in Stuyvesant Plaza Albany, 489-4761, which keeps a good selection of current books for adults and children and is developing a worthy collection of classics in fiction and non-fiction. Book House also features maps of local and general interest. Similarly comprehensive is the inventory at **UNION BOOKS**, 131 State St. Schdy, 393-2141, and Clifton Country Mall, 371-7616.

BOULEVARD BOOKSTORE, 12 Northern Blvd. Alb., 436-8848, has the best collection of serious contemporary fiction and books on women and women's issues. **THE OPEN DOOR,** 136 Jay St. Schenectady, 346-2719, a charming bookstore giftshop, serves what the owners call the "discriminating reader" with carefully selected hardcover and paperback books. They welcome special orders. **BURNT HILLS BOOKS,** 810 Saratoga Rd. Burnt Hills, 399-7004, is also well stocked with carefully selected books.

CLAPPS, 1032 Madison Ave. Albany, 482-4136, and Twenty Mall Guilderland, 456-5772, emphasizes current best sellers and books of local interest. **PLAZA BOOKS,** Empire State Plaza, 465-1807, boasts a broad-ranging inventory of current books and classic titles as well as a carefully selected collection of records and games. A new branch of **PLAZA BOOKS** in Saratoga (in the mall opposite Congress Park), 587-9633, is similarly stocked, with a slight emphasis on children's books. **TEN EYCK BOOKS,** Ten Eyck Plaza, Albany, 463-6207, emphasizes current books. This small, interesting store gives personal attention to all readers' needs.

THE MUSEUM SHOP at the New York State Museum, 449-1404, carries a broad array of books about nature, wildlife, culture, and civilization in New York State. It also stocks unique and interesting children's books, most of them geared to creative or educational activity. **HODGE PODGE BOOKS,** 272 Lark St. Albany, 434-0238, as the name implies, playfully caters to serious young readers, offering hard and softcover books for children and young adults. **LINCOLN HILL BOOKS,** 163 Delaware Ave. Delmar (Delaware Plaza), 439-8314, specializes in children's books and books of general interest. **CHILDREN'S BOOKSTORE,** Crossgates, carries many titles for children.

NORTH RIVER BOOKS, 356 Delaware Ave. Albany, 463-3082, operates on an interesting concept. The owner of this recently opened store shelves paperback and hardcover books, new and used, side by side. The selection, small but excellent, appeals to a wide range of knowledgeable readers.

DISCOUNT BOOK CENTER, Northway Mall, 482-3300, and Rte 9 Latham, 783-6352 (these stores are part of a national chain of Friar Tuck stores), has current best sellers and remaindered books at reduced prices.

Used books are sold at **BRYN MAWR BOOK STORE,** 19 Dove St. Albany, 465-8126, **TURNING OVER A NEW LEAF,** 457 Broadway Troy, 273-8277 (specializing in architecture and science), and **BOOK NOOK,** 1606 Union St. Schenectady, 346-0075. These stores are very helpful for the serious reader and for the collector.

Out-of-print books (the ones you meant to buy when they first came out but never got around to or the ones you have recently discovered) are available at **W. SOMERS BOOKSELLER,** 841 Union St. Schenectady, 393-5266.

Two superior bookstores within reach of the region deserve mention. **THE OWL PEN,** Riddle Road, Greenwich, Washington County, 692-7039, is a remarkable place. In two barns located along a remote country lane, more than 40,000 books stand neatly stacked along the walls, easily accessible to browsers. This eccentric store is open only from May 1 to November 1 on Wednesday through Sunday from noon to six. **NORTHSHIRE BOOKS,** Main St. Manchester Center, VT, (802) 362-3565, has the strongest collection of literary titles in the region, combining up-to-date works of contemporary writers with an in-depth collection of quality work from the recent and distant past. Browsing in this store is fun and instructive.

Costumes:

THE COSTUMER, 444 State St. Schenectady, rents and sells costumes for a wide variety of purposes, serious or comic.

Clocks and Watches:

THE CLOCKWORKS, 1726 State St. Schenectady, sells and repairs quality clocks and movements. **FRANK ADAMS,** 58 N.Pearl St. Albany, has carried and serviced handsome, finest quality watches for men and women for three generations. **COHOES SPECIALTY STORES,** 43 Mohawk St. Cohoes, carries major brand name watches at discounted prices.

Floral Arrangements: Several area florists seem particularly creative
and responsive to special requests:

Dankers
658 Central Ave.   Stuyvesant Plaza
Albany 489-5461   Albany 438-2202

Felthousen's Country Florists
and Greenhouses
1537 Van Antwerp   250 Columbia St.
Schenectady 374-4414   Cohoes 237-2100

Meagher's
1144 Western Ave.
Albany 482-8696

Rudy Grant of Flower Design
Incorp
1956 Watt St.
Schenectady 377-0697

Silver Strawberry
830 Hoosick Rd.
Troy 279-1277

Verstandig's
454 Delaware Ave.
Delmar 439-4946

Garden Equipment and Supplies: Probably because summer months in the Capital District are ideal for the development of productive gardens, the region is replete with stores providing equipment, supplies, and plants for the gardener. The list below surveys the area, noting the special strengths of each merchant:

Agway Cottage
1158 Troy Schenectady Rd.

Wholesale and retail farm and garden supply; bird food

Faddegon's Nursery
1140 Troy Schenectady Rd.

All around garden supplies, plants and equipment; landscaping available

Garden Shoppe
Feura Bush Rd/Glenmont
3699 Carman Rd/Schdy

All around garden supplies, plants, and equipment; landscaping available

Gardenway Living Center
102nd St and 9th Ave/Troy

Power equipment Troybilt rototillers logsplitters, lawn mowers

Price Greenleaf
14 Booth Rd/Elsmere

Excellent selection of bulbs; all around garden supplies, plants and equipment

**Schultz Greenhouse and
  Garden Center**
136 Wolf Rd/Colonie

All around garden supplies, plants and equipment

Utica Seed Co.
Menands Market
Broadway/Menands

Wholesale and retail; bulk seed; supplies for farmers, backyard gardeners, and hobby greenhouse owners

Garden Plants: These excellent shops prepare plants for the gardener who does not wish to grow everything from seed.

Brizzel's
562 New Loudon Rd.
Loudonville

Open for Christmas, Easter, Spring and Fall; home grown house and garden plants, garden mums; home made balsam wreaths

Cedar Hill Iris Garden
Rte 144 (6 mi south of Alb.)

Perennials, with an emphasis on peonies and irises

Helderledge Farm
418 Picard Rd/Altamont

Trees, shrubs and plants; specializing in perennials, particularly day lilies; Christmas shop; display gardens; design-oriented use of materials

Menands Market
Broadway/Menands

Different vendors selling plants and bushes at low prices

Siesel's Flower Farm
488 Loudonville Rd/Loudonville

Annuals and perennials; vegetable plants; summer only

White Flower Farm (see Not Far Away, east)	Specimen varieties of hard-to-find plants and bushes; Display garden, beautiful, instructive catalog

House Plants: All these stores carry a good selection of carefully nurtured plants.

Creative Nature Center
411 New Karner Rd (Rte 155)
Colonie

Faddegon's Nursery
1140 Troy Schenectady Rd.

**Felthousen's Country Florists
and Greenhouses**
1537 Van Antwerp/Schdy

**Schultz Greenhouse
and Garden Center**
136 Wolf Rd/Colonie

Valoze Greenhouses
Rte 9 (North of Circle)
Latham

Verstandig's
454 Delaware Ave/Delmar

Gifts: These shops carry interesting, good quality gifts for the home or the individual.

Albany Institute Shop	Museum related gifts: books, prints, cards, reproductions
Albany Inst Shop Two	Annex to Luncheon Gallery
Bed, Board and Bath Stuyvesant Plaza/Albany	Fine accessories and gifts for the home
Carriage Trade 475 Albany Shaker Rd/Albany	Gifts for the home from playing cards to lamps
Cottage Herb Shop 311 State St/Albany	Imported and handmade gifts; Rare teas, herbs and spices
Crabtree and Evelyn Stuyvesant Plaza/Albany	Toiletries and cosmetics for men and women
Dansk Factory Outlet 50 Mohawk St/Cohoes	Decorative cookware, glass and tableware, all at reduced prices
Difference Is 118 S. Ferry St/Schdy	Unique gifts: glass, pewter, baskets, household items, stationery, pottery, stuffed animals

Frank Adams
58 N. Pearl St/Albany

China, crystal, silver
Fine traditional jewelry

Guess What
Stuyvesant Plaza/Albany

Handcrafted American
artist designs

Iron Horse Gifts
Rte 9/Latham

Imported toys and dolls:
collectors' items

Mabou
462 Broadway/Saratoga

Wide variety: gifts, kitchenware,
clothing, tableware, gourmet
foods, jewelry, baskets

New York State Museum Shop
Cultural Education Building
Albany

Natural artifacts—geodes, shells,
stones, plus books, stationery
and prints, jewelry, scarves and
other items made in NYS

Open Door
136 Jay St/Schdy

Stationery, hard-to-find records;
small but choice selection

Owl's Nest
164 Jay St/Schdy

Jewelry, chocolates, crystal,
paper goods

Pearl Grant-Richman
Stuyvesant Plaza

Fourteen shops in one;
excellent, changing selection;
Bridal Registry

Perfect Present
110 Wolf Rd/Colonie

Crystal, brass, gourmet foods,
baby boutique,
decorative accessories

Pier I
120 Wolf Rd/Colonie

Imported housewares, clothing,
candles, home furnishings,
artprints

**Rensselaer County
  Historical Society Shop**
59 2nd St/Troy

Museum-related gifts plus select
toys, books, gifts for the home

Rumplestiltskin and Friends
33 2nd St/Troy

Hand-produced leather goods

Schenectady Museum Shop
Nott Terrace Heights
Schenectady

Artifacts, souvenirs
reproductions from around the
world, books on nature, science,
and cooking

Shuttle Hill Herb Shop
241 Delaware Ave/Delmar

Cooking and fragrance herbs
and spices; stationery, homemade
teddy and piggywinklebears

Traditions
Stuyvesant Plaza/Albany

Select choice of decorative
home accessories; excellent prices

Verstandig's
454 Delaware Ave/Delmar

Decorative items, furniture,
imported gifts

Wit's End Giftique Parkwood Plaza/Clifton Park	Wide variety of merchandise and price ranges: music boxes, crystal, country kitchen et al

Handicraft Supplies: These helpful, well stocked shops cater to the person actively engaged in making objects by hand as well as those seeking a hobby.

Crafts Plus Stuyvesant Plaza	Kits and loose supplies for beginners or pros
Mardel Hobbies and Crafts 351 Altamont Ave/Schenectady	Radio control specialists
Needlework Center 1796 Rte 9/Clifton Park	Wide selection of patterns and supplies
Rayge Display 230 Broadway/Albany	Decorations for parties Custom displays

Hardware Stores: There are scores of good hardware stores in the Capital District, but three of them are more comprehensive than the rest. They offer the widest selection and the most expert advice.

Terminal Hardware
1157 Central Ave/Albany

Trojan Hardware
96 Congress St/Troy

Wallace Armor
225 Erie Blvd/Schdy

BROOKSTONES in Crossgates Mall is yet another story. This branch of the famous Boston-based store is as much a museum of human ingenuity as a shop. Featured are gadgets to eliminate inconvenience, stress and petty annoyances from ordinary tasks—or to make life more comfortable in heretofore unimagined ways. It allows for browsing at its best.

Jewelry: These reputable jewelers specialize in selling, repairing, and appraising beautiful ornaments.

American Indian Treasures 2558 Western Ave/Guilderland	Handsome items handmade by various tribes; predominantly silver and turquoise
Cohoes Specialty Stores 43 Mohawk St/Cohoes	Watches, adornments; discounted
Drue Sanders Clifton Country Mall Stuyvesant Plaza/Albany	Handcrafted silver and gold; will custom craft
Frank Adams 58 N. Pearl St/Albany	Traditional; fine jewelry; appraisals and repairs

Fritz Jewelry	Manufacturing and repairing
1659 Central Ave/Albany	
Kelly's Jewelers	Traditional; fine jewelers;
88 Central Ave/Albany	appraisals and repair

Newspapers and Magazines: A full range of local and out-of-town periodicals are stocked at these locations, all of them open around the clock:

Central News
980 Central Ave/Albany

Colonie News
1797 Central Ave/Albany

Coulson's
420 Broadway/Albany

Tyger's News
1 First St/Troy

Uptown News and Variety
136 N. Allen St/Albany

Newspapers (Out of Town) Delivered:

G.T. Taylor
482-1730 Albany

Paint: Most nationally distributed paints are available throughout the region and are listed by manufacturer in the telephone directory. Residents should also be aware of Passonno/PC Paint, an excellent brand produced locally and marketed exclusively through its own factory outlets, one at the plant in Watervliet and one in Albany.

Passonno/PC Paint
1438 Western Ave/Albany
500 Broadway/Watervliet

Picture Frames:

Framers Workshop
1710 Central Ave/Colonie
(See also Galleries in chapter on Arts)

Sporting Goods: Three stores cater to the general needs of the athlete; these are supplemented by highly recommended merchants who carry an in-depth selection of equipment for a few sports.

Generalists:
Andy's
688 New Loudon Rd
(Rte 9)/Latham
Stuyvesant Plaza/Albany

Goldstock's
121 N. Broadway/Schdy
Herman's
20 Wolf Rd/Colonie

Specialists:

DeRossi Sports 1823 Western Ave/Westmere	Hockey, soccer, lacrosse, rugby, tennis
Down Tube 466 Madison Ave/Albany	Cycling: supplies and repairs
Down-to-Earth Bike Works 54 Cohoes Rd/Watervliet	Cycling: supplies and repairs
Johnny Evers 330 Central Ave/Albany	Team sports: uniforms and equipment
Kemp's Rte 9/Latham 1527 15th St/Troy	Hockey
Klarsfeld 1370 Central Ave/Albany	Cycling: supplies and repairs
Orvis Manchester, VT	Fishing
Phoenix Ski Shop 1057 Troy-Schenectady Road	Downhill ski equipment and clothing
Ski Market 600 Troy-Schenectady Rd.	Cross country and downhill equipment and clothing; cycling
Taylor and Vadney 303 Central Ave/Albany	Camping, trapping, hunting; licenses, maps, equipment
Tough Traveler 1012 State St/Schdy	Ski and boot bags, backpacks, knapsacks, luggage
The Mountaineer Keene, NY	Mountaineering, hiking, expedition outfitting, camping

Stationery and Office Supplies: These shops have the best selection of items essential to make the office (and the home) function efficiently.

Gavit and Co. 50 Trinity Place/Albany	Fine hand-engraved stationery
Green's 374 Broadway/Albany Stuyvesant Plaza/Albany	
Hill, Robert and Co. 451 Broadway/Troy	
Paper Cutter Westgate Plaza/Albany	Discounted

Paper Mill
Delaware Plaza/Delmar

Schatz Stationery Stores
Colonie Center,
Latham Circle Mall
Mohawk Mall,
50 N. Pearl St/Albany

Union Book Co.
131 State St/Schdy
Clifton Country Mall

Libraries

General Libraries

THE PUBLIC LIBRARIES in Albany, Schenectady, and Troy are more than repositories of books and papers; they are vibrant cultural forces in the community. Each has a collection of materials on local history and well-trained, knowledgeable staff. They all offer special programs that appeal to various groups in the community—from preschoolers to octogenarians, from the erudite to the learning disabled. All their services are free of charge.

The libraries invite citizens to be Friends of the Library by making a small donation each year. Members receive a monthly calendar of events and notices of special programs. The branches and telephone numbers are listed below:

Albany

Main Branch, 161 Washington Ave. 449-3380
Delaware Branch, 328 Delaware Ave. 463-0254
New Scotland Branch, 369 New Scotland Ave. . . . 482-6661
John A. Howe Branch, Schuyler and Broad St. . . . 472-9485
Pine Hills Branch, 1000 Madison Ave. 482-7911

Schenectady

Main Library, Liberty & Clinton 382-3511
Duane Branch, 1331 State St. 382-3504
Pleasant Valley, 1026 Crane St. 382-3505
Quaker St., Quaker St. 895-2719
Scotia Branch, 14 Mohawk Ave. 382-3506
Wingate, 2558 Guilderland Ave. 382-3507
Woodlawn, 3002 Albany St. 382-3508

Troy

Main Library, 100 Second St. 274-7071
Lansingburgh, 114th St. & 4th Ave. 235-5310
Sycaway, Hoosick & Lee 274-1822

Troy Public Library
Michael Fredericks, Jr.

Specialized Libraries

THE MCKINNEY LIBRARY, in the Rice Building at the Albany Institute of History and Art, 125 Washington Ave, Albany, 463-4478, is in possession of an important collection of papers, diaries, letters, manuscripts, maps and prints of Albany's past. Open: T-F 9-3.

THE NEW YORK STATE LIBRARY, 474-7646, located in the Cultural Education Building of the Empire State Plaza, is a research library serving the government and the people of New York State. The collection of 4.5 million items, including some rare books and manuscripts, is available for use within the building. Those presenting a library card, a privilege reserved for persons professionally engaged in research, may borrow material.

The library uses a microfiche catalog; a folder explaining its use is available near the information desk. Four separate reference desks are staffed by librarians: (1) Law and the Social Sciences; (2) Science, Health Science and Technology; (3) Humanities; and (4) History and Geneology.

The library also provides other important services: statewide interlibrary loan, database service, legislative and governmental service, and special facilities for the blind and visually handicapped. Also located in the building are the archives of New York State Government. Open: M-F 9-5.

Academic Libraries

All of the colleges in the Capital District have libraries designed primarily to serve the needs of their own students and faculty. This purpose has been expanded recently to include other faculty and students as well, for the Capital District Library Council has established an interlibrary loan which allows full access to all holdings by all students and faculty members affiliated with any member institution. Another cooperative venture has been the creation of a common pool of periodicals. Students and faculty members can receive copies of articles they need for research, even if the library at their own institution does not own the source.

Residents not attached to a campus may apply to the loan desk at the library to learn what privileges are offered to the general public. Most of the libraries are willing to assist visitors and residents in any way they can. Expert librarians will answer questions in person or on the telephone.

The libraries vary in the breadth and depth of their holdings. The SUNYA library is the largest and most comprehensive; other campus libraries excel in fields in which their curriculums concentrate. Descriptions of these specializations can be found in the chapter on Education.

Professional Libraries

The three professional colleges in the area have specialized collections available to their own faculty and students as well as to practitioners of the profession.

THE ALBANY LAW SCHOOL LIBRARY, 445-2340, has summer hours and winter hours. Summer: M-F 9-9, Sat 9-5, Sun 12-6; winter: M-Th 8-midnight, F 8-10, Sat 9-9, Sun 10-midnight.

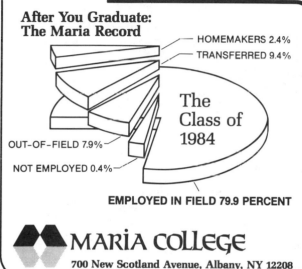
THE ALBANY COLLEGE OF PHARMACY LIBRARY, 445-7217, has summer hours and winter hours. Summer: M-F 8-4; winter: M-Th 8-10:30, F 8-5, Sat 1-5, Sun 1-10:30.

THE ALBANY MEDICAL COLLEGE LIBRARY (SHAEFFER LIBRARY), 445-5532, has a special telephone, 445-5534 with recorded information on open hours. At press time these were as follows: summer: M-Th 8-9, F 8-6, Sat 9-1, Sun 6 pm-10 pm; winter: M-Th 8 am-midnight, F 8 am-9 pm, Sat 10-6, Sun 2-10.

Museums

The Museums and Historic House Museums presented in this chapter are within the Capital-Saratoga region. Other museums are covered in the chapter *Not Far Away*.

MUSEUMS

ALBANY INSTITUTE OF HISTORY AND ART, 125 Washington Ave Albany, 463-4478, presents a permanent display and mounts a variety of temporary exhibits throughout the year. The permanent display, which emphasizes the cultural heritage of the region, includes antique silver, glass, porcelain, pewter, portraits, and furniture. One special section, the Dutch Room, is a replica of a home of the early Dutch settlers of the city. The collection also features miscellaneous objects bequeathed by local residents. These range from mummies (always a favorite with children), to posters and handbills from long ago.

Temporary exhibitions range from dazzling contemporary art by regional artists to somber portraits of Puritan forebears. Free. Open: T-Sat 10:00-4:45; Sun 2-5.

DISCOVERY CENTER OF THE CAPITAL REGION, P.O. Box 2235, Empire State Plaza, 12220, 474-5801 or 439-6705, will be an innovative science center for young people and their families. Planners for the museum, who conceived of the facility in 1984, hope to open in 1986-87. The center will draw on the plentiful resources of the region's educational, arts, and business communities to build a lively, contemporary site where children can engage in experiments to discover the meaning and impact of natural laws. Also on display will be demonstrations and explanations of recent innovations in science.

Adirondack Exhibit, NYS Museum
Michael Fredericks, Jr.

MUSEUM OF EARLY AMERICAN DECORATION, 19 Dove St Albany, 462-1676, is located in the Harmanus Bleeker Center. This museum houses a rare collection of American and British decorated furniture and accessories. There are frequent special exhibits. Free. Open: W-F 9:30-4; Sat noon-3; closed holiday weekends.

FORT CRAILO, 9½ Riverside Ave Rensselaer, 463-8738, was the house of the descendants of Kiliaen Van Rensselaer until the mid-19th century when it served as a school for boys and as a church rectory. It is now a New York State historic site and houses a museum on the history of Dutch culture in the Hudson River Valley. Free. Open: W-Sat 10-5, Sun 1-5.

NATIONAL BOTTLE MUSEUM, Verbeck House, 20 Church Ave., Ballston Spa, 885-7589, has a display of antique bottles, jars, containers, insulators, and glassblowing tools. Attached is a library with reference books, research materials, and slide programs. Admission. Open: Daily first weekend in June-Labor Day 10-4. Opening weekend includes great festivities.

THE NATIONAL MUSEUM OF RACING, Union Ave. Saratoga Springs, 584-0400, is entertaining for the entire family. On display are such artifacts from thoroughbred racing as trophies, portraits of great horses and famous owners, and the costumes and equipment of leading jockeys and renowned stables. The explanatory notes throughout the museum tell of the role of Saratoga in the growth of racing in America and describe the impact of various men of wealth on the sport. In summer, films of great races are shown. A gift shop with items pertaining to horses is in the museum. Free. Open: Year round as follows: Jan-April M-F 10-4; May-Dec M-F 9:30-5, Sat 12-5, but June 15-Sept 15 add Sun 12-5, and August racing season hours go to daily 9:30-7. Directions: Take Northway to Exit 14. Take Union Ave (Rte 9P) west to museum, which is opposite the Flat Track.

THE NEW YORK STATE MUSEUM, Cultural Education Building, Albany, 474-5877, is a vibrant cultural center. It offers films, permanent and temporary exhibits, and special programs. The award winning film *Chronicles of Change*, which plays every half hour on the quarter hour, sets the theme of the museum—humans' interaction with their surroundings in response to and as a cause of change. There are at present five permanent exhibits, with another—Upstate New York—scheduled to open soon. Open: Daily except Thanksgiving, Christmas and New Year's Day.

Permanent Exhibits

1. **ADIRONDACK WILDERNESS** shows what that region was like before people began to use it for recreation and for profit, analyzes the impact of humans, and explains contemporary attitudes toward conservation and thoughtful development. The exhibit is handsomely mounted with life-sized models of loggers, fishermen, and North Country guides.

2. **NEW YORK METROPOLIS** shows the emergence of the city of New York from a small port into a major world center of commerce, art, and finance. Included are handsome diaramas which recreate memorable places like Delmonico's Restaurant, South Street Sea Port, Chinatown, Broadway, Ellis Island and even Sesame St. Also of interest are preserved originals of the "A" train, an Otis elevator, a turn of the century classroom, and the New York Stock Exchange. Films and photographs supplement the written text.

3. **THE WORLD OF GEMS** is a breathtaking array of precious and semi-precious stones in all stages of presentation, from raw, inert rocks to beautifully mounted jewelry. The exhibit also explains how people labor to transform raw stones into finished pieces and how they make artificial stones.

4. **BIRDS OF NEW YORK** presents mounted models of birds residing in the state. Above the cases are speakers through which the calls and songs of the various birds sound.

5. **FIRE FIGHTING** traces the growth of the ability to control fire from the times of bucket brigades to the era of high pressure pumps. Included are some magnificent antique fire engines and hose carts.

Changing Exhibits

On the terrace level (fourth floor), the museum mounts changing exhibits, always described in newspapers or at the information desk at the main entrance. This level also affords a splendid view of The Mall. The grand staircase at the front of the building provides seating for open air entertainment on the Mall in the warm weather.

Special Programs

The museum building houses an accoustically superb, richly comfortable auditorium with seating capacity of 460. Adjoining this room is a student center with smaller, well-equipped spaces for classes or meetings. The museum sponsors courses for children and special programs throughout the year. Groups wishing to participate in classes should call 474-5843. Those wishing to use the facilities for groups should call 474-5141.

RENSSELAER COUNTY JUNIOR MUSEUM, corner Fifth Avenue and 106th Street, North Troy, 235-2120, is a wonderful little spot. Permanent collections include snakes, "touch me" objects and a fascinating sand pendulum. A small planetarium is housed downstairs in this converted firehouse, and temporary exhibits open from time to time. Suggested donation. Open: Sat-W 1-5.

SCHENECTADY COUNTY HISTORICAL SOCIETY, 32 Washington Ave Schenectady, 374-0263, is both a museum and a center of research. On display are artifacts of early life in the area — paintings, dolls, guns, costumes, furniture,

Hart-Cluett Mansion, Troy
Michael Fredericks, Jr.

and household goods. Of particular interest are the doll house which belonged to Governor Yates' family, the letter-books, notes, and memorabilia of electrical wizard Charles Steinmetz, and collections of beautiful objects of prominent Schenectady families over the years.

The Society houses books, manuscripts, maps, photos and recordings and invites the general public to do research on regional history. Over the years they have developed slide-tape programs which are available for use by individuals and groups. Free. Open: M-F 1-5. Closed holidays.

THE SCHENECTADY MUSEUM AND PLANETARIUM, Nott Terrace Heights, Schenectady, 382-7890, features permanent and changing exhibits in arts, crafts, science and natural history as well as several annual events—the Crafts Festival, Festival of Nations and Museum Ball. Of particular note is the Museum/Union College Council Series, long known for the excellence of the artists invited. Planetarium shows are offered each weekend for a nominal fee. Works of regional artists are on display and available for sale. Free to members. Minimal fee non-members. Open: T-F 10-4:30; Sat-Sun 12-5. Directions: Rte 5 (State Street) to Nott Terrace then to Nott Terrace Heights.

HISTORIC HOUSE MUSEUMS

CHERRY HILL, South Pearl St. Albany, 434-4791, is a charming colonial building built in 1787 by Philip Van Rensselaer and lived in by his family until 1963. It offers the visitor a rare opportunity to see the continuum of life in Albany for almost two hundred years. As each generation passed, it handed down the possessions it had accumulated; thus the house acquired vast collections of furniture, portraits, china, documents, textiles and other items. The accumulation of belongings came to possess a great deal of interesting variety and historic value. When Emily W. Rankin, the last member of the family, died in 1963, she left the house and its contents to Historic Cherry Hill, which opened the museum in 1964. The visitor will enjoy the warm, inviting atmosphere of this pleasant museum. On a Sunday early in December the house is decorated with family ornaments and toys, and refreshments made from family recipes are served. Admission. Open: T-Sat 10-4, Sun 1-4; closed in January and on some holidays. Tours on the hour.

HART-CLUETT MANSION, 59 Second St Troy, 272-7232, is owned by the Rensselaer County Historical Society. This late Federal style townhouse, built in 1827, has on display for the public an important collection of early 19th century furnishings and artifacts including works by Phyfe, Galusha, Hidley and Moore. The adjoining building houses changing exhibits, a museum shop, and a meeting room. The library holds maps, genealogical sources, broadsides, and photographs. Free. Open: (Museum, Shop, and Library) T-Sat. 10-4.

SCHUYLER MANSION STATE HISTORIC SITE, Clinton St. between Catherine St. and Fourth Ave. Albany, 474-3953, is the once splendid home of Philip Schuyler, general in the Revolution. Known in its day as "The Pastures," the brick building was once surrounded by ten to twelve acres of rolling lawns and carefully tended gardens through which strolled many heroes of the Revolution and "Patricians" of the era, most notably LaFayette and Alexander Hamilton, son-in-law of the general. Visitors may walk through the house, which contains beautiful furniture, a unique stairway, portraits and accessories of the time. Behind the building is an herb garden duplicating that once tended by the Schuylers. A parking lot is available behind the building. Free. Open: Apr-Dec W-Sat 10-5; Sun 1-5. (Phone for winter hours). Closed holidays except Memorial Day, Independence Day and Labor Day. Directions: Drive east on Madison Ave., turn right on Eagle St., left on Morton Ave., right on Elizabeth St. and then left on Catherine St.

TEN BROECK MANSION, 9 Ten Broeck Pl. Albany, 436-9826, a beautiful home of the Federal period, was built as a residence for Abraham Ten Broeck and his wife, Elizabeth Van Rensselaer, in 1797-8. Ten Broeck was a member of the Colonial Assembly, a delegate to the Continental Congress, Brigadier General in the Revolutionary Army in the battle of Saratoga, member of the State Senate, mayor·of Albany and first president of the Bank of Albany. The house, also called Arbor Hill, served for a short time as a boys' school and then was reconverted to a private home by the Olcott family, who occupied the house for four generations. In 1948 the Olcotts presented this lovely mansion to the Albany County Historical Association. An interesting stir was created when a wine cellar of great value was unearthed beneath the building. Proceeds of the sale have been used to further restoration. Free. Open: Year round except holidays, T-Sat 10-4; Sun 1-4.

Schuyler Mansion, Albany
Michael Fredericks, Jr.

The Arts

One of the most endearing characteristics of the Capital District is that in all the arts—music, theater, dance, art, and film—residents are welcome to produce their own work, to participate in an ensemble, or to serve as members of an audience. Throughout the year, local individuals and groups actively engage in creating artistic products, and season after season—with particular flamboyance in summer—internationally acclaimed artists come to display their talents. The visits are frequently short-lived, so the lover of the arts must be vigilant.

Information About The Arts

ALBANY LEAGUE OF ARTS, 19 Clinton Avenue Albany, 449-5380, is a regional arts service organization which provides financial, legal, promotional, and administrative services to independent artists and art organizations as well as to the general community. It runs the Community Box Office, provides a free day-by-day calendar of events, and serves as a clearing house for groups scheduling events (this last to help avoid conflict and duplication of effort).

THE CAPITAL REGION CENTER FOR ARTS EDUCATION is a program for area teachers who want to include the arts in their teaching. Run by the College of Humanities and Fine Arts at SUNYA and the Capital District Humanities Project, the program includes instruction in a summer institute, assistance in developing a program for the school year, and year-long consultation on art in the classroom. Teachers meet persons from the area art institutions, learn what resources are available to them, and study methods of making arts accessible to their students. Information is available at CDHP, SUNYA, Hu 314, Albany 12222, 442-4236.

Merrill Ashley, NYC Ballet
Carolyn George/SPAC

CLEARINGHOUSE FOR ARTS INFORMATION, INC, 625 Broadway, New York 10012, produces an annual booklet, SUMMER ARTS, which contains annotated calendars of events presented by geographic area. This handsome, clear brochure is available at no cost. The number in New York is (212) 677-7548.

COLLEGE AND UNIVERSITY BOX OFFICES provide information and tickets for the many excellent programs sponsored by student organizations throughout the year. Below is a list of colleges and the numbers to call for information for a particular campus:

CSR	454-5171
JCA	445-1725
HVCC	283-1100
Maria	438-3111
RPI	270-6505
Sage	270-2000
SCCC	346-6211
Siena	783-2383
Skidmore	584-5000
SUNYA	442-3995
Union	370-6153

NEWSPAPERS cover events and carry ads for upcoming performances. Of particular interest are the following:

KNICKERBOCKER NEWS	"The Entertainer" on Friday night
METROLAND	Weekly review of arts and entertainment
SCHENECTADY GAZETTE	Saturday edition
SOUTH END SCENE	Monthly which covers arts news not included elsewhere
TIMES RECORD	"Steppin Out" on Friday night
TIMES UNION	"Weekend" section on Friday.

PERFORMING ARTS CENTERS which serve the region include "The Egg," the Palace, Proctor's, Saratoga Performing Arts Center, and Troy Music Hall. Information about programs and tickets is available at Community Box Offices, listed at the end of this section.

SCHENECTADY ARTS COUNCIL, Proctor's Arcade, 432 State St Schenectady, 374-3321, has been a moving force in Schenectady since its birth in 1964. The principal impetus for restoring and reviving Proctor's Theater, the Council continues its work by presenting classes to help artists work more effectively, by sponsoring the Empire State Youth Orchestra, by organizing a Spring Showcase for young audiences, by supporting Art in Public Places, and by operating Gallery 400 (in Canal Square).

Tickets

COMMUNITY BOX OFFICES, run by the Albany League of Arts, handle ticket sales for most area performing arts events. Offices are located at:

Colonie Center 458-7530
Empire State Plaza 473-8122
432 State St Schdy 370-0047
Stuyvesant Plaza. 438-0721

TICKETRON, a nationwide service which uses a computer to reserve seats for arts and entertainment events, is situated at all four Community Box Office locations, at RPI Field House, and at other sites which you can learn by calling (212) 977-9020.

Special Programs Embracing all the Arts

THE HALF MOON CAFE, which hosts readings, presentations, and musical performances, is described in the chapter Other Things to Do.

NEW YORK STATE SUMMER SCHOOL OF THE ARTS is a government-sponsored summer experience for students 14-18 years old. It consists of six schools— visual arts, media studies, dance, orchestral studies, theater and choral study—each held on a campus within New York State. Information about programs and the application procedure is available at the State Education Department (Room 681) Albany 12234, 474-8773.

SPENCERTOWN ACADEMY is a community-sponsored arts and educational organization based in the 1847 schoolhouse in Spencertown. Throughout the year, members bring artists to present dramatic performances, poetry readings, film series, and musical evenings of all varieties, from chamber music concerts to old time band renderings. Art work of many forms is on exhibit. Information about the programs of this Hudson Valley/ Berkshire institution is available through the Academy at Box 171 Spencertown NY 12165.

MUSIC

Orchestras

THE ALBANY SYMPHONY ORCHESTRA offers a fine program each year, including various subscription series at the Palace Theater and at Troy Music Hall, special benefits, youth and tiny tot concerts, and out-of-town performances. Information is available at 465-4755. Tickets can be purchased at the Palace, at Community Box Office locations, or by mail—Albany Symphony Orchestra, 19 Clinton Ave Albany 12207. The orchestra is assisted by an auxiliary group, Albany Vanguard.

THE BOSTON SYMPHONY makes its summer home in Lenox, Mass, a renowned center of music education. Concerts of the full orchestra are conducted generally on weekends. Saturday morning rehersals are open for an admission fee. During the week, performances by music students of the Tanglewood Music Center, a school where talented young musicians study with the members of the orchestra, are scheduled along with appearances of popular artists, a festival of contemporary music, and a concert of the Boston Pops. The school, a summer academy for advanced music study, is open to applicants ages 18-35. Nationwide auditions run from January to March. Competition for fellowships, with cost underwritten by the Boston Symphony, is keen.

The full BSO summer calendar is printed mid-Spring in the "Arts and Leisure" section of THE NEW YORK TIMES or may be obtained before June 1 through Symphony Hall, Boston, MA 02115 and subsequently through The Box Office, Tanglewood, Lenox, MA 01234, (413) 637-1940. Lawn seats are available and picnicking is something of a tradition. (The picnickers at Tanglewood are notorious for their tendency to talk, walk, and eat during the performance. Those who enjoy this atmosphere can relax into its charms, but those who wish to listen carefully to the music should secure seats under the shed, for no amount of "shushing" will silence Tanglewood's indomitable audience.)

The Wizard of Oz
Fred Ricard/ESIPA

EMPIRE STATE YOUTH ORCHESTRA, founded in 1979, is made up of talented musicians through high school age from the greater Capital District Region. The orchestra plays regularly scheduled concerts in Albany, Troy, and Schenectady and travels to other cities for festivals and performances. The venture has been so successful that **THE JUNIOR ORCHESTRA** was formed in 1981 to accommodate more players and to serve as a training ground for the Youth Orchestra. Both are funded by private donations. Auditions are held yearly. Information about all the activities of these groups is available at ESYO, Box 211 Empire State Plaza, Albany 12220, 861-8753.

THE PHILADELPHIA ORCHESTRA makes its summer home at the Saratoga Performing Arts Center. This orchestra is internationlly acclaimed for its extraordinary discipline and cohesion, especially in the string section. The program is available in early spring at SPAC, Saratoga Springs 12866, 587-3330.

Tickets are available at the box office, either in person, by mail or by telephone if using a credit card. Lawn seats are available at the time of, or in advance of the performance. Because of the coolness of evenings, those selecting lawn seating should dress warmly.

SPAC hosts major popular musical performers throughout the summer. Artists such as Frank Sinatra, Judy Collins, the Grateful Dead, Billy Idol, Genesis, and Bruce Springsteen attract thousands of enthusiastic fans. Tickets for seats at these performances often sell out hours after the box offices open, but there are thousands of lawn seats. These are held until the day of the performance unless the security forces anticipate that the demand will create a safety problem. At this point they place a ceiling on lawn seats and offer them in advance. Over the years SPAC has earned a reputation for careful, thoughtful handling of crowds.

SPAC welcomes support through several levels of membership and rewards that participation by benefits, including advance mailing and priority ticket orders. It is also possible to request the season program and announcements by paying a small fee ($3) to have your name placed on the Preferred Mailing List write SPAC, PML Saratoga Springs N.Y. 12866.

SCHENECTADY SYMPHONY ORCHESTRA is a community orchestra which annually presents four full concerts and two children's concerts at Proctor's Theater. The League of the Schenectady Symphony, a volunteer agency, holds previews, sponsors the children's concerts, and helps to raise money for the orchestra and for a musical scholarship. Information is available at 108 Union St Schenectady, 372-2500.

Chamber Performances

CAPITOL CHAMBER ARTISTS present eight concerts each year. The members design programs deliberately mixing new and old, well-known and unknown.

Albany performances are held at Albany Institute of History and Art or the Recital Hall at SUNYA; Troy performances take place at the Troy Music Hall. Subscriptions are welcome. Information is available at 263 Manning Blvd Albany, 489-0507.

FRIENDS OF CHAMBER MUSIC INC in Troy has delighted music lovers for over 35 years by offering well-known chamber ensembles in concert four times each year. The performances are given in Kiggens Hall at the Emma Willard School. Information is available at 274-4452 or through Community Box Office.

THE INTERNATIONAL FESTIVAL OF CHAMBER MUSIC, sponsored by the Schenectady Museum and Union College, present concerts featuring some of the most renowned ensembles in chamber music. Performances are given in the lovely Union College Memorial Chapel. Subscriptions and single tickets are available through Schenectady Museum, Nott Terrace Heights, Schenectady 12308, 382-7890.

THE STRING PROGRAM, an eight week educational experience for talented young musicians who want to work in ensemble, is held each summer using the facilities of the Emma Willard School in Troy. The excellent concerts, which are not widely promoted, are open to the public. Information is available at 274-4440.

Concert Series

SIENA COLLEGE MUSIC SERIES presents concerts of vocal and instrumental artists performing solo or in small groups. Information about these on-campus concerts is available through Siena College, 783-2300.

TROY CHROMATICS CONCERTS is a series of four superior musical performances scheduled throughout the fall, winter, and spring. The accoustically superb Troy Music Hall, State and Second Streets, Troy, functions as a stage for the concerts. Information and subscriptions are available at 10 123rd St North Troy 12182, 235-6831.

Musical Groups

ALBANY PRO MUSICA is a community chamber chorus specializing in repertory for chamber choirs, especially Baroque, Romantic and Contemporary music. This relatively new society, established in 1981, is made up of residents of the extended Capital District who have auditioned for membership. The group presents three concerts a year. Information is available through David Janower, 573 Western Ave Albany 12203.

CAPITAL HILL CHORAL SOCIETY, a community chorus, presents four concerts of classical choral music each year. Tryouts for new members are advertised in the newspaper. For information call 463-7022 evenings or write Box 64, Albany 12201.

MENDELSSOHN CLUB OF ALBANY is an all male glee club with singers from the larger Capital District. Formed in 1909 as a part of a national group, it presents performances of light music throughout the year at Chancellors' Hall. Information is available at 256 State St Albany 12210 or 436-9849.

MONDAY MUSICAL CLUB has been a viable factor in the community since 1903 when it was formed as a "forum for the enjoyment of music." The society sponsors workshops at which members preside, holds member artist performances, supports a women's chorus, and sponsors a young musicians forum for High School students studying voice or instrument. Information is available at 456-6302.

OCTAVO SINGERS, established in Schenectady in 1933 as a community chorus, presents a minimum of three concerts a year—two with the Schenectady Symphony Orchestra. The group, composed of 90-100 vocalists, presents concerts of classical sacred music at Proctor's Theater or at Memorial Chapel on the campus of Union College. For information contact George Moross at 381-9444.

Calder Stabile, Empire State Plaza
Michael Fredericks, Jr.

SARATOGA POTSDAM CHORAL INSTITUTE was established to provide a chorus for the Philadelphia Orchestra's visit to its summer home in Saratoga Springs. It makes its own base on the campus of Skidmore college for the three weeks in August when the orchestra is in residence. The appeal of the site and the eminence of the orchestra have attracted people from around the world to apply for the chorus, which now numbers 300 members, a considerable number of whom are gifted local residents. Application for membership should be directed to N. Brock McElheran, Crane School of Music, SUNY Potsdam 13676.

SCHENECTADY CHORAL SOCIETY is a small community chorus of mixed voices which performs classical and contemporary works at two concerts a year. This organization, like so many of the other musical groups, has been in existence for more than half a century. Information is available at 377-7198.

SCHENECTADY ETUDE CLUB is a group of women from the tri-city area, well-trained in music, who are interested in performing at monthly meetings or at public events. Membership is open for instrumentalists and vocalists by audition only. The group sponsors the Junior Etude Club for high school students. Information is available at 399-2753.

TROY MUSICAL ARTS is a member chorus established in the Thirties as a women's choir and expanded recently to include men's voices. One of their goals is to bring to their audience musical selections not usually performed by other groups or played on the radio. The society gives two concerts a year at the Julia and Howard Bush Memorial Center on the Russell Sage Campus. For information call 235-8814.

Opera

AMERICAN LYRIC THEATRE, formed in 1981 as part of the **LAKE GEORGE OPERA FESTIVAL,** offers a two year apprentice program for American artists to develop acting skills with musical theater. It presents showcases of scenes from plays, operas, and musicals, using as its stage the Blenheim Mansion on Rte 9N in Lake George. Information is available through the Lake George Opera Festival described below.

GLIMMERGLASS OPERA THEATER presents very fine renderings of operatic masterpieces during a summer season. The cast, accompanied by a strong orchestra, performs all the operas in English translation. Information is available from M-Sat 10-5 at the theater: The Hedges, 139 Main St Cooperstown, (607) 547-2255. Tickets are available through P.O. Box 191 Cooperstown 13326.

LAKE GEORGE OPERA FESTIVAL is a summer season of operas performed in English at the festival auditorium and a musical cruise featuring selections from operas and musicals. Artists working with the American Lyric Theater also perform with this group. Information is available from Lake

George Opera Festival, P.O. Box 425, Glens Falls 12801, 793-3858. Directions: Take I-87 to Exit 19. Turn left onto Aviation Road. Queensbury High School Auditorium is on right.

WAMC (90.3 FM) broadcasts the Metropolitan Opera live on Saturday at 2:00 during the season.

Organ Music

THE KING OF INSTRUMENTS SERIES brings organists of national and international prominence to perform on the best instruments in the area. Recitals occur at different places throughout the year. For information call 861-5370.

CATHEDRAL OF ALL SAINTS, Swan Street at the corner of Elk in Albany, presents concerts at 4:30 each Sunday November-April (except at Christmas and Easter). There is no charge for admission.

PROCTOR'S THEATER puts its Golub Mighty Wurlitzer Organ to use throughout the year with live accompaniment to silent films, organ concerts by world-renowned organists, and lively sing-a-longs.

THE ROUND LAKE ORGAN, an 1847 Ferris Tracker pipe organ located in the Round Lake Auditorium, is an historical artifact as well as an extraordinary musical instrument. Each summer the Round Lake Historical Society, which is in the process of restoring the organ and its housing, sponsors six recitals. Information is available at 899-2130. Directions: Northway (I-87) to Exit 11. Go one half mile east to Round Lake.

Other Items of Interest Regarding Music

CAFFE LENA is described in the chapter Other Things to Do.

THE CARILLON in Albany's city hall has an interesting history described by William Gorham Rice in a booklet, "The Albany Singing Tower," available in the McKinney Library. Most of the sixty bells are named after their donors, and many bear inscriptions such as that on bell thirty-eight

> O Albany! O Albany!
> Far fairer city shall you see
> Yet non that seems so fair to me.

The bells of the carillon chime gallantly over the city each noon.

EIGHTH STEP COFFEE HOUSE is described in the chapter Other Things to Do.

LUZERNE MUSIC CENTER is a summer program for youth ages 11-19. It combines supervised recreational activities with serious study of music. Orchestra, chamber music, and theory are taught by members of the Philadelphia Orchestra and faculty from area colleges. Recreation is

Troy Savings Bank Music Hall
S. Blanchard/Troy Liveability Campaign

supervised by students from major music schools or graduate music students who are skilled in sports or recreation. Student campers prepare to perform, either alone or in ensemble. They watch members of the Philadelphia Orchestra rehearse and perform. Information is available through Bert Phillips or Toby Blumenthal, Luzerne Music Center, 5 East Brookhaven Road Wallingford PA 19086, (215) 566-1475 or (518) 696-2771.

MUSIC MOBILE is a traveling music program for children begun in 1977 by Ruth Pelham to bring songs to areas where the low income of families prevents children from traveling to music. The blue van goes on schedule to playgrounds, vacant lots, housing projects, schools and other similar sites. Ms. Pelham there performs and teaches the children how to make their own instruments from scrap materials—boxes, wood, rubber bands, egg cartons, old bottle caps and fabric. The unique project is funded by grants and donations from groups and individuals.

SUNDAY ACOUSTICS PERFORMANCES AT EL LOCO are described in the chapter Other Things to Do.

WAMC (90.3 FM) is a listener-supported station affiliated with National Public Radio. Its principal focus is classical music with some jazz, folk, and opera (as well as strong news, commentary and arts features).

WMHT (89.9 FM) is a listener-supported station devoted to continuous classical music. Members receive a monthly program and may participate in the listener request program each Saturday.

THEATER

ALBANY CIVIC THEATER, 235 Second Ave Albany, 462-1297, resides in a converted turn of the century fire house. In this intimate theater all seats are orchestra seats, and every audience member can appreciate fully the sounds and actions occurring on stage. The theater offers four productions each year, including a musical, a drama, a children's play and another selection. Tryouts, advertised in the Albany newspapers, are open to all. Tickets to productions (especially the weekend performances) often sell out, so it is wise to reserve seats in advance.

CAPITAL REPERTORY COMPANY is a professional regional theatre located at the Market Theatre, 111 North Pearl St Albany. The annual program is ambitious and challenging; Capital Rep is a company willing to take risks. Each year's schedule includes at least one classic, one contemporary work, and a new play. Subscriptions are available for the full season, and patrons may arrange to sponsor particular performances or bring groups to the theater. The Company also makes attractive Before Theater dinner arrangements with various downtown restaurants. Information is available at 462-4531.

THE EMPIRE STATE INSTITUTE FOR THE PERFORMING ARTS (ESIPA) produces and presents events in theatre, dance and music. Making its home in the Egg at the Empire State Plaza, this regional theatre with its own resident professional theatre company performs classical and contemporary works for the stage and also serves as a center for the development of new works by American playwrights—all open to the public at surprisingly affordable prices.

As part of the State University of New York, ESIPA offers a variety of arts-in-education programs, takes its productions to schools throughout the State of New York using theatre as an educational tool and provides curricular materials for use by students and teachers. Other programs and services include a Theatre Arts School for children and adults, an accredited Internship Program and Arts Accessibility services to make theatre available to the widest possible audience. Information is available at 474-1199 or 473-3750.

HERITAGE ARTISTS LTD, (HeArt), a non-profit arts organization founded in 1983 to revitalize and restore significant national landmarks and stimulate the cultural, educational and economic climates of regions, has taken as its principal enterprise the support of a professional music theatre repertory company at the Cohoes Music Hall. Subscriptions are available through the box office at 58 Remsen St, Cohoes, 235-7969.

PROCTOR'S THEATER, Schenectady, hosts short runs of major theater productions by first rate road companies. The presentations, many of plays still running on Broadway, are usually excellent. In addition, it is fun being part of a large and appreciative audience in this grand old theater. Proctor's publishes its schedule a full year in advance and then advertises the events just prior to the opening. Tickets are sold at the box office or through Community Box Office. Information is available at 382-1083; tickets at 346-6204.

SCHENECTADY CIVIC PLAYERS is a community theater group celebrating in 1985 its 58th season. It mounts five productions—dramas and comedies— annually, presenting seven performances of each offering. The players vary their material, taking on a range of types of plays and musicals. Tryouts for all roles are open to anyone interested in auditioning. Information is available at 12 South Church St Schenectady, 393-2408.

SCHENECTADY LIGHT OPERA COMPANY is a volunteer group which produces four Broadway shows each year—two on a small scale at their own State Street building and two on a large scale at Proctor's. Tryouts for all shows—open to the public—are advertised in the local papers. The company grants two awards each year to young members of the community who are aspiring singers. Information is available at 826 State St Schenectady, 393-5732.

Summer Theater

In June, July and August some summer regulars come to town to entertain. The Albany League of Arts coordinates the calendars of most of these companies and makes information available through Community Box Offices.

THE COLISEUM THEATRE, P.O. Box 41 Latham 12110, 785-3393, welcomes summer stock companies and a series of musical performers throughout the spring, summer, and fall. Subscription prices are available.

THE LITTLE THEATRE, Saratoga Performing Arts Center, offers drama and modern dance productions during the summer. The theater itself is the perfect size for intimate productions. Information about the schedule and tickets is available at 587-3330.

THE MAC-HAYDN THEATER presents lively renderings of the most popular Broadway musicals from the past and the present. Plays are produced "In the Round" in a rustic theater situated on a hill just outside Chatham. Because it operates from the end of May till the middle of September, the Mac-Haydn is able to mount eight plays each season. Tickets are reasonably priced, so this is ideal family entertainment. Information is available at the theater, Route 203 Chatham 12037, 392-9292.

SHAKESPEARE AND COMPANY, located at The Mount—Edith Wharton's home in Lenox, Massachusetts—is a summer theater company which makes use of its unusual setting to present a unique production of a work by Shakespeare. At this outdoor theater, the witches in Macbeth cavort and chortle in the woods behind the house, Romeo actually climbs the balcony to reach his love, and the ghost of Hamlet's father hovers hauntingly above the trees. The overall effect is usually most entertaining and provocative. (As the evening proceeds, it can grow chilly, so audiences should dress warmly and bring blankets and tarpaulins on which to sit.)

In addition to the Shakespeare play, the company usually presents an original work dealing with the life of Ms. Wharton. The Mount, which is described in detail in the chapter "Not Far Away," offers tours in summer: Th-F noon-4; S-Sun 10-4.

SHAKESPEARE IN THE PARK is a fledgling organization, the brainchild of local residents who wished to make outdoor summer theater available to all. The company invites local actors, stage technicians, and other theater experts to develop and display their skill by presenting two productions a summer—one a Shakespearean drama, one an American play—in the Lake House in Washington Park in Albany. Information is available at the City Arts Office, 409 Madison Ave Albany. All performances are free.

WILLIAMSTOWN THEATER FESTIVAL is considered one of the finest regional summer theaters in the East. This judgment is based on the nature of the plays undertaken as well as the quality of acting and directing. The theater has been the springboard of many famous theatrical figures, some of whom return each summer to contribute to the continuing excellence of the festival. Information and tickets are available at P.O. Box 517 Williamstown, MA 01267, (413) 458-8146.

WOODSTOCK PLAYHOUSE in Woodstock NY is the oldest continuously operating summer stock theater in the state. From Mid-June to early September the playhouse presents a series of plays, a set of children's theater productions, and a series of single performances by major dance companies. Tickets are very reasonable, especially through subscription. Information is available at (914) 679-2436.

DANCE

NATIONAL DANCE HALL OF FAME was conceived in 1984 to be headquartered in rehabilitated Washington Baths at Saratoga Spa State Park. The purpose of the museum will be threefold: first, to establish a center for the preservation and display of artifacts and memorabilia about dance; second, to make films, books, and records on the dance available to those studying this complex art form; third, to recognize outstanding contributions by principals in dance in the United States.

BERKSHIRE BALLET COMPANY is an interesting one which performs regionally throughout the year. One of the highlights of the winter season is the Christmas presentation of THE NUTCRACKER SUITE, for which the company recruits area students of the ballet to complement the regular ensemble. Programs and tickets are available through the Ballet, 210 Wendell Ave Pittsfield MA 01201.

eba CENTER FOR DANCE AND MOVEMENT, Chapter House Theater, 351 Hudson Ave Albany, 465-9916, offers classes in ballet, jazz, and modern dance plus programs for health and fitness. The teachers are members of MAUDE BAUM AND COMPANY DANCE THEATRE, a resident professional touring dance company, which also performs locally.

JACOB'S PILLOW, Box 287, Lee, MA 01238, is a summer dance festival featuring major dance companies from around the country. As the oldest such festival in the country, Jacob's Pillow offers a wide spectrum of dance events and attracts some of the world's finest dancers. The performances are held in the Ted Shawn Theater, the first stage in America designed specifically for the dance. Schedules and reservations are available at the

Sculpture at Schenectady Museum
Michael Fredericks, Jr.

above address or at (413) 243-0745. Directions: Take I-90 east to Mass Turnpike. Take Turnpike Exit 2. Take Rte 20E eight miles. Go left onto George Carter Rd. Theater is seven-tenths of a mile down this road.

THE SCHOOL OF DANCE AT JACOB'S PILLOW, which functions during the festival, offers training in ballet, jazz, and modern dance for qualified students from around the country. Students live in rustic cabins and study with prominent artists. The schedule of the school runs concurrent with the dance festival, so students also have informal access to leading dancers.

THE NEW YORK CITY BALLET takes up residence at SPAC, in Saratoga, during the month of July, presenting a mixed program which includes established favorites as well as world premiers of new or re-written works. The Corps is famous for its discipline, and among the principals are some of the world's greatest dancers. Much of the repertory derives from the work of its former director, the late George Balanchine.

ART

The Capital District has access to a wide variety of art collections, many of them located within easy traveling distance. Described in the chapter "Not Far Away" and listed in the index are the following museums and galleries:

Bennington Historical Museum
Chesterwood
Clark Institute
The Hyde Collection
Malden Bridge Arts Center
Munson Williams Proctor Institute
National Museum of Racing
Olana
Storm King Art Center
Tyringham Gallery
William College Museum of Art

(And, of course, the many superior museums of Boston and New York which are also listed in the chapter Not Far Away.)

Within the Capital District several serious galleries combine permanent collections with occasional shows.

GALLERIES

CENTER GALLERIES, 75 New Scotland Ave Albany, 462-4775, is the only gallery in the area dedicated to presentation of the best of area artists. Since its opening in 1977, the gallery has mounted 54 major comprehensive exhibitions. It plans to continue its schedule of eight exhibits each year, including all media. (Most works on display are available for purchase.) Open: T-Sat 12-5 or at other hours by request.

DAY SPRING GALLERY, 458 Broadway Saratoga Springs, 587-9812, is a relatively new gallery, having opened in 1975 as a place for the display and sale of paintings, pottery, and contemporary jewelry. The gallery also features limited edition prints of work by regional artists as well as those of national and international repute. In the summer season the gallery reflects the interests of the area by featuring portrayals of dancers in July and of horses in August.

GALLERY 400 in Canal Square, Schenectady invites local artists to exhibit their work. Most items on display are available for purchase.

THE NELSON A. ROCKEFELLER EMPIRE STATE PLAZA ART COLLECTION is an assemblage of contemporary paintings and sculpture commissioned or chosen by a panel of experts appointed by the government of the State of New York. The works, which are owned by the citizens of the state, are on display throughout the enormous complex of buildings and parks that constitutes the Empire State Plaza. The stated purpose of the collection is to "symbolize the spirit of free inquiry and creative integrity which are so vital to modern society—and the duty of governments everywhere to protect and promote the right of the creative individual to live and work in freedom." In addition, the art works decorate the areas to which thousands of people come each day to work or visit. The pamphlet "The Empire State Plaza Art Collection," available free of charge at the information booths on the concourse level, identifies each of the items on a very clearly marked map.

"Art At the Plaza" is a program organized to stimulate appreciation for and understanding of contemporary art, particularly for the works in the collection. The program includes:

1. Tours (one Hour)—Wed at 10:30 and 2:30 at Visitors Services, or daily by arrangement at least one week in advance.
2. Films—at noon in winter and spring.
3. Lectures—in spring and fall as announced.

Information on these activities is available through Curatorial Services, NYS Office of General Services, 29th Floor—Room 2937 Tower Bldg, Albany 12242, 473-7521.

SUNY PLAZA GALLERY, located in the arcade of the State University of New York Plaza (at the foot of State Street), exhibits the work of graduates, faculty, students, and scholars of the University. The brochure notes that it is offered to the community as "an opportunity for cultural enrichment and as a demonstration of the vitality and diversity of the State University of New York." This statement is actually an apt description, for the works do display a depth, skill, and range that the University, as a multi-purpose educational institution, aims to cultivate. Open: M-F 9-6.

THE UNIVERSITY ART GALLERY, SUNYA Fine Arts Building, 1400 Washington Ave Albany 12222, hosts a variety of shows throughout the year. The versatility in both lighting and wall space of the gallery itself allows it to be suitable for the display of large, sweeping modern canvases one week and small, detailed work the next. The skilled staff prepare handsome, helpful brochures and pamphlets to guide the visitor through the exhibits. It is best to call the gallery (442-4035) to check for hours of opening. To reach the gallery, drive into the University's main entrance on the Washington Avenue side of the campus, park in the visitors' lot immediately south of the Great Circle (the large grass plot), and walk onto the podium through the central opening (directly in front of the fountain and bell tower). The Gallery will be on your left.

Exhibition Space

Several institutions provide exhibition space for artists' work. Because each of these institutions is described elsewhere in this book and listed in the index, we will merely mention them here with the telephone number to call for information:

Albany Institute of History and Art 463-4478
Chapel and Cultural Center at RPI in Troy 274-7793
College of St. Rose (at the Picotte Gallery)
    on State St in Albany 454-5185
Congregation Beth Israel Education Center
    in Schenectady 377-3700
Emma Willard School in Troy 274-4440
Rensselaer County Council on the Arts in Troy 273-0552
Russell Sage College in Troy 270-2395
Schenectady Museum 382-7890
State Museum of New York in Albany 474-5877
Union College in Schenectady 370-6201

Sales Galleries

In addition to these exhibition centers the region has several sales galleries— shops which display the works of artists which it is offering for purchase. Browsers are always welcome at these galleries.

SUNYA Gallery
Michael Fredericks, Jr.

ALBANY GALLERY, Stuyvesant Plaza Albany, 482-5374, emphasizes 19th and 20th Century Marine art and also carries a good selection of local prints. It mounts contemporary exhibits of local artists with the same interest. Open: M-F 10-9; Sat 10-6; Sun 12-5.

ALBANY INSTITUTE OF HISTORY AND ART, 125 Washington Ave Albany, 463-4478, sponsors a Sales/Rental Gallery with a wide variety of selections. Open: T-F 11-3 except in summer. Included in the yearly activities of this gallery are two juried shows.

ARLENE SHULMAN displays her sculpture and paintings at her own studio by appointment (674-3044). Information about other individual artists is available through the Albany League of Arts, 449-5380.

CLEMENT FRAME AND ART SHOP, 204 Washington Ave Albany, 465-4558, and 39 2nd Ave Troy, 272-6811, displays mounted and framed prints.

HAMM-BRICKMAN GALLERY, 240 Washington Ave Albany, displays artistic photographs, drawings and lithographs.

MCLEAN GALLERY, 231 Lark St Albany is open T-F 11-4, Sat 10-3 (and by appointment) for visitors to view paintings, drawings, and prints.

POSTERS PLUS GALLERY, Stuyvesant Plaza Albany, 482-1984, is a full service art gallery. As its principal function it displays and sells art posters and reproductions of original works of art. It also presents three to five exhibits of original art each year, featuring the work of artists of local reputation as well as those of international renown. In all this the shop offers art investment counseling as well as corporate and residential wall decor and space planning. They will even send an expert to hang the works to insure that it is done appropriately.

"Doing Art"

In addition to the places described for patrons to view or purchase art, several centers cater to those who wish to learn more about art, to develop their own artistic talents, or to buy the works of others.

ALBANY SCHOOL OF VISUAL ARTS, 1237 Central Ave, Albany, 459-1318, staffed by graduates with degrees in art education, combines the study of art appreciation with the study of studio art. There is a wide range of classes, divided on the basis of interest and ability as well as age.

ART COLONIE BARN, 141 Old Loudon Road, Latham, 785-8220, offers lessons in oil painting for children and adults.

THE CRAFT GUILD, 790 Madison Ave Albany, 489-4115, and Ten Eyck Plaza, Albany, 465-0023, is a non-profit organization created by the Catholic Diocese of Albany to offer workshops in a variety of handicrafts and to provide a market for the end products.

THE HARMANUS BLEECKER CENTER FOR HISTORY AND ART, 19 Dove St Albany, 462-4261, a branch of the Albany Institute, serves adults and children by running various programs of instruction in art, crafts, home industries and museum skills. Schedules of upcoming events are mailed to those who have placed their names on the mailing list.

JUNIOR COLLEGE OF ALBANY presents a summer art program in the month of July for students grades 9-12. Offerings include drawing, painting, photography, ceramics, 3-D sculpture, and commercial art. Information is available at 445-1717.

THE MALDEN BRIDGE SCHOOL, described in the chapter "Not Far Away," offers excellent instruction.

RENSSELAER COUNTY COUNCIL FOR THE ARTS, 189 Second St Troy, 273-0552, sponsors workshops and classes in many art forms throughout the year.

SCHENECTADY MUSEUM, Nott Terrace Heights Schenectady, 382-7890, offers arts and crafts instruction during two segments coinciding with the two semesters of the school year.

FILM

The Capital District now has dozens of screens showing the latest the American film industry has to offer. In addition to these theaters, all listed daily in local newspapers, are other cinemas and sources of films.

THE THIRD STREET CINEMA, 1573 3rd St Rensselaer, 436-4428, and the **SPECTRUM THEATER,** 290 Delaware Ave Albany, 449-8995, offer classic and art films. These two small theaters publish a monthly schedule of films. At these theaters, popcorn has been replaced by homemade cakes and cookies, and coffee and herbal teas take the place of soda.

 In addition to the commercial movie houses, area film buffs can turn to several other sources.

THE COUNCIL OF LIBRARIES has an impressive collection of 16mm films available for home use for no charge to those who pay a small annual film-borrower fee. A catalog of their own film holdings is available at the main desk of the main branches of the public libraries as are the listings of other sources from whom films are available through interlibrary loan. All the libraries regularly show classic films from the collection. The schedules are available at least one month in advance at the library branches.

AREA COLLEGES have film clubs which periodically show second run box office smashes, "golden oldies," or foreign films. Schedules are available from the numbers published at the beginning of this chapter.

PROCTOR'S, State St Schenectady, runs film festivals periodically throughout the year. In summer, internationally respected virtuosos of theater organs bring life to classics of the silent screen by performing live on the Golub Mighty Wurlitzer Organ. In winter, film festivals featuring major stars or directors run whenever the theater is available. There is always a film festival at Christmas time. Information is available at 382-1083.

Sports and Recreation

Overview

The location of the Capital District at the confluence of two rivers (the Mohawk and the Hudson) and in the juncture of three mountain ranges (the Adirondacks, the Catskills, and the Berkshires) makes it a natural paradise for the lover of sport. The abundance of lakes, ponds, and rivers makes water sports—from sailing to ice fishing—possible year round. The hills and mountains allow for woodland sports—from hunting to snowshoeing—January to December. In addition, the fieldhouses, playing fields and gymnasiums of area colleges and universities serve as excellent arenas for area players and fans. Probably because of the long tradition of regional spectator and participant sports, area residents have also insisted that their civic parks and playgrounds be carefully tended. As a result, the system of state recreational sites in New York is extraordinary, the three area cities take justifiable pride in their beautifully landscaped, immensely enjoyable parks, and suburban towns continually upgrade their recreational facilities.

This chapter has two major parts. The first describes sports; the second deals with general recreation and use of the land. Throughout, emphasis is placed on facilities available to all citizens. Therefore, the excellent facilities maintained by suburban communities for their own residents are not described.

SPORTS

Auto Racing

FONDA SPEEDWAY is a half-mile dirt track located on the Fonda Fairgrounds in Fonda, New York. The speedway features modified and street stock car racing every Saturday night from April to September. The schedule of

Playground, Empire State Plaza
Michael Fredericks, Jr.

specific events is available at P.O. Box 231, Fonda NY 12068, 853-4235. Directions: Thruway to Exit 28; ¼ mile along Mohawk River.

LEBANON VALLEY SPEEDWAY AND DRAGWAY in West Lebanon N.Y. (1-794-9606) features stock car races every Saturday night from the end of April to the middle of September and drag races every Sunday night from early April to late October. Special events (like demolition derbys) highlight the program occasionally, drawing enthusiastic spectators who love the tension and the glamour (and the noise and the dust). Directions: I-90 East to Exit 11 East; left on Rte 20; 6 miles to West Lebanon.

Baseball

Because the Capital District is equidistant from Fenway Park, Shea Stadium and Yankee Stadium, area fans used to fall into fairly even camps— Red Sox fanatics, Mets maniacs, and Yankee devotees. No more. In 1985, with a new Yankee farm team in town, the scale appears to be tipping in favor of the Bronx Bombers. The newcomers are the **ALBANY-COLONIE YANKEES**, an Eastern League minor league franchise. They play at the newly constructed Heritage Park on Watervliet Shaker Rd (adjacent to the Albany County Airport).

In addition to taking pleasure watching professionals, area afficionados play the game themselves in a variety of leagues. Each city and town has Little League and Babe Ruth League ball and dozens of semi-organized sandlot groups. Information about these activities is available at the nearest city office of Parks and Recreation.

Basketball

The **ALBANY PATROONS**, a minor league affiliate of the New York Knickerbockers, is a community-supported team begun in 1981. It was something of an experiment to determine what degree of interest the region would display toward professional sports. The answer is clear: the team has set league attendance records, often packing its home court at Washington Avenue Armory in Albany. Schedules, season tickets and individual tickets are available at the box office, 465-5366.

In addition to professional ball, the region is filled with superior college and high school play. Siena, SUNYA, and Union generally post winning seasons in seriously competitive leagues and combat each other fiercely in an annual Christmas tournament. The regional high school council pits the best area players against one another in play which draws enthusiastic fans throughout the season.

Biking

Class I (pedestrian and bicycles only) bike paths in Albany, Colonie, Niskayuna, and Schenectady follow along the Mohawk and Hudson Rivers. Signs mark the paths.

The Town of Colonie guides peddlars along its section of the trail with an excellent booklet—complete with identification of flowers, birds and wildlife likely to be encountered.

The Uncle Sam Bikeway (Class I) in Troy runs through North Troy. It can be found by going east on 125th Street and watching for signs.

N.B. The Capital District Transportation Committee is planning publication of a Bike Atlas, which will give details of bike trails (predominantly Class I) in the Capital District. It will cover the approximately 50 miles of trails from downtown Albany to Lock 7 of the Barge Canal.

THE HUDSON-MOHAWK WHEELMEN is a touring bicycle club. During the season it runs two regularly scheduled rides each weekend, including weekend trips, a picnic, and a Century Weekend (100 mile event). Some events are "tours" (20-50 miles at 12 m.p.h.); others are "casuals" (7-15 miles at 8 m.p.h.); on occasion the club runs a "sportsman" (50-100 miles at 16 m.p.h.). Information is available at area bike shops and through Betty Lou Bailey, Schuyler 16, Netherlands Village, Schdy 12308.

CAPITAL BICYCLE RACING CLUB arranges bicycle races in the area. For information about CBRC, write P.O. Box 7254 Albany, 12224 or call 767-9730.

Boating

The Capital District is a haven for boating enthusiasts. Lake George and the Mohawk and Hudson Rivers accommodate sizeable vessels, and lakes suitable for small craft abound.

Boat launching sites are listed and described in a brochure free for the asking from the New York State Parks and Recreation Bureau, Empire State Plaza 12238, 474-0456.

A map of **NEW YORK STATE INLAND WATERWAYS** is available from the National Survey, Chester, Vermont 05143.

Competitive rowing is described later in this chapter.

Bowling

The presence of over three dozen local bowling lanes testifies to the regional popularity of this year-round sport. Many of the facilities are reserved regularly for league bowling, so occasional bowlers should call ahead. Knowledgeable advice on the current bowling scene is available at Bob Daubney's Bowling Enterprises, 1904 Central Ave. Albany 456-7858.

Cricket

THE ALBANY CRICKET CLUB, founded in the early 1970's, is open to anyone who wishes to play cricket or learn about the game. The club, though not part of any formal league, hosts matches against opposing teams from throughout New York, Connecticut, Massachusetts, and Canada. Practices are scheduled regularly for 5:00 Friday afternoon from May through September, with games set for Saturdays and Sundays. Spectators are welcome at any time. In addition to fielding its own team, the club conducts a clinic once a week, supervises exhibition matches, and runs a Cricket Field Day. All events take place on the field behind the Training Academy out New Scotland Avenue—almost at Albany's city line. Information is available through Jai Miser, 489-2775.

Curling

Curling, the game in which two teams of four players each slide special "stones" over a stretch of ice toward a circular target, is enthusiastically played and watched at two area centers:

Schenectady Curling Club
    Balltown Rd, Schdy 372-4063
Albany Curling Club
    McKown Rd, McKownville 456-6272

Fishing

Some of the best trout fishing in the country is found along the Battenkill, Kaydeross, and Kinderhook Creeks and the Ausable River.
Salmon, smallmouth bass, trout and pike can be fished from Lake George. Pike run in Saratoga Lake, and large mouth bass inhabit all major lakes in the area. For good advice about wise use of all facilities in the Catskills and Adirondacks, check Taylor-Vadney (303 Central Ave Albany, 472-9183) or Goldstock's (121 N. Broadway Schdy, 382-2037).

Superior advice, instruction, equipment and expert fishing "chat" are available at Orvis Co Inc, Manchester VT, (802) 362-3622. The experts here are renowned for their knowledge of fly-fishing techniques and equipment. They also provide a commentary on daily fishing conditions.

Football

The **METRO MALLERS**, an Eastern Football League team, play home games at Bleecker Stadium in Albany in a season running from July through September. Information about the team's schedule is available at 438-2166.

Area college and high schools field respectable teams in an intensely competitive Fall season of Saturday afternoon games.

Golf

In part because the Capital District enjoys such pleasant summers, golf thrives. Ardent enthusiasts swing their clubs on sunny April mornings and push the season well into October. As is the case elsewhere, a network of members-only clubs features the sport and hosts serious competition. In

Empire State Plaza
Michael Fredericks, Jr.

addition, the region maintains competitive public courses—some government sponsored, some run for profit. The following is a list of these courses, presented in alphabetical order.

Name	# Holes	Open	Shop	Rentals	Comments
Albany Municipal New Scotland Ave. 438-2209	18	dawn-dusk	yes	clubs/ pullcart	
Colonie Town 418 Consaul Rd. Schdy. 374-4181	27	8 am-7 pm	yes	yes	
Frear Park Lavin Ct. Troy 270-4553	18	dawn-dusk	yes	yes	Putting green/ driving range
Hiawatha Trails State Farm Rd. Guilderland 456-9512	18	7 am-dark	yes	yes	3 par
Northway Heights Rte 146A Ballston Lake 877-7082	18	dawn-dusk	yes	yes	
Pine Haven P.O. 544 Guilderland 456-7111	18	*M-F 10-dusk	yes	yes	Open to public *on weekdays off season
Schenectady Muni Oregon Ave Schenectady 382-5155	18	dawn-dusk	yes	yes	
Stadium 333 Jackson Schenectady 374-9104	9	dawn-dusk	yes	yes	Expanding to 18
Sycamore Rte 143 Ravena 756-9555	18	dawn-dusk winter: 8-5	yes	yes	Driving range/ putting green
Saratoga Spa Saratoga Spa St. Pk. Saratoga Springs 584-2000 (day) 584-2008 (night)	27	7-7 weekdays 6-7 weekends	yes	yes	Championship park

Horseracing

Harness Racing

Saratoga Harness Track hosts trotters M-Sat from mid-April to mid-November, and Th Sat from January to March. The track has a comfortable enclosed grandstand and a pleasant dining room. Post time is 8:00, but the grandstands and restaurant open at six. For dining room reservations, the number is 584-2110. Directions: Northway (87) to Exit 13N; Rt 9N to second blinker; turn right and follow signs.

Thoroughbred Racing

Saratoga Race Track, the nation's oldest track, merits the lavish praise it receives. The splendour of the grounds, the accessibility of the paddocks, and the pervasiveness of tradition make a visit to the track an exciting and pleasurable experience. Races are held W-M during the month of August, with featured events being the eighth race on Saturday. The first of nine races begins at 1:30. Even those who do not like to bet will enjoy spending an afternoon watching magnificent animals, proficient jockeys, and unpredictable spectators.

In addition to the actual racecard events, Saratoga's morning activities provide a source of interest and pleasure. From 7:30 to 9:30 each morning, there are starting gate demonstrations, backstretch tours, and paddock talks open to all. Near the finish line, visitors may listen as an expert comments on the lineage, performance record, and idiosyncracies of each horse taking morning warm-up on the track. Afterwards, lectures on horse care and betting techniques are given. (Those who visit the track at this early hour must then exit and re-enter for the day's races.) Patrons may have breakfast at the track while enjoying the morning workout. Information about this is in the chapter on Restaurants.

Horseback Riding

A surprising number of area residents train, maintain, and show horses. Most stables which board horses also make several of their own available for public use with instruction. All the stables listed below offer boarding services and riding lessons (English saddle) for adults and children. Some run summer programs which are described in the chapter on summer activities.

Dutch Manor*
1641 Western Ave.
Guilderland
456-5010
(Moving Soon)

Sunday Stables
2681 River Road
Schenectady
370-2321

Horsemen's Choice
5940 Veeder Rd.
Slingerlands 869-1196

Hot Air Ballooning

Two regional centers provide rides, lessons, or equipment for this thrilling sport. **ADIRONDACK BALLOON FLIGHTS** (P.O. Box 65 Glens Falls; 1-793-6342) offers 45 minute to one hour journeys in a valley between the Adirondack Mountains and the Green Mountains every day from May through October. **STAR BALLOONS** (Chatham; 392-3208) sails over the upper Hudson Valley.

On the third weekend in September, hot air balloon enthusiasts (spectators as well as flyers) gather for a festival at Warren County Airport, Glens Falls. The assemblage of colorful balloons floating gracefully above the field makes a wonderful backdrop for picnics and family gatherings.

Hunting

Experts at Taylor-Vadney's (303 Central Ave Alb) and Goldstock's (121 N. Broadway Schdy) can provide up-to-date information about seasons and regions for those who enjoy hunting animals with weapons.

The genteel sport of pursuing dogs who are in turn pursuing another animal is organized by two groups: the traditional mounted English fox hunt is conducted with great flourish by the Old Chatham Hunt Club, the oldest fox hunting club in the country. (The hunt is open to members.) Kindred spirits, the members of the Old Chatham Beagle Hunt Club, engage in beagling adventures—mad chases on foot after beagles pursuing rabbits. (This hunt, too, is open only to members.)

Lacrosse

The **MOHAWK LACROSSE CLUB** organizes a league which uses the playing fields of SUNYA for its summer schedule. The newspapers report on recruiting and playing activities.

Ice Hockey

Hockey is an intensely popular winter sport in the area. On the professional level, the **ADIRONDACK RED WINGS**, an NHL team, make their home at the Glens Falls Civic Center (to be joined, Albany leaders hope, with another pro team if the Albany Civic Center comes into being soon.)

On the college level, RPI and Union put superior teams on the ice; in fact, RPI took the National Division I championship in 1985.

In addition to school leagues, there are independent leagues for children and adults. Information about this level of play is available at regional sporting goods stores, especially those listed in the shopping section of this book as specializing in hockey equipment. The various leagues schedule practice sessions and games at area rinks as follows:

Youth Leagues

TROY ACADEMY YOUTH HOCKEY, using Albany Academy, Frear Park Rink, and RPI.

SCHENECTADY YOUTH HOCKEY, using Achilles Rink at Union College and the rink at Center City.

WATERVLIET YOUTH HOCKEY, using Veterans Municipal Rink in Watervliet.

Adult Leagues

CAPITAL DISTRICT HOCKEY LEAGUE, using Veterans Municipal Rink in Watervliet.

HUDSON VALLEY HOCKEY LEAGUE, using Frear Park Rink.

MOHAWK HOCKEY LEAGUE, using Achilles Rink at Union College.

In addition to these formally organized leagues, there is fine pick-up hockey played wherever amateurs find a bit of frozen water during December and January. Many town and city custodians mark off areas on ponds described in the section on iceskating to protect recreational skaters from injury should they intrude on the fast paced play of these games.

Ice Skating

Ice skating is an increasingly popular winter sport in the area, and facilities are expanding to keep pace with the demand.

ARTIFICIAL ICE is maintained at the following sites, listed in alphabetical order:

Name	Open	Comments
Achilles Rink Union College Schdy 370-6134	Oct-Mar M-Sat 1-3 Sun 1-2:30; 3-4:30	Rentals available Instruction available
Center City Rink 433 State St Schdy 382-5105	Oct 15-Mar 31 M-Sat noon-1:30 Th-F 7-8:30 Sat 3:30-5 & 10-11:30 Sun 3:30-5	Rentals available Lessons and programs Weekend parking in rear
Empire State Plaza Near State St Alb 474-6447 (rink) 474-8860 (office)	Nov 15-Mar 17 M-F 12-2; 6-9 Sat 3-5 Sun 3-5; 6-9	Rentals Lockers Sharpening Instruction Holidays add 3-5 session

Center City, Schenectady
Michael Fredericks, Jr.

Frear Park Rink Park Blvd Troy 270-4557 (rink) 270-4553 (shop)	Nov 1-Mar 31 M 12-1 T 9-12; 12-1 W 12-1; 7:30 9:30 Th 9-12; 12-1; 3-5 F 12-1; 3-5:30; 7:30-9:30 Sat 2:30-5:30; 7:30-9:30 Sun 2:30-5:30	Rentals Instruction Sharpening
Houston Field House RPI Peoples and Burdett Ave Troy 266-6262	Depends on practice schedule of team Call for info	Rentals
Saratoga Springs **Youth Community Rink** Excelsior and East Ave 584-6590	Mid-Nov thru March M closed T 4-5:30 W closed Th 4-6:30 F 6:30-8 Sat 12-4 Sun 1-5	Fig Skating Club M 4-6 T closed W 4-5:30 Th closed F 4-5:30 Sat closed Sun 5-7:30
Swinburne Park Clinton Ave at Manning Blvd Alb 438-2406 (rink) 438-2447 (office)	M-F 3-5; 8-10 Sat & Sun 12:30-10	May be reserved for parties Rentals Sen Cit Th 10-12
Veterans' Memorial 2nd Ave & 13th St Watervliet 270-3824	M-F 12-4:30 Sat 12-2; 9:30-11 for adults Sun 3-6	No rentals

NATURAL ICE at the following areas is tested for safety and plowed:

Albany:

Buckingham Pond (also called Rath's Pond) at Berkshire Blvd between Western and New Scotland Aves off Euclid.

Washington Park Lake on the south side of Washington Park.

Colonie:

Colonie maintains 14 natural skating sites. Ann Lee Pond, adjacent to the Albany County Airport, is one of the best in the area. For information and conditions for all Colonie sites, call 785-4301.

Loudonville/Menands:

Little's Lake, Van Rensselaer Blvd near Menands Rd (Rte 378).

Saratoga:

Three rinks (recreational, speed, and hockey) at Saratoga Spa State Park. Open daylight, Mid-Nov to Mid-Mar. Rentals and sharpening are available at recreational rink. For information call 584-2000.

Schenectady:

Iroquois Lake in Central Park and Steinmetz Lake in Steinmetz Park (near Lenox Road).

Troy:

Beldon's Pond, near the junction of Routes 2 and 66; and Knickerbocker Park, at 103rd St and 8th Ave.

Parasailing

In this exciting new sport, bold novices sail hundreds of feet above a body of water (in this area, Lake George), held aloft by a parachute drawn by a motorboat. The sensation is gripping, the view spectacular. Rides are available May 15 through October 15, 9 am to dark, weather permitting. Details are available through Aqua Sports Plus, c/o King Neptune Lounge, 1 James St Lake George, 668-3280. (Prices range from $18-22, depending on length of ride.)

Polo

Polo is a serious sport in the Capital District. Two organizations maintain facilities and supervise competition:

SARATOGA POLO ASSOCIATIONS LTD., P.O. Box 821 Saratoga Springs, presents some of the best high goal polo in the world during the month of August. Top players from England, Argentina, and the U.S. contend in sponsored cup matches. The association welcomes spectators and encourages them by having the narrator explain the sport throughout play. The matches are played on fields famous for their quality. (From 1901-1935, the sport was popular in the area. Then it declined. In 1978 the field was redone and polo promoted once more.) Matches—which last about 1½ hours—are played on Tuesdays, Fridays and Sundays at 5:30. Local newspapers note any variation is schedule. Picnic facilities are available.

OWL CREEK POLO CLUB, 123 Hetcheltown Road Glenville, 399-4804, was established in 1966 by Paul Kant. It is the only year-round polo club within 200 miles of the Capital District. Lessons in the sport are held regularly, and cup games are held twice a week at 5 (June-Sept, Tues and Thurs; Oct-May, Wed and Sun). Mr. Kant is happy to provide more information.

Rafting

ADIRONDACK WILDWATERS INC., Box 801 Corinth NY 12822, offers rafting on the Hudson River Gorge and the Sacandaga River. There are two levels:
For high adventure (passengers must be 15 or older), rafting during spring runoff (April and May) starts at Indian Lake.
For pleasant family outings in summer (passengers must be 9 or older), rafting starts at Lake Luzerne. The numbers to call for information are: summer (518) 696-2953; winter (518) 654-2640.

HUDSON RIVER RAFTING CO., Rte 28 North Creek (just before south entrance to North Creek, at Cunningham's Ski Barn), offers rafting on the Hudson River Gorge from the first weekend in April through the first weekend in June. The 16 mile trip takes from four to five hours. It is open to rafters age 12 and up. In summer, this company runs rafts on the Sacandaga River and the Black River at Watertown. Information is available at 251-3215 or 251-2466.

Courtesy Norstar Bancorp

Roller Skating

Residents of the Capital District have taken the 50's sidewalk sport and converted it into a challenging entertainment practiced indoors and out. The following is an alphabetical list of centers for skating.

EMPIRE STATE PLAZA, in Albany is a skaters' paradise. The smooth, unobstructed walkways allow skaters to gather considerable momentum. On warm sunny days, independent trucks parked along Madison or State provide rentals. Information is available at the convention office, 474-0549.

GUPTILL ARENA INC, Rte 9 in Latham, 785-0660, the largest indoor arena in the area, hosted skaters long before the coming of the modern vinyl-wheeled skate. Open W-Sun, Guptill's offers a wide variety of skating programs. Musical accompaniment includes live organ selections as well as top 40, disco and rock. Adjacent to the arena is a disco with a lighted dance floor. Information on programs and parties is available at 785-4214.

ROLLERAMA, 2710 Hamburg St Schenectady, 355-2140 or 355-2410, offers an interesting array of programs, of which this is just a sampling:

Sun and Tues: skate-dancing to live organ music
Jan-April: special girl scout skating
3rd Mon of month: skating to Christian music
Thurs 7-10:   cheap skate (full family for one adult ticket)
        Open: T 8-10:30 (adults)
               W 7-10 (adults)
               Th 7-10 (family rate)
               F 7-11:30
               Sat 10:30-12:30; 2-4:30; 7:30-midnight
               Sun 2-4:30; 7-9:30

STARBURST ROLLER SKATING, Rte 146 P.O. Box 441 Clifton Park, 371-1567, opens for public sessions Th-Sun and for private parties M-W.
        Open: Th 7:30-10
               F 7:30-11
               Sat 10-12; 1:30-4:30; 7:30-11:30
               Sun 1:30-4:30; 7:30-10

Rowing

Rowing, the traditional Hudson River sport which had disappeared in the twentieth century, is staging a comeback as dramatic as the revival of downtown Albany. A boat launch site (including a boat house and docks) is located near the Colonie Street section of the Corning Riverfront Preserve. Individuals and groups (including Union College and SUNYA) are purchasing sculls and sponsoring teams. The sport promises to return with a flourish, with intensely competitive teams cheered on by spectators lining the riverfront parks. To forward the progress of the sport, the Empire State Regatta Committee will promote open regattas to lure the world's best rowers to the site. For information write Box 94, New Scotland, NY 12127 or call (518) 765-2025.

Rugby

This sport has grown in popularity in recent years, both for participants and spectators. Local city and college clubs, all members of USARFU (the United States of America Rugby Football Union) play in spring and fall. The **ALBANY KNICKERBOCKERS RUGBY AND FOOTBALL CLUB** arranges matches in Lincoln Park in Albany. The **SCHENECTADY REDS RFC** play at Windover Park on Grooms Road in Clifton Park. This park has 10 fields and hosts many rugby clubs in games, tournaments, and national events. Information about all rugby events is available through Tom Selfridge, 120 S. Church St. Schenectady, 370-3155.

Running

Running enthusiasts can use college campus paths and the riverfront bike and pedestrian paths for safe, predictable running. Those who enjoy running with others or training for competition can contact **HUDSON MOHAWK ROAD RUNNERS CLUB (HMRRC)** Box 12304 Albany 12212, 370-4275. The group publishes a monthly magazine on area running events and helps organize two major runs:

1) the Price Chopperthon, a 30K from Schenectady to Albany, held on the 3rd Sunday in March.
2) the Stockade-athon, a 15K in Schenectady, held on the 2nd Sunday in November.

The third major run in the region is Freihofer's Run for Women, a 10K held in spring organized by the Adirondack TAC.

Of course many area runners train for the traditional marathons in nearby New York or Boston.

Skiing/Downhill

The Capital District is in the enviable position of being surrounded by the Adirondacks, Catskills, Berkshires, and Vermont Mountains. As a result, the community of accomplished skiiers in the region expects and receives comprehensive services.

There are four telephone numbers for current ski conditions:

For New York State	1 (800) CALLNYS
For Catskills (24 Hour)	1 (800) 852-5500
For Massachusetts	1 (800) 342-1840
For Vermont	1 (800) 229-0531

Printed material is available for New York State at 474-4116 and for Vermont at SKI VT, 134 State, Montpelier 05602. The following is a list of popular ski centers presented according to driving distance from the Capital District. [Rentals and snow making are standard at all sites. Those which feature night skiing are preceded by an asterisk (*)].

One Hour or Less

*BRODIE MOUNTAIN**, Rte 7 New Ashford Ma, (413) 443-4752 or (413) 443-4753 (for conditions). Directions: I-90 East to Exit 7 (Defreestville). Turn left on Rte 43 to New Ashford.

*CATAMOUNT**, Hillsdale NY, (518) 325-3200 or (413) 528-1262. Directions: Taconic State Parkway south to Hillsdale Exit onto 23 East; 11 miles to Catamount.

*JIMINY PEAK, Hancock MA, (413) 738-5431 or (413) 447-7088 or (413) 458-5771. Directions: I-90 East to Exit 7 (Defreestville); left on Rte 43 to Hancock MA; right at Jiminy Peak sign to Brodie Mountain Rd. (Jiminy is ¼ mile on right.)

*MAPLE RIDGE, Rte 159 Rotterdam (4 miles west of Schenectady), 377-5172. A great place to learn to ski in classes conducted by the Schenectady Ski School.

Open: T-Sat 6:30 pm-10
Sat-Sun 9-4:30
Holidays 9-4:30

*WEST MOUNTAIN, R.D. 2 West Mt Road Glens Falls NY, (518) 793-6606. (N.B. Night skiing is limited to weekdays; West closes Sat and Sun at 6:00.) Directions: Northway (87) to Exit 18; left on Corinth Rd; three miles to sign on right; entrance is ¾ mile on left.

*WILLARD MOUNTAIN, R.D. 3 Greenwich NY, (518) 692-7337. Directions: Northway (87) to Exit 9 (Clifton Park); left on 146; right on 67 in Mechanicville; left on 40N; 3-4 miles to Willard.

SKI WINDHAM, Windham NY, (518) 734-9850. Directions: Thruway to Exit 21, to Rte 23 West.

One and One Half Hours

GORE MOUNTAIN, Box 105 North Creek, (518) 251-2411, is a New York State operated facility also offering ice-skating and cross-country skiing. Directions: Northway (87) to Exit 23; bear right; 9N to Warrensburg; left onto 28; proceed 18 miles; left onto Peaceful Valley Rd; Gore is 1 mile on right.

HUNTER MOUNTAIN, P.O. Box 629 Hunter NY (518) 263-4223. Directions: Thruway to Exit 21; east on 23 and 23A West. Alternate directions: Thruway to Exit 21B; 9W South to Catskill; 23A East to Hunter.

Two to Two and a Half Hours

BROMLEY MOUNTAIN, P.O. Box 1130 Manchester Center VT, (802) 824-5522. (Shuttle buses link Bromley with Stratton, which can be skied on the same lift ticket.) Directions: NY Rte 7 to Rte 9 in Bennington to Vermont Rte 7; at Manchester, right onto Rte 11; two miles into Peru and Bromley.

KILLINGTON, 400 Killington Rd, Killington VT, (802) 422-3333 and (802) 422-3261 (24-hr report). Directions: Northway (87) to Exit 20 (Fort Ann, Rutland); NY 149 East to US 4; left on 4 East to Killington (12 miles east to Rutland).

MOUNT SNOW, 100 Mountain Road, Mount Snow VT, (802) 464-3333 or (802) 464-2151. Directions: Rte 7 East to Bennington VT where it becomes

9; Rte 9 to Wilmington VT; left at stoplight onto 100 North; nine miles to Mount Snow.

STRATTON, Stratton Mountain V1, (802) 297-2200 or (802) 297-2211 (ski report). This site also has an indoor sports center and a cross-country center. (Shuttle buses link Stratton with Bromley, which can be skied on the same ticket.) Directions: VT Rte 7 North to Manchester Vt; north to Rte 11 to Rte 30 South to entrance in Bondville; follow Stratton Mountain Rd 4 miles to ski area.

WHITEFACE, Box 1980 Wilmington NY, (518) 946-2223. Whiteface was the site of the 1980 Winter Olympic Alpine events. Cross-country skiing in village. Directions: Northway (87) to Exit 30; left onto Rte 9; follow signs to Whiteface.

Three to Three and a Half Hours

STOWE, Stowe VT, (802) 253-7311. (Cross country skiing also.) Directions: Northway (87) to Exit 20; Rte 149 East to Ft. Ann; US 4 North to US 4 East at Whitehall; crossing into Vermont at Fair Haven, take 22A North to Vergennes; north on US 7 to Burlington; Interstate 89 South to Exit 10; left onto 100N; 9 miles to Stowe.

SUGARBUSH VALLEY SKI RESORT, Sugarbush Valley VT, (800) 451-5030 or (802) 583-2381. (Indoor sports center and cross-country trails as well.) Directions: Northway (87) to Exit 20; 149 East to Whitehall; on Rte 4 go eight miles past Rutland; left on Rte 100 North to Sugarbush.

Skiing/Cross-Country

Capital District residents have access to excellent cross-country skiing facilities. This section will be divided into two parts: first, nearby public sites, open to all at no charge; second, nearby and distant sites which charge a fee. This second group is organized according to driving distance. Before turning to those listings, it is important to note that detailed information on cross-country skiing is available from four sources.

NYS Department of Environmental Conservation Bureau of Preservation, Protection and Management, 50 Wolf Rd Albany, 457-7433, publishes an excellent booklet, "Nordic Skiing Trails in NY State," complete with maps and thorough information on each site.

NYS Department of Environmental Conservation Region 4 Headquarters, 2176 Guilderland Ave Schenectady, 382-0680, is also an important source of information.

Albany County Department of Public Works, Rte 85A Voorheesville 12186, will provide information about opportunities in the immediate vicinity.

Capital Area Ski Touring Association (CASTA), c/o Robert E. Fager, 20B Glenwood St McKownville 12204, 438-6544, is a membership organization of Nordic skiing enthusiasts. It organizes tours and publishes a newsletter and a valuable booklet describing almost 100 skiing areas. (Published in 1979, it is currently being updated by CASTA.) N.B. The following downhill sites, described in the previous section, offer cross-country skiing as well: Gore, Stowe, Stratton, Sugarbush, and Whiteface.

Free Skiing

Free Skiing Less than an Hour Away
(These sites do not offer rentals unless otherwise marked):

ALBANY MUNICIPAL GOLF COURSE, New Scotland Ave Albany, 438-2209. Open: daylight in season. Directions: First left after Whitehall Rd when headed west.

BURDEN LAKE COUNTRY CLUB, Totem Lodge Rd Averill Park, 674-8917. Rentals and sales. Open daily. Directions: Totem Lodge Rd is south of 150 at Sliters Corners.

FIVE RIVERS ENVIRONMENTAL EDUCATION CENTER, Game Farm Rd Delmar, 457-6092. Open: 9-4:30. Directions: Off Rte 443, eight miles from downtown Albany.

GLENS FALLS INTERNATIONAL, Crandall Park, 624 Glen St Glens Falls, 793-5676. Includes lighted trails. Open: daily till 11 pm. Rentals. Directions: Northway (87) to Exit 19; right to main intersection; right onto 9S (at third light); ½ mile down on 9S.

INDIAN LADDER FARMS, Rte 156 Voorheesville, 765-2956. Hot cider and warm cider donuts in barn. Open: T-Sat 9-5; Sun 10-5. Directions: Rte 20 to 155 South; at end of 155 bear right on Maple Ave in Voorheesville; right onto 156; Indian Ladder 2½ miles on left.

JOHN BOYD THACHER STATE PARK, Rte 157 Voorheesville, 872-1237. Open: daily. Directions: New Scotland Ave (Rte 85) to Park. From Schenectady take Rte 146 South to Rte 156 in Altamont, go up the hill. Turn left on Rte 157A opposite Highland Farms Restaurant. Go to end, turn left on Rte 157.

PARTRIDGE RUN WILDLIFE MANAGEMENT AREA, Sickle Hill Rd Berne, (607) 652-7364. (Cited by CASTA to have the most reliable snow conditions locally.) Directions: Rte 443 through Delmar to 146 through Altamont; west on 157 through Knox and south on 156; at Berne Knox Central School bear left and go one half mile; right onto Sickle Hill Rd; at top of steep hill, turn onto High Point Rd or Beaver Rd (just past church ruin) to Partridge Run.

SARATOGA SPA STATE PARK, Saratoga Springs, 584-2000. Rentals, sales, service, and lessons. Several miles of lighted trails. All trails well-groomed. Open: daily in daylight. Directions: Northway (87) to Exit 13N; left onto 9N to park.

SARATOGA NATIONAL HISTORIC PARK, between Rte 4 and Rte 32, Stillwater, 664-9821. Open: 9-5 except Thanksgiving, Christmas, and New Years. Directions: Northway (87) to Exit 12; follow signs to park, using routes 9N, 9P, 423 and 32.

SCHENECTADY MUNICIPAL GOLF COURSE, Oregon Ave Schenectady, 382-5152 (Parks Dept.) or 382-5155 (golf course). Some lighted areas open till 10. Directions: Thruway to Exit 25 to Rte 7; right onto Golf Rd at fourth light; left onto Oregon Ave.

TOWN OF COLONIE GOLF COURSE, 418 Consaul Rd Schenectady, 346-5940 or 783-2760. (Small fee for adults on weekends). Rentals. Well-groomed trails.

WHISPERING PINES GOLF COURSE, 2208 Helderberg Ave Schenectady, 355-2724. Rentals, sales and instruction. Open: daily in daylight. Directions: Thruway Exit 25 to Rte 7 West (Curry Rd) for 3 miles; left onto Helderberg Ave; Whispering Pines is 1 mile on left.

Places to Ski which Charge a Fee

Less Than One Hour Away

BERESFORD FARMS, Chadwick Rd Delanson, 895-2345. Second largest center in region (Mt. Van Hoevenberg being largest). Rentals, sales, tours, instruction. Open: daily. Lighted trails open W-Sat. Directions: Rte 20 to Duanesburg; west on Rte 7 two and a half miles; south one mile on Chadwick Rd.

FO'CASTLE FARMS, Kingsley Rd Burnt Hills, 399-2900. Rentals. Family season rate available. Open: daily 9-4. Directions: Northway (87) to Exit 9 (Clifton Park); west on 146; right onto Blue Barn Rd; farm is 3 miles on right.

HELDERBERG FAMILY, R.D. 1 Box 400A Voorheesville, 872-2106. Rentals and instruction. Open: Sat and Sun 10-dusk. Directions: Rte 443, bear right to East Berne ⅛ mile; turn right on Pinnacle Rd, county Rte 303; 2 miles on left.

MOUNTAIN GARDENS, R.D. 1 Box 115, Troy, 279-3760. Rentals and instruction. Open: daily. Directions: Rte 7 through Troy to Flower Road (7 miles east of Troy).

HOWE CAVERNS, Rte 7 Howes Cave, 296-8990. Rentals and instruction. Open: daily. Directions: Thruway to Exit 25A; I 88 West to Howes Cave exit; right onto Rte 7 and follow signs.

IN THE WOODS, Doolittles, R.D. 1 Cobleskill, 234-2109. Rentals and instruction. Night skiing in moonlight. Open: daily. Directions: West on Rte 20 to Carlisle; 1 mile west of light, turn left onto Becker Rd to ski area.

LAPLAND LAKE, R.D. 2 Northville, 863-4974. Rentals, sales, and instruction. Lodging available. Open: daily. Directions: Thruway to Exit 27; Rte 30N to Northville; west on Benson Rd for 6 miles.

PUTNAM MAPLE FARM, Beards Hollow Rd Richmondville, 294-7278. This working maple farm invites skiers on trails through the sapbush. Maple products and deerskin leather items are for sale. Skiers can visit the sap house Th-Sun 10-5. Ski rentals. Open: Th-Sun 10-5. Directions: I-88 South to Warnerville; west on Rte 7 for one mile; left onto Beards Hollow Rd; farm is 3 miles up road.

Two Hours

CUNNINGHAM'S SKI BARN—NORTH CREEK, 251-3215. Rentals, instruction, guided tours. Open: daily in season. Directions: Northway (87) to Exit 23; north on Rte 28. (Cunningham's is 20 miles NW of Warrensburg on Rte 28.)

GARNET HILL SKI TOURING CENTER, North River NY, 251-2821. (Ten miles from Gore for those who enjoy Alpine and Nordic Skiing.) Rentals, instruction, guided tours, varied trails. Open: daily including night skiing. Directions: Northway (87) to Exit 23 (Warrensburg); north on Rte 9 for 4½ miles; northwest on Rte 28 for 20 miles to North River; left on 13th Lake Rd to Garnet Hill.

Two and a Half to Three Hours

MOUNT VAN HOEVENBERG, Olympic Regional Development Authority, Olympic Center, Lake Placid, 523-2811. Snowmaking capability. Site of 1980 Olympics and annual competitions; has 40km of groomed trails. Rentals, instruction, tours. Open: daily in season. Directions: Northway (87) to Exit 24; east on Rte 73 to seven miles east of Lake Placid.

SAGAMORE LODGE AND CONFERENCE CENTER, Sagamore Rd Raquette Lake NY, (315) 354-5311 or (518) 587-8770. Cross-country skiing recreation weekends include instruction, guided tours, evening entertainment, moonlight skiing, skating and sledding. Rentals available. Directions: Northway (87) to Exit 23 (Warrensburg); North on 28 to Raquette Lake. Reservations required.

Skiing/Special Cross-Country

Wilderness ski tours are two or three day excursions in which skiers leave a Central Adirondack lodge in the morning and travel to another point, staying at a different lodge each night. Fees include meals, lodging, guides, and the transfer of luggage between lodges. Information is available at **ADIRONDACK HUT TO HUT,** R.D. 1 Box 85 Ghent NY 12075, 828-7007 or 449-5098.

Skydiving

ALBANY SKYDIVERS, INC, Knox Airport, 895-8140, serves as base for both a club and a school. Affiliated with the U.S. Parachute Association, its members, many of whom have hundreds of jumps on record, jump for festivals, carnivals, and exhibitions—but mostly for fun. The company owns its own aircraft. Members pay a fee for each lift, depending on the elevation.

Members serving as instructors have trained over 10,000 students since 1973. They conduct lessons each Sat, Sun and holiday year round at 10 am, weather permitting. No appointment is necessary. (It is possible to make arrangements for lessons at other times.) Equipment is available.

Swimming

There are numerous supervised swimming facilities in the region, some seasonal and others year round. Pools in outlying districts usually restrict use to verified residents. Information regarding hours and rules for these pools is available at the appropriate village or town hall. The three major cities open their facilities to the general public. Information about swimming opportunities and programs in the three cities is available at the following numbers:

Albany 438-2447
Schenectady 382-5152
Troy 270-4600

SWIM SCHOOL INC, 172 1st St Troy, 274-8677, gives lessons on all levels— from competitive racing and synchronized teamwork to exercise, therapy and recreation. Pool is also available for pool parties.

Some area hotels and motels quietly open their pools to the general public through **SWIM CLUBS,** informal arrangements whereby local residents may pay an annual fee and swim when the pool is open. Details are available at each facility.

STATE SUPERVISED PARKS AND PRIVATE BEACHES: Because specific information on state run parks and private beaches open to the public is not so easy to find, the remainder of this section will present details.

Capitol Park, Albany
Michael Fredericks, Jr.

Parks with Lakes: State Operated

These parks are free but a modest fee is charged for parking.

CHERRY PLAIN STATE PARK, off Rte 22 north of Stephentown is open 10-6 daily from late June through Labor Day.

GRAFTON LAKE, Rte 2, Grafton, is open 10-6 daily late June through Labor Day. CDTA (482-8822) runs a bus to and from this park on a regular schedule.

MINEKILL STATE PARK, off Rte 20 south of Middleburgh, is open 10-6 daily late June through Labor Day.

MOREAU STATE PARK, Exit 17S off Northway (87), Moreau, is open 10-6 late June through Labor Day.

THOMPSON'S LAKE CAMPING AREA, Rte 157 off Rte 85 Berne-Knox, is open 10-6 daily late June through Labor Day. There is also a pool here.

TAGHKONIC STATE PARK, 11 miles south of Hudson, Rte 82 at Taconic State Parkway, is open 10-6 daily, late June through Labor Day.

Parks with Lakes: Privately Operated
BROWN'S BEACH, Saratoga Lake. Open Memorial Day through Labor Day.

KAYDEROSS BEACH, Saratoga Lake. Open 10 to 6 late June through Labor Day. Amusement Park on grounds.

SCHOLZ-ZWICKLBAUER BEACH, Warners Lake Berne. Open daily 11 am-dark July 4 through Labor Day.

TIFTS BEACH, Rte 66 Glass Lake. Open 10-dusk Memorial Day through Labor Day.

Parks with Pools
JOHN BOYD THACHER STATE PARK, Voorheesville. Open 10-6 late June through Labor Day. Modest fee.

SARATOGA SPA STATE PARK, Rte 9 Saratoga Springs [Exit 13N off Northway (87)]. There are two pools here, the Victorian Pool and the larger Peerless Pool. Open 10-6 late June through Labor Day. Car gate fee and pool fee.

Tennis
The three cities maintain and oversee tennis courts at various locations, some lighted. The numbers to call for information are:

Albany 434-4181
Schenectady 382-5152
Troy 270-4600

Schenectady offers league tennis in Central Park. It is open to all Schenectady residents.

Tennis is played throughout the year at several indoor clubs. Membership, which is open to the public, entitles members to full use of the facilities and participation in leagues and tournaments. However, non-members are welcome to rent available courts. These clubs are listed in the telephone directory.

Water Racing
WHITE WATER DERBY on the Hudson River is an annual event guaranteed to provide exhilaration to contestants and spectators alike. The race, sponsored by the Johnsburg Fish and Game Club, takes place early in May in North Creek. The first day of the two day contest is the slalom; the second day is downhill.

Most spectators and photography buffs gather at Spruce Mt. Rapids where the boats must maneuver with great skill to stay upright. Directions: Northway (87) to Exit 23; Rte 28 to North Creek. (One and one half hours.)

GENERAL RECREATION

Sources of Information

The New York State Office of Parks, Recreation and Historic Preservation and the New York State Department of Environmental Conservation operate dozens of historic sites, parks and preserves. All are centered in beautiful locations and maintained with scrupulous attention to preservation and comfort. The two agencies split their duties thus: EnCon oversees the Catskill and Adirondack Forest Preserves; Parks and Recreation oversees all other state supervised parks. The addresses and telephone numbers are as follows:

NYS Parks, Recreation and Historic Preservation
Agency Bldg 1,
Empire State Plaza
Albany 12238
474-0456

Ask for the pamphlet
A GUIDE TO NYS PARKS,
RECREATION, AND
PRESERVATION

Environmental Conservation
50 Wolf Rd
Albany 12233
457-2500
(For fish and wildlife—457-5690)

State Parks

The parks are open to all citizens for minimal fees, with three special packages available.

An **EMPIRE PASSPORT** offers unlimited year-round entry to all NYS parks and recreational facilities. It is sold at all state parks or by mail from Passports, State Parks, Albany NY 12238.

A **GOLDEN PARK PASS** is free to NYS residents 62 or over, providing lifetime free admission for day use of state parks (M-F, except holidays.) It is available at the address listed above.

An **ACCESS PASS** is available for state residents with permanent physical disabilities. It provides free vehicle access to state parks and historical and recreational facilities. It is available at the address listed above.

The Parks

THE ADIRONDACK PARK is a vast area (6 million acres) of publically and privately owned land carefully overseen by the Adirondack Park Agency, whose aim is to protect the area and advise vacationers on wise and full use of available facilities.

The region offers a wealth of recreational opportunities, for the southern and western areas have gentle slopes whereas the northeast features jagged faced, high-peaked mountains. Thus horseback riding, camping, picnicking, hiking, mountaineering, hunting, snowshoeing, and skiing can be practiced at all levels of difficulty. Moreover, sheltered amidst the mountains, a multitude of lakes and streams invite boating of all kinds, swimming, scuba diving, waterskiing, fishing—even icefishing. The air and water everywhere have always been known to be crystal clear and pure. (The fact that acid rain threatens this purity is a major concern upon which many New Yorkers are determined to act.)

Pamphlets, brochures and general information are available at no cost through Adirondack Park Association, Adirondack NY 12808.

The beautiful magazine ADIRONDACK LIFE is described in the section on sources of information.

FIVE RIVERS ENVIRONMENTAL EDUCATION CENTER, Game Farm Road, Delmar, 457-6092, is a branch of the NYS Department of Environmental Conservation. The Center, which has been honored with a National Park Service Award, provides an opportunity for people to learn the interdependence of natural phenomena, either on their own as they walk the clearly marked trails using guidebooks or through classes and workshops presented at the site. One trail has been especially adapted to be accessible to the handicapped, and tape recorded descriptions of two trails make it possible for a visually handicapped visitor to tour in the company of a sighted companion. The Center publishes a newsletter, *The Tributary.* One may receive further information or register for the mailing list by using the number or address above. Directions: South on Delaware Ave; right onto Orchard; ½ mile to Game Farm Rd on left.

JOHN BOYD THACHER STATE PARK, located 18 miles west of Albany (out New Scotland Avenue), offers splendid views of the Hudson-Mohawk Valleys and the peaks of the Adirondack and Green Mountains. Thatcher, as it is called, has fine picnic areas and an olympic swimming pool, but its most popular attraction is the Indian Ladder Geologic Trail, a naturally formed ledge along the Helderberg Escarpment, an area described by geologists and paleontologists as one of the richest fossil-bearing formations in the world. The half mile walk along this trail is truly awesome. The park is open June 16 through Labor Day, 8 am to 10 pm, with the Indian Ladder Trail open 8-8 and the pool open 11-7, weather permitting. In winter, the park is open for ski-touring, snowshoeing, tobogganing and snowmobiling, with heated comfort stations along the trails. Directions: New Scotland Ave (Rte 85) out of Albany to park. From Schenectady, take Rte 146 South to Rte 156 in Altamont. Go up hill, turn left on Rte 157A opposite Highland Farms Restaurant. Go to end; turn left on Rte 157.

SARATOGA SPA STATE PARK, a beautifully landscaped stretch of ground, has outstanding athletic and health facilities. Two golf courses—an 18-hole course and a 9-hole course—two swimming pools and a dozen well-maintained picnic spots are available as are tennis courts, a speed skating rink and cross country ski trails. Also open to the public are the two bathhouses which offer massage, mineral baths and hot packs. This practice of "bathing," very fashionable in the 20's and 30's, declined for a while but has been regaining popularity in recent years. Those who have taken advantage of this local facility claim that there is no doubt the process makes one feel invigorated and renewed.

Information about the hours and fees for all the park's features is available at Saratoga Spa State Park, P.O. Box W, Saratoga Springs 12866 or at the bathhouses:

> Roosevelt Bath Pavilion
> (open all year) 584-2011
> Lincoln Bath Pavilion
> (open July and August) 584-2010

Directions: Northway (87) to Exit 13N; 9N north to park entrance (on left).

Private Preserves

THE EDMUND NILES HUYCK PRESERVE AND BIOLOGICAL RESEARCH STATION in Rensselaerville harbors housing and laboratory space for twenty year-round students of the natural sciences and forty summer residents participating in research on the lands and waters which make up the compound. The preserve is open to the public throughout the year for picnicking, fishing, canoeing, and rowboating. Visitors should, however, follow the posted regulations carefully to avoid intruding on wildlife for whom this is a habitat.

Hikes are scheduled for Sunday afternoons from mid-May to mid-September. Information is available from P.O. Box 188 Rensselaerville 12147, 797-3440. Directions: New Scotland Ave (Rte 85) to Rensselaerville; at end of road in the town, turn right; proceed to end of road to sign for Preserve.

THE MOHONK TRUST, Mohonk Lake, New Paltz, (914) 255-0919, is open to the public for general recreation—including walking, hiking, camping, horseback riding, bicycling, snowshoeing and ski touring. The setting is beautiful. Directions: Thruway to Exit 18; left on Rte 299; through New Paltz; right after bridge over Wallkill; bearing left, follow Mountain Rest Road to Mohonk gate.

Camping

New York State maintains and administers an extraordinary array of campsites. Two agencies supervise their operation: **DEPARTMENT OF ENVIRONMENTAL CONSERVATION** (50 Wolf Road Albany 457-2500) oversees camping in the Catskill and Adirondack Forest Preserves; **OFFICE OF PARKS, RECREATION, AND HISTORIC PRESERVATION** (Agency Bldg 1 Empire State Plaza 474-0456) oversees all other sites. Campsites are available on a first-come-first-served basis. Reservations (which can be made through Ticketron, mail or telephone with credit cards) are required at some areas. Detailed information is presented in a free brochure, *A Guide to New York State Parks, Recreation and Historic Preservation*, available at either office. Also available are brochures about certain areas or about types of campsites ("Island Camping," for example).

City Parks

The cities and towns of the region maintain dozens of parks and playgrounds which area residents use both for organized activities and personal leisure. Town and city employees organize and supervise programs, lessons, competitions and leagues throughout the year. Information on facilities and schedules is available at the office listed in the blue pages of the telephone book. The principal numbers for the three major cities are as follows:

Albany
General Information 434-4181
Recreation Dept and Scheduling 438-2447
Schenectady . . . . 382-5151 or 382-5152
Troy 270-4600

Albany

In the center of the capital city sits **WASHINGTON PARK,** a model urban park situated on 90 acres of rolling land designated as parkland by foresighted city planners in 1869. Remnants of the original formal park remain in the bridal paths, the unusual and exotic trees, and the traditional statues. But in the 1980's the park is an up-to-date place with benches, picnic tables, walkways and playgrounds filled with casually dressed urbanites relaxing or participating in the growing number of concerts, festivals and fairs to which the park plays host.

LINCOLN PARK, the center of which resembles a pair of vast unembellished saucers, is the perfect place for any sort of ball game. The park, located along Morton Avenue just below Delaware Avenue, also has tennis courts and a swimming pool.

ERASTUS CORNING 2nd RIVERFRONT PRESERVE runs along the west bank of the Hudson all the way to the city line. It features a pedestrian/bike path, picnic tables, and a series of exercise stations. Specially commissioned sculptures are found throughout the park.

WESTLAND HILLS PARK, off Colvin Avenue between Central and Lincoln Avenues, maintains eight diamonds to serve its Little League program with over 2,000 participants. (There are also lighted tennis courts, a supervised junior swimming pool, and a multi-leveled playground.)

Schenectady

On Monday July 8, 1985, the *Schenectady Gazette* published a comprehensive list of the parks and recreational areas in the city and the sur-

Cohoes Falls
Michael Fredericks, Jr.

rounding towns. This extremely valuable compilation (to be found on page 34) describes each facility, gives directions where needed, and notes what hours the gates open and close. Also included is a full list of boat launch sites and bike trails.

The largest of Schenectady's parks is **CENTRAL PARK,** 500 acres of rolling land in the middle of the city. This park has lots to offer: a rose garden, paddle boats, a duck pond, a train ride, 26 tennis courts, an imaginative playground, and terrain suited for a wide variety of winter and summer sports. In 1984-85 the city engaged in a major effort to revitalize Iroquois Lake and beautify the fountain.

The other principal parks in Schenectady are **HILLHURST, QUACKENBUSH, ROTUNDA, STEINMETZ** and **WOODLAWN.**

Troy

FREAR PARK is Troy's largest park, with ball diamonds, playing fields, picnic areas, and a skating rink. **KNICKERBOCKER PARK** and **PROSPECT PARK** are the two other major recreational parks.

RIVERFRONT PARK, along the banks of the Hudson, is the site of planned public, cultural and ethnic activities.

Other Recreational Facilities

JEWISH COMMUNITY CENTERS in Albany (340 Whitehall Road, 438-6651) and Schenectady (2565 Balltown Road, 377-8803) offer a wide variety of programs in recreation. Membership is open to the entire community regardless of religious affiliation. Programs range from Yoga and belly-dancing to ballet and basketball. The centers always offer Red Cross swimming programs.

The **Y's** (**YMCA** and **YWCA**) have very active centers in the Capital District, offering good facilities and programs at reasonable prices to anyone who wishes to subscribe. (The Y will never deny access to a program because a person cannot pay the fee.) The numbers for the major centers are:

	YMCA	YWCA
Albany	449-7196	438-6608
Schenectady	374-9136	374-3394
Troy	272-5900	274-7100
Cohoes		237-6001

The summer camp run by the Schenectady YMCA (Camp Chingachgook, located at Pilot Knob on Lake George) is widely respected. More information is provided in the chapter on summer activities for children.

Other Things To Do

This chapter describes activities which have eluded categorization in other chapters. It is organized by time of year, beginning with year-round activities and then turning to seasonal.

YEAR-ROUND

BRIDGE AND GAMES can be played every afternoon and evening at **THE STUDIO OF BRIDGE AND GAMES** at 1639 Eastern Parkway, Schenectady, 346-3773. Participants play scrabble, chess, backgammon, bridge, adventure games (Dungeons and Dragons, for example) and, of course, duplicate bridge. The studio, directed by Bill and Norma Shelly, organizes tournaments for gamesters of all ages and levels. It is open to the public; a table fee is levied per session.

Duplicate Bridge is sponsored regularly at Regency Park Albany or Bethlehem Terrace Apartments in Slingerlands. Partnerships can be arranged. Information is available at 482-3800.

DANCING is organized by two groups:

SKYWAY COUNTRY, 14 Saratoga Rd Schenectady, 399-4922, presents live dancing music year-round according to a fixed schedule:

Rock and Roll   F-Sat 9-3
Ballroom and Polish American   Sundays 4-8 in fall, winter, and spring

Refreshments are sold. Schedules of planned events are available upon request.

CAPITAL DISTRICT SQUARE AND ROUND DANCE ASSOCIATION (CDSRCA) coordinates the activities of approximately 30 regional clubs which meet regularly from September to May. The Association is responsible for maintaining a schedule of events, providing callers and music, supervising lessons and, in general, promoting the pleasures of country dancing. Information is available through Dick Ellis, 765-4011.

Apple Picking
Michael Fredericks, Jr.

FOLK MUSIC CONCERTS AND POETRY READINGS are held at four area cafes:

CAFFE LENA, 45 Phila St Saratoga, 584-9789, has been the launch site for many renowned performers, many of whom lovingly return on occasion to perform for their acknowledged patroness, Lena. The program is available at the caffe.

THE EIGHTH STEP COFFEE HOUSE, First Presbyterian Church Albany, is a "Free Stage" performance space which allows local talent to try their skills before a live audience. All members of the community are invited to participate either on stage or in the audience.

EL LOCO, 465 Madison Ave Albany, 436-1855, presents "Sunday Acoustic Performances," a series of musical evenings featuring international figures from the world of the "peoples' " tradition.

THE HALF MOON CAFE, 154 Madison Ave Albany, 436-0329, welcomes writers of all media to present their material to a listening audience. Poets and fiction writers read; composers play and sing. Audience discussion is welcome.

ENTERTAINMENT CENTERS regularly program events open to the public:

1. The two **ARMORIES** in Albany and the Washington Avenue Armory in Schenectady host major spectator events—exhibitions, entertainments and sports competitions, for example. Information is available at the following numbers:

> Albany
> Washington Ave 455-0204
> New Scotland Ave 449-1575
> Schenectady
> Washington Ave 377-8581

2. **EMPIRE STATE PLAZA** and **CONVENTION CENTER** host scores of open events each year. These include displays like the college fair, the home show, and the ski show as well as numerous ethnic festivals, road races, fund-raisers and the like. Information on forthcoming events is available through the New York State Office of General Services.

3. **GLENS FALLS CIVIC CENTER** provides a stage for such events as rock concerts, the circus, the ice show, and family shows. Information is available at 1-761-3852.

4. **HOUSTON FIELDHOUSE** at RPI was renovated in 1983 to provide improved seating and acoustics for rock concerts, cabaret shows, sporting events and such displays as the home show, the boat show, the auto show, the antique show, and the flower show. The capacity of this civic center ranges from 5300 to 7600, depending on stage setting.

5. **NOONTIME** downtown Albany is a time of vitality. As thousands of people pour from offices, several downtown institutions program educa-

tional and cultural activities—from concerts to lectures and slide shows. Publicity for these events appears on bulletin boards throughout downtown and in the entertainment sections of the Friday KNICKERBOCKER NEWS, TIMES UNION and TIMES RECORD and the Saturday section of the SCHENECTADY GAZETTE.

TRIP-TAKING has been made palatable by three area residents who have inaugurated a unique business called **AT YOUR SERVICE, INC.** This company conducts regular trips to New York City and other points of interest in the region. They also make arrangements for any group for any occasion. They charter buses, confirm reservations, and purchase tickets, all according to the specifications of the client. Groups short on ideas and anxious for something innovative can ask for suggestions. Information is available at P.O. Box 517 Slingerlands, 12159. Contacts are Margie Reilly, 274-0720, Helen Casey, 439-5952, and Maureen Klein, 434-6723.

WORKPLACE TOURS are conducted at the following sites of manufacture:

Freihofers Bakery
Prospect Road/Albany
438-6631

Bread Bakery Tour
Daily 9:30 and 11
Advanced notice required

Hudson Mohawk Industrial Gateway
457 Broadway/Troy
274-5267

Arranges tours of area
factories for groups

Vermont Teddy Bear
153 Central Avenue/Albany.
434-3448

M-F 8-4
Glass windows in showroom
into sewing room

William S. Newman Brewing Co
32 Learned Street/Albany
465-8501

Sat 12

SPRING

ALBANY TULIP FESTIVAL and **PINKSTERFEST**, annual events commemorating Albany's Dutch heritage and welcoming Spring, are scheduled for the second weekend in May, when thousands of tulips come into blossom in the city's parks. The general schedule is as follows: on Thursday morning, the mayor reads an opening proclamation and young Albanians scrub State Street with traditional broad brooms. On Friday, tulips of many varieties are on display at the Lake House in Washington Park. On Saturday morning, the Tulip pageant begins, leading up to the crowning of the year's Tulip Queen at about noon in Washington Park. On Saturday afternoon and Sunday, the outdoor fair—Pinksterfest—takes over the

Park, with Kinderkermis (the children's carnival) running concurrently in the Park. The weekend also features the Tulip Ball and the Tulip Luncheon, both open to anyone wishing to purchase a ticket. The City Arts Office oversees the celebration.

GARDENING delights many residents from April through September. Community Gardens, plots of land available for cultivation by residents, are described in the food section of the chapter on shopping. Stores catering to the needs of pleasure gardeners are described in the goods section of the shopping chapter.

THE GRECIAN FESTIVAL is held each year on the third weekend in May at St. Sophia's Greek Orthodox Church, 440 Whitehall Rd Albany, 489-4442. Thousands flock to this unique event, savoring the Greek dinners and desserts and enjoying the traditional music and dancing of Greece and the Greek islands. Parishioners display, explain, and sell imported Greek merchandise in booths throughout the parish house.

MAPLE SUGARING, the laborious process of drawing sap and converting it to syrup and candy, requires extraordinary patience and watchfulness, particularly in the weeks around March 15 to April 15 when the sap is running. Five regional farms welcome curious visitors and, of course, invite them to

sample the syrup and to take some home. (Because operations are some-what dependent on weather conditions, it is best to call ahead to check open hours and to get directions.)

Columbia Hill Farm
RD 2, Averill Park 283-2896
H. Tyler Farms
Westford . . . . (607) 638-9474
On Sundays during sugaring time,
pancake dinners are served from 12-6.
Putnam Maple Farm
Beards Hollow Rd, Richmondville 294-7278

SCHENECTADY COUNTY AIR SHOW is Schenectady County Airport's tribute to the art of flying. In 1985 the show included a ground display of over 40 civilian and military aircraft as well as in-flight demonstrations by more than 20 planes. The event has grown steadily in recent years, and planners anticipate continued expansion. Information circulars are published in April and distributed throughout the Capital District.

SUMMER

ALPINE SLIDES, rides that slalom down mountains, usually on the site of ski trails, are maintained at West Mountain (793-6606) and at Jiminy Peak (738-5431). Directions appear in the section on skiing.

THE ALTAMONT FAIR usurps the picturesque Helderberg village of Altamont each August. It combines a genuine country fair (including serious farm competitions—animal husbandry contests, cooking and sewing displays, and art shows) with a midway, live entertainment, an antique auto show, a circus museum, a carriage museum, and a fire equipment museum. The result of this variety is that the fair is one of the best there is.

THE ARTS FESTIVAL is held on the Saturday and Sunday of the first week in June in Riverfront Park in Troy. Selected works of area craftspersons stand in competition in a juried show on display throughout the weekend. Ethnic food booths, arts activities for children, diverse entertainers— from tumblers and clowns to serious musicians—attract an enthusiastic audience on both days. The works of the winning artists are shown in subsequent weeks at the headquarters of the Rensselaer County Council of the Arts, sponsor of the event. Information is available at the Council, 189 2nd St Troy, 273-0552.

CATSKILL GAME FARM is a wonderful place for a family to spend a day. The founders, whose principal concern was the conservation of rare and vanishing animal species, designed a suitable habitat for each, hoping they would live and breed. The result is an expansive wooded shelter through which visitors may walk and observe a great variety of interesting animals, sheltered but not really confined. Favorites for children are the nursery where newborn animals are kept, the petting and feeding area where deer, goats, and llamas roam uncaged, and a rather spectacular playground. A single admission fee covers most of the activities offered, though additional charges are imposed for mechanical amusements at the playground. Refreshments are sold at concessions, and picnic tables are available for those who bring their own food. Directions: Thruway to Exit 21; Rte 23 West to Rte 32 South. Route is well marked.

CLEARWATER, the sloop which sails the Hudson River piloted by environmentalists committed to heightening citizen awareness of the importance of keeping the river free of industrial and urban pollution, occasionally puts in at the Port of Albany. On those occasions, folk singer Pete Seeger, the inspiration for the project, performs. The ship's arrival in port is usually announced in area newspapers.

FIREWORKS of the first magnitude are set off on the Fourth of July and other celebratory occasions at the Empire State Plaza. It's a perfect stage: the tower windows reflect the dazzle, and the architectural hollows echo the collective sighs of the delighted spectators. Moreover, the platform comfortably accommodates great crowds, assuring all an unobstructed view. Price Chopper has been the host at Fourth of July celebrations in recent years.

FRONTIER TOWN, North Hudson, features rides and shows about life on the early American frontier. Families can participate in intrigues and adventures they have seen in classic Western films. Open spring and fall 10-5; July-Labor Day 9:30-6. Directions: Northway (87) to Exit 29; turn right and follow signs.

FRUIT PICKING, an annual activity of families who like to can and preserve (or simply gorge themselves on the abundance of fruit in season) goes on all summer long and well into the fall. Information on places for picking is presented in the section on shopping for food.

GASLIGHT VILLAGE, Lake George, offers rides and shows about the theme of zesty life at the turn of the century. Admission includes over three dozen rides and all shows. One favorite attraction is the Cavalcade of Cars— classic, antique, and celebrated cars, including Greta Garbo's $250,000 Dunsenberg, Jackie Gleason's limousine, Clark Gable's Mercedes, and Chitty Chitty Bang Bang. Food and beverages abound. Information is available at 668-5459. Open: daily June 14-Labor Day. Directions: Northway (87) to Exit 21; Rte 9 North.

GREAT ESCAPE FUN PARK, Rte 9 Lake George, is a wonderful family amusement park. Well-kept gardens and immaculately maintained walks thread

Jackson Gardens, Union College
Michael Fredericks, Jr.

their way through carefully run, imaginatively designed rides geared for all levels of fun-seekers—from daredevils to rail clingers. Different sections of the park also offer entertainment and refreshments; picnic tables are open to those who bring their own food. The admission fee includes all rides and all shows. Information is available at 792-6568. Open: Memorial Day to Labor Day 9:30-6 daily. Directions: Northway (87) to Exit 19; follow signs.

HOFFMAN'S PLAYLAND, Rte 9 Latham, is a small, clean, well-run amusement park with rides, miniature golf, a driving range, and snacks of various kinds. Tickets purchased by the book offer substantial savings.

INDIAN LADDER FARMS, Rte 156 Voorheesville, lures natives to an annual summer-autumn orgy of fruit-picking and general overindulgence in the fragrance of fresh baked pies, cookies, and cider donuts. Information is available at 765-2956. Open: mid-July to the end of May, M-Sat 9-5; Sun 10-5. Closed Mondays Jan 1 to end of May. Cider mill open mid-Sept to end of year.

KAYDEROSS PARK, Saratoga Lake, is a small, clean, carefully run family beach and amusement park, which includes a swimming pool, miniature golf, and paddle boats. Information is available at 584-3719. Directions: Northway (87) to exit 14; follow signs.

NATURE WALKS in any of Schenectady County's five Nature Preserves— Christmas Sanctuary in Duanesburg, Plotter Kill Nature Preserve in Rotterdam, Handers Preserve in Glenville, Amy Lemaire Woods in City of Schenectady, and Schenectady Museum Nature Preserve in Niskayuna— are possible any day. Information is available in two booklets, **NATURAL AREAS OF SCHENECTADY COUNTY** and **ENVIRONMENTAL TRIP TIPS**, published by the Environmental Clearinghouse of Schenectady.

A NEW LOOK AT OLD ALBANY is a house and garden tour held on the first Saturday of June under the cooperative sponsorship of Historic Albany Foundation and several downtown neighborhood associations. During this well-organized event, participants visit selected private homes in the historic regions of the city. A carefully detailed tour brochure enables participants to travel at their own pace. Hosts are present in each house to answer questions about its architecture, design, or decoration.

RIVERSIDE PARK, in Agawam, Massachusetts, is an enormous supermarket of an amusement park. The 150 acre site presents rides, shows, games, food, merchandise, and attractions of all kinds (from arcades to stock car races, merry-go-rounds to hamburger stands). But the unchallenged stars of this thrill-seekers' paradise are the roller coasters: the Cyclone boasts the steepest climb and drop of any in the United States; the antique wooden Thunderball creaks and squeals in concert with its passengers; the new Black Widow loop defies not only death but description. Admission to this fun-park, which first opened its doors in 1939, can be purchased in various combinations. Information is available at (413) 786-9300. Directions: Thruway to Mass Pike Exit 4, Rte 5 South (5 8 mi) to Rte 57; Rte 57 to Rte 159 South (Main Street, Agawam); 2.9 miles to park.

WATERFORD FLIGHT is a set of lift locks that raise boats from the Hudson River to the Mohawk River above the Cohoes Falls. Each of the five locks lifts the craft 33 to 35 feet. Each boat therefore climbs a staggering 168.8 feet. The trail is well marked and facilities are maintained by the Department of Parks and Recreation. A brochure with more information is available through the Waterford Historical Museum (open Saturday and Sunday afternoons) or the New York State Department of Transportation, Region I office, 474-6715.

Lake and River Cruises

On The Hudson River:

CAPE ISLANDERS CRUISE, P.O. Box 1604, Troy, 274-2545, operate a two-hour cruise on Saturday and Sunday afternoons from April 15-October 31. The boat leaves from Riverfront Park by the Green Island Bridge and takes one of two routes—round trip to the Port of Albany or round trip through the first canal lock to Waterford. The boat is available for private cruises Monday through Friday and for moonlight cruises on Saturday evenings. (The moonlight cruise comes complete with live entertainment.) Meals can be arranged.

THE DUTCH APPLE, 463-0220, is the newest river boat offering cruise service on the Hudson River. The boat leaves from the Snow Dock at the foot of Broadway and Quay, near the U-Haul building in Albany, and goes to Hudson and back four times a day, on Friday, Saturday and Sunday. The sightseeing cruise takes two hours, and can include meals and entertainment. Call for reservations.

On Lake George

Three steamships make regular trips along the lake.

STEAMBOAT MINNE-HA-HA takes a one hour trip six times a day. An evening "Moonlight Cruise" with a Dixieland Jazz Band runs Sat-W in summer, Sat-Sun in spring and fall.

TICONDEROGA takes a two and a half hour cruise twice daily, a dinner jazz cruise from 6:30 to 8:30 and a "Moonlight Cruise" with a Dixieland Jazz Band on Th-Fri-Sat evenings.

MOHICAN takes a full day cruise from Lake George to Ticonderoga and back. In spring and fall, the boat takes two island cruises daily. Information, schedules, and fees are available through Lake George Steamboat Company, Steel Pier, Lake George, 12845, 668-5777. Directions: Northway (87) to Exit 21; Rte 9 North; right at base of lake.

On The Mohawk River:

RIVERBOAT CRUISES, 201 2nd St Troy, present three-hour narrated cruises along the section of the river between locks 6 and 7. In 1985, a new boat, the Nightingale II, joined the fleet. The cruise embarks at the northeast end of the Rte 9 bridge at Crescent every day except Monday. Dinner is served on the evening cruise, 6-9. Riverboat Cruises may be chartered for private parties. Information is available at 273-8878.

FALL

APPLE PICKING has become an annual tradition for many Capital District families. Most area orchards invite patrons to climb the trees themselves in search of the perfect fruit. As a result, residents have become quite knowledgeable in the subtleties of species; they argue the virtue of their favorite variety and discuss vehemently the best weeks to pick each. From mid-September on, local newspapers carry orchard announcements of what trees are ready for picking.

COMMUNITY UNIVERSITY DAY is SUNYA's open house. Scheduled to coincide with Homecoming—complete with football game and other fall festivities—Community University Day is an opportunity for area residents to get a feeling for campus life. Faculty, staff, and students are available to conduct tours of the campus and to play host at events designed to allow the community to see the university at work—and play. Programs vary from year to year but often include art exhibits, computer and laboratory demonstrations, musical performances, and lectures. Information is available through the Community Relations Office, 442-3300.

FOLIAGE TOURS, though not generally organized, are part of the fall ritual in the Capital District. This has become true in large part because the area is the perfect center for touring: glorious colors appear in every direction over a period of five weeks or more. As autumn approaches, media report the progress of color. Although exact dates depend somewhat on the summer rainfall, the "North Country" generally peaks in the last week of September, the Capital District—including the Helderbergs—by Columbus Day, and the Catskills during the last two weeks of October. The New York State Commerce Department, 99 Washington Ave Albany, 474-4116, distributes a brochure of suggested tours. One of the most spectacular is the three-state triangle—Capital District to Bennington VT to Williamstown MA and back.

Festival of Trees
Albany Institute of History and Art

LARK FEST, Lark Street Albany, has become Upstate's largest street festival. From 9 to 5 on a September Saturday, Lark Street from Central to Madison becomes an urban fair grounds. "With it" Lark Street merchants display their wares, in friendly competition with invited street venders, fast food impressarios, and performing musicians for the attention of the thousands of visitors. Arrangements are explained in detail in METROLAND, one of the event's sponsors.

THE MEDIEVAL FAIR is a weekend festival arranged by the Cathedral of All Saints in Albany. Parishioners remove the seats and convert the nave into what the medieval cathedral in fact was—a center for art, music, entertainment, and commerce as well as the focus of religious solemnity. The variety of its offerings—which include caligraphy, puppetry, tumbling, juggling, music, and medieval food—attracts a wide range of people.

THE WALKABOUT is an annual house and garden tour conducted each September by the Schenectady County Historical Society and the Stockade Association. Participants pay a fee and receive a well illustrated map and brochure to guide them in a walking tour of various homes, churches, and buildings in the historic district of the Stockade. Information is available at the Schenectady County Historical Society, 32 Washington Ave Schenectady, 374-0263.

WINTER

THE ANNUAL CHRISTMAS GREENS SHOW at the Rensselaer County Historical Society, 57-59 Second St Troy, 272-7232, offers an opportunity to tour the lovely Hart-Cluett Mansion and view beautifully rendered Christmas decorations.

THE FESTIVAL OF TREES at The Albany Institute of History and Art, 125 Washington Avenue Albany, 463-4478, presents scores of trees, each sponsored and decorated by a community group or business. Many things make this show appealing, not least of which is the variety—the blend of sleek, trendy, witty, innovative, simple and traditional decorations combining to make a wonderful show.

Not Far Away

The Capital District is within easy reach of many beautiful towns, exciting cities, interesting sites, and lively amusement centers. This chapter describes principal attractions at a distance of one half hour or more from the tri-cities. It is divided into four parts on the basis of general direction. In each instance, estimated driving times are given. Times are measured from the center of Albany. All places represented in the chapter were found to be well worth the journey required.

NORTH OF THE CAPITAL DISTRICT

Saratoga

In August, Saratoga Springs is a fascinating place to be. The world's most spectacular thoroughbreds gather for a brief season and lure with them a dazzling assemblage of some of the world's most colorful individuals— third generation multi-millionaires, world champion jockeys, internationally respected trainers, and glittering entertainment personalities. Mansions which sit empty for eleven months shimmer well into the night; stables desolate from September to July bustle from before dawn to dusk; the performing arts center, dormant from September to June, fills with music as the summer sun goes down. In town, the hotels and restaurants honor reservations made months in advance and the Fasig-Tipton Pavilion quietly responds to bids in the hundreds of thousands of dollars.

When the horses leave and the musicians pack up, Saratoga changes. It becomes again a quiet, charming city. In both of its states, Saratoga is a pleasant place to be.

Below are descriptions of things to do and see in Saratoga year round. (The chapters on sports, on arts, on restaurants, and on shopping describe the major attractions in Saratoga in those fields.)

Olana
Michael Fredericks, Jr.

TOURS: THE SARATOGA CIRCUIT TOURS INC. offers a two hour tour which departs from the Drink Hall opposite the entrance to Congress Park during July-August, daily 10 A.M. Information is available at the Tours office, 417 Broadway, Box 38, Saratoga Springs 12866, 587-3656.

SARATOGA SPRINGS PRESERVATION FOUNDATION, 465 Broadway P.O. Box 442 Saratoga Springs, 12866, 587-5030, offers tours of architecture, parks, sculpture, and burial grounds in Saratoga Springs. Tours are by appointment only, except the annual fall house tour.

CONGRESS PARK AND THE CANFIELD CASINO. In the center of Saratoga Springs sits a thirty-three acre park which houses handsome sculptural pieces, landscaped ponds, mineral springs, and the **CANFIELD CASINO,** an elegant nineteenth century gambling hall. The casino, which features domed windows, and stained glass panels, is owned by the city of Saratoga Springs and may be rented. On the second and third floors the Historical Society of Saratoga Springs runs a museum of local history.

THE DRINK HALL, Broadway and Congress Street, Saratoga Springs, is a handsome building which has served as a trolley station and a pavillion where spring waters were served. It will be the site of the Visitors Center for Saratoga Springs.

GIDEON PUTNAM HOTEL is a charming old resort nestled amidst tall pines on the grounds of the Saratoga Spa State Park. It is a center of activity during August when the flat track is in action. The general public is welcome in the dining room and the gift shop which displays an interesting selection of antique jewelry. Reservations are suggested in high season, 584-3000. Bikes are available for rental at the Gideon Putnam in July and August, 9 AM-6 PM weather permitting. The terrain throughout the park is level and the surroundings are beautiful so it is the perfect place for casual peddling or serious racing. Directions: Take I-87 to Exit 13N. Take 9N. Follow signs. (Thirty minutes.)

The **LINCOLN AND ROOSEVELTS BATHS,** Saratoga Spa State Park, function throughout the year. Men and women are welcome to take the baths. This consists of relaxing in a deep tub filled with warm effervescent water and then, wrapped in an oversized towel, moving to a cot for a massage and rest. The personnel at the baths are congenial and gracious.

Everyone who tries this luxury reports feeling greatly restored and refreshed. The fee for the bath is reasonable. Information is available at 584-2010 or 584-2011. Directions: Northway (87) to Exit 13N; 9N north to entrance.

NATIONAL MUSEUM OF RACING, Union Ave., is described in the chapter on Museums.

SARATOGA SPA STATE PARK is described in the chapter on Sports and Recreation.

YADDO is a Victorian estate in Saratoga Springs set aside by Spenser Trask as a retreat for invited artists, writers and composers. Among those whom Yaddo has served over the years are such luminaries as Robert Lowell, Flannery O'Connor, Aaron Copland, Jessamyn West, William Carlos Williams, Carson McCullers and Saul Bellow. The house is not open to the public, but it is possible to drive through and visit the grounds. Directions: take I-87 North to Exit 14. Go west on Union Street. Watch for sign on left after crossing over I-87.

Stillwater

SARATOGA NATIONAL HISTORIC PARK, Rtes 4 and 32 between Stillwater and Schuylerville, 664-9821, is an historic area marking the site of the critical encounter of the Revolution, the Battle of Saratoga. A visitor center provides information about the historical moment and guidance for a complete driving tour of the battlefield. Free. The park is open from April 1-November 30 from 9-5; July-Aug. 9-6. The center is open daily except Thanksgiving, Christmas and New Year. Directions: Take I-87 North to Exit 12. Follow clearly marked signs to park. (Forty minutes.)

Nearby is **SCHUYLER HOUSE,** beautiful home of General Philip Schuyler and Elizabeth Schuyler. Free. Open mid-June to Labor Day, 10-5.

Glens Falls

THE HYDE COLLECTION, 161 Warren St., is a small fine arts museum housed in a Florentine style villa willed to the town of Glens Falls by Charlotte Hyde. Works include pieces from twenty-five centuries including works by major artists. Guided tours are led by residents of the town. Admission. Open: T-Sun 12-5. 1-792-1761. Directions: Take I-87 North to Exit 18. Take Hudson Ave. into the center of town. At light, Hudson Ave. becomes Warren St. (One hour)

Lake George

LAKE GEORGE is a sensationally beautiful natural lake on which many local residents rent or own summer homes. The village at the foot of the lake has become a center for summer entertainment. Some of the attractions offered are described in the chapter "Other Things to Do." The public beach along the foot of the lake gives a lovely view of the water and mountains. Sailing on the lake can be exciting and challenging, and the width of the lake makes it a wonderful place for waterskiing. Directions: Take I-87 North to Exit 21. Follow Rte 9 North. (One hour)

MARCELLA SEMBRICK MEMORIAL STUDIO, Lakeshore Drive, Rte 9N, Bolton Landing, is a treasury of opera memorabilia. Located in the summer studio used by the famous soprano, the museum displays letters, photographs, and awards of Ms. Sembrick and other noted opera stars. Free. Open July 1-Labor Day daily 10-12:30; 2-5:30. 1-644-9839. Directions: Take I-87 North to Exit 22. Follow 9N towards Bolton Landing. (One hour and fifteen minutes)

Cambridge

NEW SKEET MONASTERIES are houses of religious orders of monks and nuns originally affiliated with the Russian Orthodox Church. They support their chosen life of prayer by practicing various arts and making the fruits of their labors available to the public. The monks train dogs, craft icons, and operate a butcher shop and bakery. The nuns make icons, sew liturgical vestments, and prepare marzipan and cheesecakes. The foodstuffs are available at the monasteries, 1-677-3928 (for the monks) and 1-677-3810 (for the nuns), and through SYSCO, Fuller Rd., Albany and DeFazio Imports, Troy. Directions: Take Rte. 7 East to Rte 22 North. (One hour)

Ticonderoga

FORT TICONDEROGA is a splendid historic site. The stone fortress situated on a hill at the juncture of Lake George and Lake Champlain provides not only a spectacular panorama, but also a glimpse of what it must have been like both to attack and to defend a fort. The holdings of the military museum complement the fort's impressive structure, as do well-staged cannon drills, musketry shows, and fife and drum presentations. Guided tours are available on the hour from 9-5 in July and August. Admission. Open mid-May to mid-October 8-6 (to 7 in July and August). 1-585-2821. Directions: Take I-87 North to Exit 29. Turn right. Follow signs. (Two hours.)

Helderberg Escarpment
Michael Fredericks, Jr.

Adirondack Mountains

ADIRONDACK MUSEUM, Blue Mountain Lake, is a compelling portrayal of man's relationship with this giant region of the country. It tells through displays how man initially used the mountains to live simply and make a living from the animals and natural resources he found there, how he was joined by others seeking recreation, and how others came who sought commercial gain and began to abuse the region. It explains that now, under careful supervision, the Adirondack Park is a composite of commercial success, recreational haven and wilderness preserve. Displays show lifestyles, transportation and use of leisure time, the scenes predictably ranging from primitive to lavish. (It is interesting to note that the term "camp" came to be applied in the Adirondacks to all mountain dwellings, tent or palace.) Admission. Open June 15-October 15 from 10-6. 1-352-7311 or 7312. Directions: Take I-87 North to Exit 25. Take Rte. 28 to Rte. 28N. (Two hours.)

SOUTH OF THE CAPITAL DISTRICT

West Side of the Hudson

BRONCK HOUSE MUSEUM, Coxsackie, is a cluster of buildings and fields in which the settlement of the area is commemorated. The oldest structure is the 1663 stone house built by Pieter Bronck to establish the claim on the enormous stretch of land. The surrounding buildings and cemeteries show what life was like in this home lived in by nine generations of Broncks. Admission. Open: Last Sunday in June-Labor Day, T-Sat 10-5; Sun 2-6. 731-8862. Directions: Take N.Y.S. Thruway to Exit 21B. Take 9W south 3¾ miles to Pieter Bronck Rd. on right at red barn. (Forty minutes.)

WOODSTOCK is a lovely little Catskill town southwest of Saugerties. The wooded setting, the privacy, and the presence of a longstanding summer arts colony have made Woodstock a place where musicians, dancers, writers, sculptors, painters—artists of all forms—feel comfortable living and working. The main street of the town houses shops in which their work can be viewed and purchased. Directions: Take Thruway Exit 20. Go west on Rte 212. (One hour.)

Information on exhibits of artwork throughout the region is available at the Woodstock Artists Association, 28 Tinker Street, (914) 679-2940. This organization also has its own gallery.

Friendly cafes and restaurants like the Little Bear (Chinese cuisine), Joshua's Cafe (Middle Eastern menu), and Deanie's (a beloved oldtimer) welcome visitors. The proprietors are always up to date on activities in town.

THE WOODSTOCK TIMES, a weekly newspaper, publishes a calendar of current events and coming attractions.

THE MAVERICK CONCERTS, performances by local musicians, are held June 30-Sept 1 at The Maverick on Rte 28. Information is available at Box 102 Woodstock 12498, (914) 679-8746 or 679-9558.

TUBING ON THE ESOPUS is a frolicking family entertainment practiced on the free-flowing Esopus Creek off Rte 28 north of Woodstock. Efforts are under way to organize this formerly casual activity, and specific details will be available in town.

The Woodstock Theater is described in the chapter on The Arts. There are also several points of interest open to the public:

BYRDCLIFFE is the summer arts and crafts colony established in 1902 by Ralph Radcliffe Whitehead. Over the years, it has supported the work of hundreds of creative persons, some of them of renown—Charlotte Perkins Gilman, Harry Hopkins, John Dewey, Thomas Mann, Wallace Stevens, and Eva Watson-Schultz, for example. Today, supervised by The Woodstock Guild, Byrdcliffe continues its mission of providing a quiet, stimulating place for artists and craftspersons to work during summer. Visitors are welcome to tour the facility. A map and further information is available through The Woodstock Guild, 34 Tinker Street Woodstock, NY 12498.

BYRDCLIFFE THEATER, part of the arts colony described above, presents theatrical entertainment in the summer, much of it of an experimental nature. Information is available through The Guild at the address above. Productions are promoted in the regional media.

OPUS 40, 7480 Fite Road Saugerties, is difficult to explain. The lifetime accomplishment of stone sculptor Harvey Fite, it is best described as an enormous spacial decoration composed of huge pieces of stone drawn from a neighboring quarry and shaped into an awesome garden. Smooth ramps lead to platforms, walls, benches—spaces enhanced by contemporary sculptural pieces. Because Fite was conscious of the relationship of his work to the surroundings, there are beautiful vistas everywhere. The impact is overpowering. Information about accommodations for visitors is available at (914) 246-3400.

SENATE HOUSE, 312 Fair St., Kingston, was the first meeting place of the government of New York in July 1776. The rooms have been carefully preserved and restored to give an accurate impression of what life was like in colonial times. Free. Open: Wed-Sat 10-5; Sun 1-5. (914) 338-2786. Directions: Take N.Y.S. Thruway south to Exit 19. At circle take exit to Washington Ave. At second light turn left onto N. Front St. Take third right onto Fair St. (One hour.)

STONE HOUSES, Huguenot St., New Paltz, is a group of 18th century stone homes and a church built by a group of Huguenot settlers from Northern France. The buildings are charmingly clustered into a little community surrounded by fine old trees and gardens. Admission. Houses open May 11 through October 30, Wed-Sat 10-4; Sun 1-4 except July and August 10-4. (914) 255-1660. Directions: Take N.Y.S. Thruway south to Exit 19. Take Rte. 299 west through New Paltz. Just before bridge turn right on Huguenot St. (One hour and twenty-minutes.)

LAKE MOHONK MOUNTAIN HOUSE is a resort hotel located on a small lake atop a mountain near New Paltz. The hotel, a Victorian wonder with turrets, porches and gingerbread, is extraordinary in its preservation of a gracious style long abandoned by most commercial hostelries. Well-maintained gardens and walking paths are open to day visitors as is the dining room. Reservations are required for the dining room. This resort has great appeal for those of all ages interested in physical activity in a healthy environment. (914) 255-1000. Directions: Take N.Y.S. Thruway south to Exit 18. Turn left on Rte. 299. Pass through New Paltz. After crossing bridge turn right. Bear left and follow Mountain Rest Road to Mohonk Gate. (One hour and forty-five minutes.)

VINEYARDS and **WINERIES** dot Ulster County. The five vineyards listed below offer tours and winetasting. Some are open only in summer but others are open year round. Because schedules change, it is necessary to call or write to learn hours of opening.

Brotherhood
Washingtonville, NY 10992
(914) 496-9101

Hudson Valley Wine Company
Blue Point Road
Highland, NY 12528
(914) 691-7296 (212) 594-5394

El Paso Winery
Rte 9W
Ulster Park, NY 12487
(914) 331-8642

Royal Kedem Winery
P.O. Box 811
Dock Road
Milton, NY 12547
(914) 795-2240 (212) 583-5800

Valley Vineyards
Oregon Trail Road
Walker Valley, NY 12588
(914) 744-3449

A map of sixteen wineries of the Hudson River region, including a guide to winery tours, is available from Cascade Mountain, Flint Hill Rd, Amenia 12501. Ask for brochure, "Winery Tours."

THE UNITED STATES MILITARY ACADEMY at West Point is a great place to visit. The **VISITOR'S CENTER**, (914) 938-2638, located just outside the gates in Highland Falls (on the campus of the former Ladycliff College), is the best place to start. It provides interesting background—the history of West Point, stories about famous graduates, replicas of the academy's past, and an explanation of the nature of the college as it currently exists.

Once within the military compound, the visitor may walk through the grounds, tour the museum, visit the Cadet Chapel and the Catholic Chapel, and enjoy the scenery. Some of the buildings of the college are open to visitors. It is of course best to plan a visit to coincide with a parade or a sporting contest. The corps of cadets parade during the school year on a schedule available at the Public Affairs Office (914) 938-2638 or 938-5261. The schedule of sporting events open to the public is released by the Sports Information Office (914) 938-3303 or 938-3512.

Food is available on the post at the Hotel Thayer. (On weekends the restaurant is very crowded and there may be a long wait.) Many visitors bring their own food and either picnic or tailgate in areas designated for public use. (Parking restrictions and all motor vehicle laws are strictly enforced.) Visitors in the company of a cadet who has made arrangements in advance may dine in the Mess Hall, and cadets may accompany a guest to Eisenhower Hall for light refreshments. The Officers Club on base is restricted to officers and their guests.

A fine gift shop is located in the Visitors Center. Directions: Take N.Y.S. Thruway south to Exit 17. Turn left on 17K into Newburgh. Turn right on 9W and then follow signs. (Two hours and a half.)

THE STORM KING ART CENTER, in Mountainville outside of Cornwall, (914) 534-3115, is a museum of modern art which features outdoor sculpture, much of it of monumental scale. The collection also includes paintings, graphics, and smaller sculptures which are displayed in a French Normandy style house. Among the artists of the over 160 pieces are David Smith, Isamu Noguchi, and Richard Stankiewicz. Suggested donation.

Open: Mid-May through October daily except Tuesday 2-5:30. Grounds open at 12 noon. When Tuesday is a legal holiday, center is open on Tuesday and closed on Wednesday.

Directions: NYS Thruway to Exit 17. Left on Rte 17K to center of Newburgh. Right onto Rte 32 South. Go six miles, through Vails Gate, and down a hill. Right on Orrs Mill Road. Go ½ mile. Left onto Old Pleasant Hill Road. Entrance ½ mile on left. (Two hours and a half.)

East Side of the Hudson

MALDEN BRIDGE ARTS CENTER consists of four units: Woods Gallery displays and sells fine crafts and pottery; Bridge Editions displays and sells paintings by Albany artist Betty Warren and prints by different artists; Malden Bridge Pottery, a studio, offers workshops; Malden Bridge School of Art offers summer painting workshops and lectures during the year. Closed Jan-Feb. Open: Sat 11-5, Sun 12-5. Directions: Take I-90 East to Exit 12. Turn right onto Rte. 9. Go approximately one mile. Turn left on to Rte. 32. Go 5 miles. Turn left onto Rte. 66. Take first left turn. (One-half hour.)

THE SHAKER MUSEUM, Old Chatham, has a collection of artifacts of the Shaker community based in this area in the 18th and 19th centuries. Furniture, baskets, and working tools are arranged in the buildings to recreate the lifestyle of simple dignity espoused by the Shakers. Admission. Open: May 1-October 31 from 10 am-5:30 pm. (Last ticket sold at 5:00). Library open year round for research. 1-794-9100. Directions: Take Rte. 20 East to Rte. 66. Turn right on Rte. 66. Go through Malden Bridge and follow signs to Shaker Museum. (Forty minutes.)

KINDERHOOK was the birth place of Martin Van Buren, the eighth president of the United States. There are several architecturally important houses to visit:

HOUSE OF HISTORY, 16 Broad St., is a Federal Period house open to the public. Admission. Open: Memorial Day to Labor Day, T-Sat 11-5; Sun 1-5. 1-758-9265. Directions: Take I-90 East to Exit B1. Take Rte. 9 South (One-half hour.)

LINDENWALD is the former home of Martin Van Buren. Major restoration is currently being conducted. A portion of the house may be seen. Free. Open: May-Sept, W-Sun for guided tours on the hour and the half hour 9-4:30. 1-758-9689. Directions: Take I-90 East to Exit B1. Take Rte. 9 South to 9H South. House is two miles south of village. (One-half hour.)

VAN ALEN HOUSE is an early Dutch house graced with Hudson Valley furnishings and paintings. Admission. Open: Memorial Day to Labor Day, T-Sat 11-5; Sun 1-5. 1-758-9265. Directions: Take I-90 East to Exit B1. Take Rte. 9 South to 9H South. (One-half hour.)

OLANA is not easy to define, for it is of interest to anyone interested in art, gardens or architecture, for anyone seeking a spectacular view of the Hudson River, or anyone wanting to picnic, hike, ski, skate or sled. Olana was the home of the American artist Frederick Edwin Church, a 19th century landscape artist of the Hudson River School and a world traveler. The structure and decor of the house, the thoughtfully planned grounds, and the objects on display in the house reflect his eclectic taste and philosophy. From the windows, especially as the sun is setting, the visitor can see landscapes which inspired Church's paintings.

The estate is now a historic site and state park. Admission. Open by guided tour only: Memorial Day weekend to Labor Day, W-Sat 10-4; Sun 1-4; Labor Day to last weekend in October, W-Sat 12-4; Sun 1-4. Grounds open year round till dusk. 1-828-0135. Directions: Take N.Y.S. Thruway south to Exit 21. Go east on Rte. 23 across Rip Van Winkle Bridge. Turn south on 9G. (Forty-five minutes.)

CLERMONT, in Germantown, is the estate of the Livingston family, many of whom played significant political roles in the birth and development of the United States and the state of New York. The core of the house dates to 1777; subsequent additions reflect the architectural and decorative tastes of varing ages.

The grounds surrounding the house offer nature walks, picnic areas and facilities for hiking, snowshoeing and cross-country skiing. Excellent literature describing the history of the house and family are available.

Clermont is now a historic site and state park. The house is open Memorial Day weekend to Oct 31, W-Sat 10-5; Sun 1-5. Grounds are open 6 am-dark all year. 1-537-4240. Directions: Take N.Y.S. Thruway south to Exit 21. Take Rte. 23 east to Rte. 9G south. (One hour.)

AMERICAN MUSEUM OF FIRE FIGHTING, Harry Howard Ave., located at Firemen's Home in Hudson, is a fascinating display of instruments of fire fighting from the primitive buckets and horse drawn pumps to the contemporary swiveling snorkel. Included in the collection are parade models used by volunteer companies for purposes of pageantry rather than fire extinction. As a result, one need not be a fire fighting buff to enjoy this museum, for the array is dazzling. It is a wonderful museum for families. Free. Open April 1-December 1, except Mon., from 9:30-4:30. 1-828-7695. Directions: Take N.Y.S. Thruway south to Exit 21. Go east on Rte 23 across Rip Van Winkle Bridge. Once in Hudson, follow signs to Firemen's Home. (Fifty minutes.)

The principal **ANEMONE** growers on the East Coast are located in Rhinebeck. Dazzling colors line the greenhouses, and great bouquets are available at reasonable prices. Ralph Pitcher's nursery is open from 8:30-4:30 weekdays mid-September to Mother's Day; from 8:30-12 on Sat.; closed Sun. (914) 876-3974. Directions: Take N.Y.S. Thruway south to Exit 19. Go east over Kingston Rhinecliff Bridge to Rte. 9G. Turn right. Take first left onto Middle Road. Turn at sign for cut flowers. Watch for red barn and greenhouses. (One hour and fifteen minutes.)

OLD RHINEBECK AERODROME is a museum and arena for aircraft. In the hangar the visitor can see planes from the World War I era and earlier, and from the stands the visitor can witness air shows featuring stunt flights, synchronized displays, and antique and customized planes in motion. The aerodrome is open May 15 through October from 10 am to 5 pm. Aerial shows Sat-Sun at 2:30. (914) 758-8610. Directions: Take N.Y.S. Thruway south to Exit 19. Go east over Kingston-Rhinecliff Bridge to Rte. 9G. Turn right onto 9G and follow signs. (One hour and 15 minutes.)

INNISFREE GARDEN, Millbrook NY, 12545, (914) 677-8000, is a man-made natural wonder, an Oriental cup garden designed and build by Walter Beck over a period of 22 years from 1930-1952. Beck literally rearranged the landscape—moving rocks, streams and waterfalls, constructing terraces, slopes and walls, decorating space with plants and vines. At this mammoth site, Beck improved on nature but eschewed artifice. Open: May-Oct, Sat-Sun 11-4; W-F 10-4.

HYDE PARK is a park, museum, library and national monument maintained on the site of the childhood home of Franklin Delano Roosevelt. The house, maintained as it was in 1945, is a charming and warm home filled with historic memorabilia and signs of human vitality. The museum houses a diverse collection of fascinating items ranging from FDR's boyhood pony cart to documents which shaped national and international events. Eleanor's years as wife of the President and as world figure in her own right are also documented. The chronological display offers a wonderful opportunity for visitors to learn—or relearn—what happened in the world between 1932-1945, and in the case of Eleanor's humanitarian activities, between 1932-1962. Admission fee to the house and museum includes admission to nearby Vanderbilt Mansion. The house is open 9-5 every day except Christmas and New Year's. The tours on tape are particularly fine at Hyde

Park. (914) 229-9115. Directions: N.Y.S. Thruway south to Exit 18. Go east on Rte. 299 to Rte 9W. Go south on 9W to Mid-Hudson Bridge. Cross Bridge. Go north on Rte. 9N. (Two hours.)

VAL-KILL, Hyde Park, was Eleanor Roosevelt's personal retreat from 1927 through her husband's first term as President. After his death in 1945, the house became her personal home. Here, eminent guests—Haile Selassie, Nikita Krushchev, John Kennedy, and Jawaharal Nehru, for example—sought her counsel. Here, too, she began an experiment in business for women. The house is open daily. It is reached by shuttle bus from Hyde Park Museum, with buses running every twenty minutes 9:20-5:00. Information is available through the Park Service (914) 229-9115. Directions: See Hyde Park.

VANDERBILT MANSION is an enormous, opulent mansion built by the American millionaire, Cornelius Vanderbilt, to provide a place to entertain and house hundreds of guests in lavish style at one time—as was the practice of many nouveau riche industrialists at the end of the 19th century. The landscaping and the view of the Hudson from the lawns are spectacular. Directions: Follow directions for Hyde Park and continue on Rte. 9N. (Two hours and fifteen minutes.)

BOSCOBEL, in Garrison, is a beautiful mansion set on the highlands of the Hudson across from West Point. The house itself is handsome, the interior is furnished with Federal furniture and china, glass, and silver imported from Europe, and the view from the lawns and gardens is spectacular. Admission. Open: Apr-Oct, W-M 9:30-5; Nov, Dec, Mar, W-M 9:30-4. (914) 265-3638. Directions: N.Y.S. Thruway south to 84 east to 9D south. (Two hours).

Camp Sugamore, Raquette Lake
Mark L. Peckham/Preservation League of New York

New York City

NEW YORK, the metropolis that hums day and night, is a second home to many residents of the Capital District. An easy three hours away by car, even closer by bus (Trailways runs frequent trips daily) or by train (Amtrak travels at 110 mph along a beautiful stretch of track on the east bank of the Hudson River) the cultural, commercial and social opportunities of New York are second to none. Once in the city the visitor has access to the efficient, relatively inexpensive mass transit system. Maps of bus routes and subways are available through *I Love New York*, 99 Washington Ave., 456-8369.

This office also will send free maps of the city and brochures on shopping, touring, dining, and enjoying the night life. Bookstores and libraries in the Capital District carry comprehensive guides to the city.

The New Yorker, a weekly magazine, lists and reviews the cultural activities current in New York. *New York Magazine*, a bi-weekly, prints "*Cue*," a full calendar of events of all kinds. The Friday edition of *The New York Times* carries a "*Weekend*" section which lists upcoming events, and the Sunday edition's "*Arts and Leisure*" and "*Sports*," further describe the current scene. And, of course, the daily *Times* carries countless advertisements for New York's great stores. All of these sources of information make it easy for the resident of the Capital District to take advantage of the proximity of this infuriating, intimidating, exhilerating, alluring, animating city. What follows are lists of some unrivaled attractions of New York which the non-resident might not know about but which cannot fail to please. *I Love New York*, 456-8369, can provide more information on each one as can The New York Convention and Visitors Bureau 212-397-8222. (Three hours by car.)

Places to Visit
Air Craft Carrier Intrepid
Bronx Zoo
Central Park and Zoo
Empire State Building
    Guinness Hall of World Records
Hayden Planetarium
New York Botanical Gardens (Bronx)
    Enid A. Haupt Conservatory
New York Stock Exchange and Commodities Exchange
Rockefeller Center
South Street Seaport
Statue of Liberty
Trump Tower
United Nations Building
World Trade Center

Libraries
New York Public Library, Main Branch

Museums
American Museum of Natural History
Cloisters
Cooper-Hewitt Museum
Frick Museum
Guggenheim Museum
Pierpont Morgan Library
Metropolitan Museum of Art
Museum of the City of New York
Museum of Modern Art
Museum of Holography
Whitney Museum

Notable Houses of Worship
Cathedral of St. John the Divine
St. Bartholemew's Church
St. Patrick's Cathedral
Temple Emmanuel
Trinity Church

Rides
Carriage Ride (Central Park)
Sightseeing Boats (Dayline)
Staten Island Ferry

Walks
Fifth Avenue (90th St. to 34th St.)
Madison Avenue (80th St.-South)
Chinatown/Little Italy
Greenwich Village/SoHo
Wall Street

Plays, Music and Dance
PLAYS: New York is still the national capital for dramatic arts. Theaters vary somewhat on show times, but the traditional hours still dominate; that is, Matinees Wed. and Sat. at 2:00; evening performances M-Sat. at 8. Half-price tickets are available day of performance at Times Square Ticket Center, Broadway at 47th St. Many Broadway theatres will accept ticket orders on major credit cards by telephone.

The theatre listing and analysis of availability of seats is published in the *Knickerbocker News* each week. Charter buses offer theater excursions. These are advertised locally. Information is available at At Your Service, Inc., 274-0720, Yankee Trails, 286-2400, Mountain View Coaches, 756-2176, and Wade Tours, 355-4500.

MUSIC AND DANCE: Half price tickets to same-day opera, concert and dance performances are sold at the Bryant Park Ticket Booth (behind the New York Public Library) seven days a week noon-7. The three principal halls are:

Carnegie Hall
City Center
Lincoln Center

ENTERTAINMENT: The world reknowned Art Deco theater, **RADIO CITY MUSIC HALL,** features family shows of many varieties.

Washington, DC

WASHINGTON DC, though not nearby, is popular with area residents as a place to visit, particularly in spring and early summer. The Travel section of the Sunday NEW YORK TIMES frequently advertises outstanding weekend specials in Washington hotels.

Residents who plan a trip to the Capital may get special visitor passes to the White House and the galleries in the houses of Congress plus helpful tips on visiting the city by calling the office of their local Congressional Representative. (Numbers are in the blue pages of the telephone directory.)

EAST OF THE CAPITAL DISTRICT

Vermont

Bennington

Bennington is a charming New England town with many things for the visitor to see and do. The approach to Bennington is itself splendid. Route 7 comes to a rise at the border between New York and Vermont, and all the beauty of rural Vermont is on display. Although the area is lovely throughout the year, it is particularly spectacular in the autumn. Directions: Take 787 North to Rte. 7 East to Bennington (One hour.)

In addition to scenic beauty Bennington offers historic sites, museums, and stores, presented here more or less in order for the visitor approaching from the Capital District.

OLD FIRST CHURCH is a beautiful, graceful church, awesome in its eloquence of line and simplicity of decor. Built in 1805, it still functions as an active center of worship. For this reason, visiting hours are somewhat dependent upon the needs of the congregation. However, even from the outside the church is a pleasure to see.

Beside and behind the church, enclosed in a splendid white fence, is Old Burying Ground, the cemetery in which rest the founders of the town, many soldiers from the American Revolution, as well as Robert Frost, the poet. The tomb markers, many of Puritan style, are of interest to students of art, history and religion.

WALLOOMSAC INN, a building which always attracts attention and invites comment, has functioned as a haven for travelers since it was built in 1764. Among its illustrious guests have been Jefferson, Madison, and T. Roosevelt. It has been run by the same family for over ninety years. It is open mid-May to early December.

MONUMENT AVENUE, the street which extends up from the inn and church, is lined with magnificent colonial homes and beautiful trees.

BENNINGTON BATTLE MONUMENT is an obelisk commemorating the defeat of British Troops by the Green Mountain Boys. A tourist office located at the base of the monument provides information and access to the tower which visitors may climb. Admission.

BENNINGTON HISTORICAL MUSEUM, (802) 447-1571, is a regional museum which features early American furniture, glass, paintings, and sculpture and a collection of Bennington pottery. At the same site is a museum displaying the works of Grandma Moses, the American primitive painter. Admission. Open: Mar 1-Dec 1, daily 9 5.

POTTERS' YARD is a collection of shops all worthy of a visit. Of particular note is **BENNINGTON POTTERS**, 324 County St, (802) 447-7531, which has both a display room-sales room and a grist mill where factory seconds and overuns of this fine pottery are sold. Also for sale are interesting candles, placemats, napkins, prints, cookware and wools. Tours of the factory are available by reservation for buses. Tours for four or more individuals are available June 15-Sept 15, 11 am and 2:15 pm. **THE BRASSERIE** in the Potters' Yard serves pleasant meals both inside and on the patio. Open: M-Sat 11:30-5, Sun 10:30-5. Information is available at (802) 447-7922.

PARK MCCULLOUGH HOUSE, North Bennington, (802) 442-2747, is both a house museum and a community center. It hosts weddings, receptions, parties, meetings, art shows, and concerts, and also welcomes visitors for tours. The interior of the 1865 Victorian dwelling features handsome wood paneling, Italian marble mantels, original furniture, and portraits and artifacts of the several generations of Parks and McCulloughs who lived here. Admission. Open for tours: late May-Oct, Sun-F 10-4, Sat 10-2. Directions: From Bennington take VT Rte. 7 North to Rte. 67A. In North Bennington turn up hill to West St. Gate is at top of hill. (One and one half hours.)

Manchester

Manchester is another beautiful old Vermont town with many interesting places to shop and to eat. The shops are well worth visiting for pleasure and/or buying. Directions: Take 787 to Rte 7 East to Bennington. Take VT Rte. 7 North. (One hour and 45 minutes).

HILDENE, the summer home of Robert Todd Lincoln, son of Abraham Lincoln, was occupied by descendants until 1975. The house contains a pipe organ and is furnished with family possessions. The formal gardens are being restored. Admission. Open: daily May 21-Oct. 30, 9:30-4:30. (802) 362-1788. Directions: Follow directions to Manchester. House is on Rte. 7A, 2 miles south of the junction of Rte. 7A and 30, in Manchester.

Massachusetts

The Berkshires

The Berkshires is a region in Western Massachusetts united as much by its common pursuits as by its geography. Chosen almost simultaneously by the 19th century artistic colony and the affluent as a center for their summer lives, the area has remained to this day a focal point of literature, music, dance, and the expressive arts. Many of the mansions built as "summer cottages" in the opulent era at the end of the last century have become schools, monasteries, convents and inns. Writers, composers, and choreographers as well as performing artists continue to flock to the area, especially in July and August.

General tours of the area are interesting, but some places in and around Stockbridge and Lenox serve as focal points.

THE BERKSHIRES LOCAL COLOR, a very helpful booklet, is available through Berkshire Visitors Bureau, Berkshire Common, Plaza Level, Pittsfield, MA 01201, (413) 443-9186.

BERKSHIRE BED AND BREAKFAST is an organization which helps travelers arrange for inexpensive lodgings in spare rooms of homes throughout the area. The accommodations vary greatly in size and style. The person to contact for further information is Terry Ross, Main St Williamstown, Mass 01096-0211, (413) 268-7244. In 1986, this group will become **BED AND BREAKFAST IN NEW ENGLAND** and will make arrangements in parts of Vermont, New Hampshire, and New York as well as western Massachusetts.

Williamstown

Williamstown is an interesting place to visit for several reasons, beauty being the first. Williamstown is so like the college town of fiction—a small New England town with splendid old trees, wide streets, beautiful colonial homes, impressive fraternity houses, small tweedy shops, well-dressed students, and ever-so-slightly rumpled professors—that it seems more like a Hollywood set than a real town.

In addition to serving as idyllic home for **WILLIAMS COLLEGE,** an excellent undergraduate college of liberal arts, Williamstown is the home of the **CLARK ART INSTITUTE,** a gallery of fine arts. The display features a major collection of the French Impressionists, as well as beautiful porcelains, silverware and works of the Old Masters. It was established by Sterling and Francine Clark, heirs to the Singer sewing machine fortune. The Institute is open Tu-Sun, 10-5. (413) 458-9545.

THE WILLIAMS COLLEGE MUSEUM OF ART mounts excellent exhibits. Because it serves a multi-purpose art department, the displays cover a full range of art forms and historical periods. Recent exhibits, for example, have included such a wide variety of titles as Helen Frankenthaler Prints, Depression Era Color Photographs, Commemorative Sculpture of the Mijikenda of Kenya, and History as Art: Prints, Letters, Documents, Books, Manuscripts and Broadsides from the Chapin Library. Museum is open M-Sat 10-5; Sun 1-5. (413) 597-2429.

Directions: Take Rte. 787 north to Rte. 7 through Troy to Rte. 2. Follow Rte. 2 to Williamstown. (One hour.)

Stockbridge

Stockbridge is a charming town in the valley. Information about its history, its points of interest and its most famed citizen, Norman Rockwell, are readily available in restaurants and stores or at the Visitor Information Booth opposite the Red Lion Inn. Directions: Take I-90 East to N.Y.S. Thruway to Mass. Pike. Take Exit 2. Go south on Rte. 102 to Stockbridge. (One hour.)

THE RED LION INN, Main Street, Stockbridge, has served travelers since 1773 when it was a stagecoach stop. The inn serves fine meals. Many travelers plan their day in the Berkshires around a stop at this historic spot.

The Inn is described further in the chapter on Lodging and the chapter on Restaurants.

BERKSHIRE GARDEN CENTER, Stockbridge, is a non-profit horticultural center established "to educate its members and the public in the art and enjoyment of growing things." On display are types of garden settings, formal plantings, vegetable plots, rock gardens, and greenhouses, including a solar greenhouse. Free.

CHESTERWOOD, the home and studio of sculptor Daniel Chester French, is a fascinating place, for on display is the plaster cast French used to model the statue of the seated Lincoln now located within the Lincoln Memorial in Washington. Admission. Open Memorial Day weekend to October 31. Directions: From Stockbridge take Rte. 102 West two miles to Rte. 183. Turn left onto Rte. 183. Go one mile to fork in road. Turn right onto blacktop road. Take next left.

NORMAN ROCKWELL MUSEUM, Main Street Stockbridge MA 01262, (413) 298-3822, displays 50 original pieces by the famed Stockbridge resident, acknowledged Dean of poster art. The collection of paintings, drawings, and sketches, which changes each year, must be seen in the company of a guide. A gift shop sells books and prints. Open: W-Sun 10-5. (Last tour begins at 4:15.)

Hancock

HANCOCK SHAKER VILLAGE, Rte. 20, Hancock, (413) 443-0188, is a restored Shaker community showing the material and ideological contributions of the Shakers to American society. The stark contrast between Shaker lifestyle and that of contemporary America makes a visit to this village very interesting. Admission. Open June 1-October 31, 9:30-5. Directions: Take I-90 East to Rte. 20. Go east, cross the Mass line and continue to Hancock.

Lee

TYRINGHAM GALLERY in Tyringham MA is a collection of contemporary art. The work of thirty artists—painters, sculptors, and potters—are on display in the gallery and the sculpture garden. Tyringham also sponsors single artist shows. Open: Memorial Day to Nov. 1, weekends 10-6; weekdays 10-5. (After Labor Day open on weekends only.) Directions: Take I-90 east to NYS Thruway to Mass Pike; Mass Pike to Exit 2; at juncture of Mass Pike, Rte 20 and Rte 102, take Tyringham Rd south for four miles.

Lenox

Lenox is a beautiful town of interest because its setting is so picturesque and because it is the site of Tanglewood, the keystone of music in the Berkshires. Directions: Take I-90 East to N.Y.S. Thruway Exit B3. Follow signs to Massachusetts Rte 102. Take 102 to Rte 183 North. Tanglewood is 4-5 miles up road. (One and one half hours.)

THE MOUNT, was the summer home of Edith Wharton, the author of *Ethan Frome, The Age of Innocence, The House of Mirth,* and others. It is currently being refurbished to serve as an historical site and as residence for a theater company, Shakespeare and Company. (The company is described in the chapter "The Arts.") Company members offer tours of the 29 room mansion which, because it is only partially restored, is of particular interest to those concerned with restoration. Admission. Open: June-August, Tu-F 12-4; weekends 10-4 (413) 637-3353. Directions: Take I-90 east to N.Y.S. Thruway to Mass Pike. Take Exit 2. Follow Rte 20W to Rte 7 south to junction of Rtes 7 and 7A—Plunkett Rd. (One hour and ten minutes.)

TANGLEWOOD, the summer home of the Boston Symphony, was the brainchild of three persons of imagination and will—Dr. Henry Hadley, Gertrude Robinson Smith and Serge Koussivitsky. They envisioned a center where young musicians could come to learn from masters and where the public could enjoy the fruits of their collaboration in the fresh summer mountain air. The center, located on an estate donated to the symphony, includes the music shed for performances and other buildings for study and practice. Information about concerts is included in the section on music.

Pittsfield

ARROWHEAD, (413) 442-1793, was the home of Herman Melville during his most prolific years as a writer. Here he wrote *Moby Dick* and *The Piazza Tales.* The house has been refurnished to represent its appearance at the time Melville was living and working under its roof. Admission. Open: June-Oct, M-Sat 10-4:30; Sun. 11-3. Directions: Take I-90 East to N.Y.S. Thruway and Mass. Pike to Exit 2. Take Rte. 20 North to Pittsfield. Right onto Holmes Rd. Entrance is ahead on left. (One hour and ten minutes.)

Springfield

THE BASKETBALL HALL OF FAME, 1150 W. Columbus Ave., Springfield, (413) 781-6500, is both a museum and a Hall of Fame. The displays trace the history of the sport from its birth at Springfield in 1891 to the present. Recent additions to the museum include a high school room honoring coaches and stars of the sport at that level and exhibits of great women players. Admission. Open: daily Sept-June 10-5; July-August 10-6. (Closed Thanksgiving, Christmas, New Years.) (413) 781-6500. Directions: Take I-90 East to N.Y.S. Thruway to Mass. Pike to Exit 6 to Rte 291 South. Watch for signs. (One hour and forty-five minutes.)

Sturbridge

OLD STURBRIDGE VILLAGE, an outdoor museum designed to recreate life in a 19th century New England town, is an interesting and entertaining spot for families to spend a day. Visitors can watch demonstrations of crafts and arts and participate in some of the events. Informative brochures outlining special occasions and giving details about hours and fees are available by mail or phone. The brochures stress that comfortable warm clothing is recommended. Admission. (617) 347-3362. Open: April 1 to November 30, 9-5 daily; winter 10-4 T-Sun. Directions: Take I-90 East to N.Y.S. Thruway to Mass. Pike to Exit 9. Follow Rte. 20 west one mile. (Two hours.)

Boston

BOSTON is only three hours away—an easy ride along the New York State Thruway and the Massachusetts Turnpike. Commercial bus lines run the route daily, and charter companies—Mountain View, Wade Tours, and Yankee Trails—offer occasional excursions to the city. The Travel section of the Sunday NEW YORK TIMES frequently carries ads for weekend packages at Boston hotels at considerably reduced prices. Additional information is listed in Boston's premier newspaper, THE BOSTON GLOBE, available at the main branches of the public libraries and at the cosmopolitan newsstands listed in the information and shopping chapters of this book.

Boston has lots to offer: excellent museums, interesting historic sites, unique entertainment centers, handsome campuses, good public transportation—and, of course, the Red Sox, the Celtics, and the Bruins. (Three hours drive.)

THE OFFICIAL GUIDE TO GREATER BOSTON, a small booklet published by the Greater Boston Convention and Tourist Bureau, is excellent. It briefly describes each point of interest, giving open hours and admission prices, and suggests hotels and restaurants. It is available for a small fee from the Bureau's office in the Prudential Tower (617) 536-4100. This office also sells a clear map of the city, "The Official Boston Map and Freedom Trail Guide."

What follows is a list of recommended things to do, places to see, and sources of information.

Recommended Walks

Boston is a city of neighborhoods, a city most rewarding to the visitor willing to walk a bit. Much of Boston developed with an unique blend of residential and small commercial architecture; the result is that the city appears divided into distinctive, self-contained pieces, manageable for residents and tourists. Below is a list of only five of many places to stroll.

Beacon Hill
Boston Common and Boston Gardens
Copley Square and Newbury Street
Freedom Trail (16 Historic Sites)
Government Center

Places to Visit
Boston Public Library
Christian Science Center
Faneuil Hall and Quincy Market
Harvard Square and Harvard University
John Hancock Observatory
John F. Kennedy Library
New England Aquarium
Skywalk (Prudential Center)
Subway
U.S.S. Constitution

Museums
Boston Tea Party Ship and Museum
Children's Museum
Harvard Museum
Museum of Fine Arts
Museum of Science

Music
Boston Pops (T-Sun in May, June, July) . . . . . . (617) 266-1492
Boston Symphony. . . . . (617) 266-1492

Sports
Boston is a college town—with thousands of students bringing vitality to both sides of the Charles River. Their highly competitive teams draw loyal supporters from the city at large as well as from the campuses. In addition to the usual centerpieces, football and basketball, Boston enthusiastically support a longstanding tradition of rowing on the Charles.
Bostonians also fiercely cheer their three professional clubs.

Boston Bruins (hockey)
Boston Celtics (basketball)
Boston Red Sox (baseball)

Connecticut

Hartford

NOOK FARM is the carefully maintained home of Mark Twain during the years he was writing *The Adventures of Tom Sawyer, The Adventures of Huckleberry Finn, The Prince and the Pauper,* and *A Connecticut Yankee in King Arthur's Court.* The mid-Victorian home includes a girls' nursery, a billiard room, and a library, all of which are furnished with original pieces or replicas. Admission. Tours take 45 minutes. Open: June-August, daily 10-4:30; Sept-May, T-Sat. 10-4:30, Sun 1-4. (203) 525-9317. Directions: Take I-90 East to N.Y.S. Thruway and Mass. Pike. Take Exit 4 for I-91 South to I-84. Take Exit 46. Go east on Sisson Ave, then right onto Farmington Ave. (Two hours.)

Litchfield

WHITE FLOWER FARM is a botanical haven. The grounds are laid out in beautiful planned gardens so that the visitor may learn at first hand the principles of good garden design. Similarly displayed are fences and borders. The gardens are particularly breathtaking in June.

All of the varieties for sale are unique or at least unusual. A beautiful, informative catalog is published four times a year; mail orders are welcome. (203) 567-8789. Directions: Take I-90 to NYS Thruway to Mass Pike. Take Exit 2. Follow Rte 8 south to Litchfield—Harwinton Exit. Follow Rte 118 to Litchfield. Take Rte 63 south about 3 miles. (Two hours and a half.)

Woodbury

MILL HOUSE ANTIQUES, Rte. 6, has a wide variety of fine quality furniture and accessories collected from country estates in England, Scotland, and Wales. Open W-M 9-5. (203) 263-3446. Directions: Take N.Y.S. Thruway to Taconic Parkway south to I-84 East to Exit 15. Take Rte. 6 North for seven miles. (Two hours and a half.)

WEST OF THE CAPITAL DISTRICT

Amsterdam

GUY PARK, 366 West Main Avenue, Amsterdam, is an historic 18th century home situated on lock 11 of the Barge Canal. It was built in 1766 by regional hero Sir William Johnson as a wedding present for his daughter Mary and his nephew Guy Johnson. Free. Open: W-Sun, 9-5. (518) 842-7550. Directions: Take N.Y.S. Thruway west to Exit 27. Go north on Rte. 30. Left on Main St. (Rte 5); left on Evelyn St. (Forty minutes.)

Esperance

THE GEORGE LANDIS ARBORETUM is both an exhibition center and an experimental outpost. Its 100 acres of land hold over two thousand species of plantings, many of them exotic trees, flowers and bushes from far lands. The Arboretum staff tend their gardens carefully, measuring what conditions are required for each planting to survive in this climate. They also cooperate with other botanical gardens and arboreta in international seed exchanges and maintain a library of botanical holdings. Visitors are welcome to tour the grounds or attend formal programs. Information is available at the Arboretum, Esperance 12006, (518) 875-6935. Directions: Rte 20 to Esperance; right onto Rte 44 (Charleston St); at sharp bend in Rte 44, straight onto Lape Rd. (Forty minutes.)

Howes Cave

HOWE CAVERNS on N.Y. Rte. 7 between Central Bridge and Cobleskill is a series of carefully lighted, interestingly presented underground caves and subterranean waterways. The one hour twenty minute tour and underground boat ride leaves at frequent intervals. Visitors should bring a sweater or jacket as the temperature in the caves is 52 degrees. Open 9-6 year round except Christmas, Thanksgiving and New Year's Day. Admission. (518) 296-8990 or 296-8900. Directions: Take Rte. 20 West to Rte. 7. Follow signs to Howe Caverns. (Forty-five minutes.)

Johnstown

JOHNSON HALL, Hall Avenue, Johnstown, is the estate of William Johnson, a fascinating and significant figure in 18th Century American History. A small building to the side of the main house displays interesting memorabilia of the man and his era. Free. Open W-Sun. 9-5. (518) 762-8712. Directions: Take N.Y.S. Thruway west to Exit 28. Turn left on Riverside Drive. Take right across Mohawk Bridge into Fonda. Go left on Rte. 5 then right on 30A to Johnstown. Go left on E. Main St. (Rte. 29W). Go right on N. Williams St. and right on Hall Ave. (Fifty minutes.)

Rensselaerville

RENSSELAERVILLE is an appealing village filled with beautifully crafted 19th century homes and the carefully preserved remnants of active though modest industry. It was in fact the original location of the Huyck Felt Mills. Within the boundaries of the village are the Huyck Preserve, a site for the study of natural habitats, and the Rensselaerville Institute, a facility which supports study of humanity's use of technology. Directions: Take Rte. 85 (New Scotland Avenue) to Rensselaerville. (Fifty minutes.) The Rensselaerville Institute is described further in the chapter on Education.

Cooperstown

COOPERSTOWN is a picturesque but vital town filled with points of interest for the visitor. Directions: Take NYS Thruway west to Exit 25A to Rte 88 west; take Emmons Exit. Take Rte 28N to Rte 80N. (One hour and a half.) The town itself, with its beautifully maintained homes and gardens, is pleasant to see.

THE FARMER'S MUSEUM depicts in believable fashion the life of early rural settlers in N.Y. State. Men and women on the staff use authentic tools to perform manual arts at which all colonists were skilled. Admission. Open daily 9-5 except Christmas, New Year's and Thanksgiving. (607) 547-2593.

FENIMORE HOUSE is a museum containing American folk art, painting and articles related to James Fenimore Cooper. Admission. Open: Sept-June, 9-5; July and August, 9-9. Closed Monday in winter, Christmas, New Year's and Thanksgiving. (607) 547-2533.

NATIONAL BASEBALL HALL OF FAME AND MUSEUM contains mementos of great moments in the sport generally believed to have been born in this little town. Great excitement fills Cooperstown on the day new members are inducted and on the day of the annual Old Timer's Game, early in August. Tickets are sold well in advance of this last event. Admission. Open Nov-April, 9-5; May-Oct, 9-9. (607) 547-9988.

OTESAGA HOTEL is a fine old resort that stands at the foot of Lake Otsego. The golf course is excellent. Buffet luncheon is served on the terrace during the summer. (607) 547-9931. The hotel is described further in the chapter on Lodging.

COOPER INN, an elegant house in the village, offers accommodations to travelers. Guests may use other facilities of the Otesaga Hotel. (607) 547-9931. The Inn is described further in the chapter on Lodging.

Utica

THE MUNSON WILLIAMS PROCTOR INSTITUTE, 310 Genesee St Utica, is a museum, a school, and a performing arts center.

The collection includes works by major artists—Cole, Pollock, Arp, Picasso, Kandinsky, Mondrian, Klee, Calder, and Moore as well as many fine works by lesser known figures. It is housed in a gallery designed by architect Philip Johnson.

At nearby **FOUNTAIN ELMS,** an 1850 Italianate house, the museum's collection of early American furniture and decorative arts is displayed.

Changing Exhibits of paintings, sculpture, graphic art and photographs are drawn from the museum's collection and from circulating exhibitions from other museums. The museum also offers a shop, a library, a sales and rental gallery, and educational programs. Open: T-Sat 10-5; Sun 1-5.

THE SCHOOL is a college level program. Offered in cooperation with area colleges, it leads to a degree in fine arts. Courses are available in painting, drawing, sculpture, metal arts, pottery, ceramics, graphic arts, photography, figure drawing, quilting, and dance.

THE PERFORMING ARTS PROGRAM of the institute functions year round, with the Great Artists Series performing in the museum throughout fall, winter and spring and with the Arts Festival in summer. This last, a combination of open air performances and sidewalk exhibitions of paintings, runs for six days mid-summer, attracting major artists from far and near. Free. Information for all Institute functions is available at (315) 797-0000. Directions: Take N.Y.S. Thruway to Exit 31. Follow signs to downtown Utica to Genesee St. Turn right 2½-3 miles on right. (One hour and a half.)

F.X. MATT BREWING COMPANY—TOUR CENTER, Court St. provides a guided one hour tour through the halls and rooms where Matts Premium, Utica and Maximus Super are brewed. This is followed by a tour of the bottling facility, a trolley ride, and a stop at the 1888 Tavern. Here, in an atmosphere characteristic of the era when this family-operated brewery was

founded, the participant may enjoy a complimentary mug of Matts Premium Beer (or root beer for those who prefer). Free.

Open: June, July, Aug, M-Sat, 10-5 (except July 4); Sept-May, M-Sat 12-4. (Reservations must be made during this period.) (315) 732-0022.

Directions: N.Y.S. Thruway to exit 31. Follow signs for downtown Utica. Proceed to Court St. Turn right. Three blocks down on right side. (One hour and a half.)

Summer Programs for Youth

The following is a list of some of the best summer programs for children ages 3-18. The central text describes regional opportunities; appended are several unusual national and international experiences recommended by numerous residents.

Day Camps

ALBANY ACADEMY DAY CAMP is an instructional day camp conducted on the campus of Albany Academy. Although the camp is co-educational, children are separated for most activities, with the boys being coached in competitive field sports, particularly baseball, soccer, football, basketball, tennis, track and field, and the girls being led in sports, dramatics, games, arts and crafts. All children receive swimming instruction in the Academy pool. The camp session runs from 8:45-4 weekdays from July 1 to early August. Bus transportation is available to some areas. Information is available through Ernest Steck, 465-1461 or 463-6762.

CAMP CE-DA-CA is a seven week program for children ages 4-14 offered by the Troy Jewish Community Center at a camp site in Grafton. A computer program is offered along with traditional activities. Information is available at 274-0700.

CAMP CHAVERIM is an eight week summer program at the Jewish Community Center in Schenectady. An integral part of all camp programs is the development of a sense of Jewish life and culture. The younger (pre-school) unit encourages social interaction through outdoor games, music, crafts, cookouts, and swimming instruction. The school age group participates in sports and activities including Israeli cultural programs. Bus transportation is provided upon request. Information is available at 377-8803.

CAMP IS SHO DA is a day camp conducted by the Hudson Valley Girl Scout Council. Is Sho Da operates on 75 acres of natural setting off Rte I 90 in

Union College
Michael Fredericks, Jr.

East Greenbush. Girls grades 1-6 may attend any or all of the seven one-week sessions and work for Brownie or Girl Scout badges. (The camp began experimenting in 1985 with a companion camp for boys.) Nonscouts are also welcome. Information is available from 750 Delaware Ave., Delmar, 439-4936.

CAMP NASSAU is a day program for boys and girls aged three to thirteen. Run by retired teacher Ben Becker, the camp blends athletics and arts with enrichment reading, mathematics classes, and nature studies. The camp, which is located in a pleasant wooded section off Rte 155 in Guilderland, has small cabins to provide shelters and play areas for the campers. Each child must enroll for a minimum of two of the eight weeks the camp is in session. Information is available at 456-6929.

CAMP SHALOM is an eight week summer program for children 2½ years to teens, conducted by the Albany Jewish Community Center. (Full day or half-day enrollment is accepted for younger children.) Daily swimming is supplemented by games, sports, and instruction in arts and crafts. A special teen camp for children in grades 7-10 is presented at Kaydeross Camp on Saratoga Lake. This program includes many waterfront activities, using the Center's fleet of power launches, sailboats and canoes. A two-week consecutive enrollment is required of all campers. Transportation is provided for a fee. Information is available at 483-6651.

GIRLSUMMER is a program in sports, computer, and the arts at Emma Willard School in July. Girls may choose from a two week or four week program and emphasize swimming, gymnastics, tennis, weaving, printmaking, ceramics, drawing, slidemaking, or computer use. Car pools are coordinated to provide transportation to the beautiful Emma Willard campus where Girlsummer takes place. Information is available through Katie Haviland, 274-4440.

HELDERBERG WORKSHOP, Picard Rd., Voorheesville 12186, 765-2777, conducts two-week, half-day sessions for children to study nature and the arts outdoors. Located on a wooded area at the base of the Helderberg escarpment, just below the southeastern corner of Thacher State Park, the workshop quietly teaches children to understand and respect the simplest, most common natural phenomena.

SUMMERDANCE is a two or four week intensive dance training session for persons aged 6 to adult conducted on the campus of the Emma Willard School. Children aged 6-12 take classes in French ballet supplemented by instruction in arts, crafts, drama and swimming. Teenagers and adults undertake intensive dance workshops which they supplement with recreation in other art forms. All participants travel to Saratoga and Jacob's Pillow to watch professional dancers perform and then prepare a presentation of their own for the last day of the session. Information is available at 274-4440.

TIPPECANOE DAY CAMP is an eight week co-educational program conducted by the YMCA of Schenectady. It uses its own woodland camp grounds on Princetown Road in the town of Rotterdam. The camp stresses nature study and appreciation of life in the outdoors. Each camper is given the opportunity to camp overnight using the cabins on the grounds. Chartered buses provide transportation. Campers may choose to participate in any or all of the eight one-week sessions. Information is available at 374-9136, ext 41-2.

Residential Camps

CAMP CHINGACHGOOK is the co-ed summer camp run by the Schenectady YMCA at Pilot Knob, a beautiful cove on Lake George. The Spartan accommodations are well maintained, and the activity centers, particularly the waterfront, are well equipped. Originally open only for boys, the recent move toward coeducation has been quite successful. A challenging wilderness unit for older campers undertakes backpacking and canoeing trips into major wilderness areas in the United States. Information for all Chingachgook programs (which fill up early in Spring) is available at Schenectady YMCA, 13 State Street Schenectady, 374-9136.

CAMP LITTLE NOTCH welcomes 800 girls each summer for one or all of five sessions. The camp, conducted under the supervision of the Hudson Valley Girl Scout Council, is located in Adirondack woodlands just east of Lake George. Children sleep in four-person tents grouped in units of 16-32 campers. The program includes waterfront activities, campcraft, nature study, and sports. Optional trip units offer bicycle trips, canoe trips, and backpacking excursions. Information is available at Hudson Valley Girl Scout Council, 750 Delaware Ave, Delmar, 439-4936.

Special Programs

ALBANY ACADEMY SUMMER PROGRAM offers Driver Education, SAT Prep, computer training, and accelerated or remedial work in levels 1-12. Information is available through Baxter Ball, 465-1461 or 465-2127.

CAPITAL DISTRICT INTERNATIONAL SOCCER CAMP is conducted at Albany Academy for Girls under the joint sponsorship of the Capital District Youth Soccer League and SUNYA. The co-educational program focuses on developing basic skills and preparing for serious competition. Children aged 7 and up are welcome to enroll. Information is available through P.O. 662 Guilderland 12084.

COLLEGE SPORTS PROGRAMS FOR MIDDLE AND HIGH SCHOOL STUDENTS (All programs are coeducational unless otherwise noted.)

COLLEGE	PROGRAM
RPI	Ice Hockey
266-8534	Hockey League
266-6685	Softball
Siena College	Basketball
783-2341	Overnight: 2 weeks boys
	2 weeks girls
SUNYA	Mostly one week sessions
Summer Sports Program	Tennis
SUNYA Div of Phys Ed Athletics	Volleyball
and Recreation	Softball
442-3030	Baseball
	Wrestling
	Football
	Ballet
Union College	Football
Continuing Education	Soccer
370-6288	Basketball
	Field Hockey
	Volleyball

COLLEGE STUDIES PROGRAMS FOR HIGH SCHOOL STUDENTS are offered at Russell Sage, Skidmore, and Union. A few typical programs are listed below, but because the opportunities for young students change each year, it is best to ask for information from the appropriate office on each campus.

Russell Sage	Special art for students
Albany Campus	Grades 9-12
140 New Scotland Ave	
445-1717	
Skidmore	Credit and non-credit courses
Office of Special Programs	in regular courses open to
Saratoga 12866	high school students
584-5000	
Union College	International study and travel
Office of Graduate Studies	On-campus living and study
and Continuing Education	in special courses
370-6288	

COMPUTER CAMP AT ST. GREGORY'S SCHOOL FOR BOYS is a co-educational program for children interested in learning more about computers. Each child works on a computer advancing his or her current knowledge of computer functioning. Information is available through George Ripicky, St. Gregory's, Old Niskayuna Road, Loudonville, 785-6621.

JACOB'S PILLOW SCHOOL OF THE DANCE is described in the dance section of the chapter on the Arts.

LEAP (Learning Enrichment Activities Program) is a two-track program for boys and girls entering Pre-K to Fourth Grade. In the morning the children undertake formal classroom study for either remediation or acceleration. Classes are kept very small. In afternoons, the children visit area sites or enjoy planned recreational activities in the facilities of the Albany Academy. The program runs for six weeks from the beginning of July to early August. Information is available through Baxter Ball, Albany Academy, Academy Road Albany 12208, 465-1434.

LUZERNE MUSIC CENTER is described in the chapter on the Arts.

NEW YORK STATE SUMMER SCHOOL FOR THE ARTS is described in the introduction to the chapter on the Arts.

RECREATIONAL AND TUTORING CAMPS are held at St. Gregory's School. Counselors lead children in games and sports, and tutors assist children in grades 1-4 on an individual basis. Information is available at 785-6621.

RIDING CAMPS are conducted at three area riding academies. Children receive riding instruction, lessons in grooming and care of the horse, supervised recreation. Information is available at the following stables:

Dutch Manor 456-5010
Horsemen's Choice 869-1196
Sunday Stables 370-2321

SCHOLASTIC FOOTBALL DAY CAMP at the Albany Academy is a five-day intensive session directed to develop the offensive and defensive skills of boys grade 5-11 who aspire to excel at football. Area coaches make up the faculty for this end-of-June camp. Information is available through Ernest Steck, 465-1461 or 463-6762.

SOCCER CAMP at St. Gregory's School for Boys is a co-educational day program with various levels. In June and mid-August, children 14 years and under who have completed first grade attend one-week sessions designed to improve skills. At the end of August, a more intensive session teaches those who will be competing in the coming season. Coaches from the highly competitive St. Gregory's team join with other area coaches in presenting this camp. Information is available at the school, 785-6621.

TANGLEWOOD MUSIC CENTER is described in the material on the Boston Symphony in the music section of the Arts chapter.

Appendix

AMERICAN FIELD SERVICE assists individuals and communities in arranging foreign study with home stays. Many Capital District families welcome international students for homestays during the summer or the academic year, and many area youngsters study abroad through AFS programs. Information about in-bound and out-bound opportunities is available through the office in New York City, 313 East 43rd St NY 10017, (212) 949-4242.

AMERICAN INSTITUTE FOR FOREIGN STUDY, INC. (AIFS) is an international educational travel organization providing supervised travel for people from middle school age to retirees. Since its founding in 1966, AIFS has assisted over 300,000 teachers and students in a wide array of ventures ranging from 10 day tours to four-year college degree programs. Many of the plans combine travel, home stays, and foreign language study. The group also sponsors home stays in the United States for foreign students, allowing host families to earn travel scholarships themselves. Information is available at 102 Greenwich Avenue, Greenwich CT 06830, (203) 869-9090 or (800) 243-4567.

EXPERIMENT IN INTERNATIONAL LIVING arranges for high school and college students to travel abroad in small groups and to live with citizens in their host country. Over the years the Experiment has earned an international reputation for the excellence of its intensive language study programs. Information is available through the office in Brattleboro VT 05301, (802) 257-7751.

NATIONAL STUDENT LEADERSHIP AND ADVENTURE TRIP is a 36 day educational and recreational program for 15 and 16 year olds. The 40 students, who are selected from among applicants, travel by chartered bus around the United States, camping in State Parks, visiting National Sites, participating in formal and informal educational experiences along the way. Students, led by experienced counselors, must work together to solve the miscellaneous problems of group travel and living. Information is available from National Student Leadership Center, 110 Spring St Saratoga Springs 12866, 587-8770.

SWISS CHALLENGE is an American-run series of programs in Zermatt, Switzerland. Applicants, who must be between the ages of 12 and 18, may choose from various programs—a ski camp, European travel, an intensive language camp, a sports spectacular program, or a combination of all. The winter base for Swiss Challenge is Stowe, Vermont. Information is available at (802) 253-8550 or (802) 253-9715.

THE ALBANY ACADEMY

"A Tradition of Excellence"

Educating young men in the
Capital District since 1813.

Grades Pre-K through 12

1813

James F. Manning
Headmaster

The Albany Academy
Academy Road
Albany, NY 12208
518/465-1461

Peter N. Shepley
Director of Admissions

Education

PRIMARY AND SECONDARY SCHOOLS

Public Schools

All three cities and all the suburban regions of the five county area have comprehensive educational systems K-12. They work together to provide active, highly competitive intermural athletic leagues and to share resources. Information regarding programs and special services is available through the local school district.

Parochial and Diocesan Schools

THE CAPITAL DISTRICT has a system of primary schools (K-8) supported by the Roman Catholic Diocese. Most are affiliated with and in part financed by local parishes. The students pay a tuition based both on ability to contribute and on the number of children of a given family enrolled at the school. The Diocese also operates four high schools— BISHOP MAGINN HIGH SCHOOL in Albany, CATHOLIC CENTRAL HIGH SCHOOL in Troy, KEVENY MEMORIAL ACADEMY in Cohoes, and NOTRE DAME-BISHOP GIBBONS in Schenectady.

No student is denied entrance to any of the schools on the basis of religion or financial status. The number to call for information regarding Diocesan Schools is 438-6681.

Private Schools

In addition to public and parochial schools, area residents may choose from a group of private schools with widely differing objectives and correspondingly diverse approaches. Because the nature of education is dependent on individual values, the descriptions of private schools

Emma Willard, Troy
Michael Fredericks, Jr.

presented here are limited to comments offered by administrators of the schools or by official catalogue copy. These descriptions should help the reader draw some sense of the school, and telephone numbers for further information have been provided. The grade levels encompassed by the schools differ, as the descriptions are presented alphabetically.

All schools in this section, even those with religious affiliation, accept students regardless of race, color or creed.

THE ACADEMY OF THE HOLY NAMES, 1065 New Scotland Road, Albany, 438-6553 and 489-2559. The Lower and Middle School is a private day school for girls (kindergarten is co-ed). The goal of the school is to "place the student in learning situations where satisfaction and self-development come through continuous, sequential progress and success." Classes are small and the curriculum is structured to permit progress at individual rates. The Upper School (grades 9-12) is a college preparatory school for girls. The Sisters of the Holy Names supervise the programs on all levels.

ALBANY ACADEMY, Academy Road Albany, 465-1434. Established in 1813 with the goal of training boys for positions of leadership and achievement, the Academy members many prominent Albanians among its graduates. Athletics are stressed as is academic progress within small classes. A full-day kindergarten and a full-day or half-day pre-school program are offered by the Academy in addition to Grades 1-12.

ALBANY ACADEMY FOR GIRLS, 140 Academy Road Albany, 463-2201. Founded in 1814, it was one of the first schools ever devoted exclusively to the education of young women. It offers a challenging college preparatory program. Housed in a splendid facility, it features small classes and warm concern for the individual. The curriculum covers kindergarten (full-day) through grade twelve.

THE BROWN SCHOOL, 1184 Rugby Road, Schenectady 12308, 346-6139, was founded in 1893 to offer "quality education in an informal, relaxed atmosphere." Enrollment is limited to ten students per grade, and the curriculum is "extremely flexible to allow each child to advance at his own rate." The school enrolls a large percentage of international students.

CHRISTIAN BROTHERS ACADEMY, 1 De LaSalle Road, Albany 12208, 462-5447. CBA is a private Roman Catholic military college preparatory school for boys grade seven through twelve run by the Brothers of the Christian Schools. Fifty percent of faculty are Brothers; the remaining members are lay teachers.

THE DOANE-STUART SCHOOL, Kenwood, Albany, 465-5222. This is a co-educational independent school created through a merger of two old Albany schools—the Roman Catholic Kenwood Academy, a member of the network of Sacred Heart schools, and the Episcopal St. Agnes School. It offers an ecumenical Christian religious program. The primary school provides individualized instruction and emphasizes the arts and humanities, with individual acceleration possible. The secondary level offers college preparatory programs for resident and day students, grades 9-12.

EMMA WILLARD SCHOOL, 285 Pawling Ave., Troy, 274-4440. One of the oldest schools for women in the country, Emma Willard offers a college preparatory program for resident and day students in grades 9-12 and post-graduate. Emphasis is placed on strong academic performance, long a tradition at Emma Willard. In addition, students can choose a varied program in the arts, including dance, fine arts, music, and photography. Independent Study provides students with an opportunity to design part or full time projects in a wide range of fields. The National Network of Complementary Schools offers specialized, short term exchanges in 30 member schools across the nation.

THE HEBREW ACADEMY OF THE CAPITAL DISTRICT, 2211 Western Ave., Guilderland, 456-6816. This is a co-educational school (grades K-12) founded to provide close study of the Judaic and secular studies for young people and prepare them to pursue both at more advanced levels. The orientation of the small classes is the approach to all subjects with an awareness of their meaning in the context of both Jewish and Western democratic traditions.

LASALLE INSTITUTE, Williams Road, Troy, 283-2500. This is a Catholic college preparatory school for boys grades 7-12 conducted by the Christian Brothers. Enrollment is about 500 students. LaSalle has an accredited Jr. ROTC program for grades 9-12. College credit courses are available through an arrangement with neighboring Hudson Valley Community College.

LOUDONVILLE CHRISTIAN SCHOOL, 374 Loudon Road, Loudonville 12211, 434-6051. This school was founded in 1960 by a group of parents concerned with the Christian education of children. It is a coeducational school with classes from pre-school through grade eight. The class schedule provides time for Chapel, devotions, and prayer. The curriculum of the school includes a course in Biblical studies and emphasizes that "secular" courses are taught from the standpoint of a Biblical view of God, man and the world. The school also takes pride in its programs in art, music and physical education.

MERCY HIGH SCHOOL, 310 South Manning Blvd., Albany, 482-1110. This school offers a four year program—either college entrance or business—for girls. It is run by the Sisters of Mercy.

ST. GREGORY'S SCHOOL FOR BOYS, Old Niskayuna Road Loudonville, 785-6621. This is a school run by Roman Catholic laymen to offer accelerated courses for boys grades 1-8. (The pre-school and kindergarten programs, both modeled after the Montessori method, enroll girls as well as boys). Grades one through eight aim at preparing students for advanced entry into the most competitive secondary schools in the country.

INSTITUTIONS OF HIGHER EDUCATION

The colleges and universities in the Capital District have formed a consortium designed to share resources and cooperate in making educational opportunities more accessible to all students. Students enrolled at any one of the colleges may use library facilities at other institutions and may enroll free of charge in any course not available on the home campus. The consortium is called the Hudson Mohawk Association of Colleges and Universities, 91 Fiddler's Lane Latham, 785-3219.

Nomenclature

The structure of the educational system in New York State is quite straightforward, but the choice of names for the units has led to confusion.

THE UNIVERSITY OF THE STATE OF NEW YORK is the term applied to the entire educational system within the state—private and public—from nursery school through the most advanced graduate degree. This body, presided over by the Board of Regents, grants and revokes licenses and oversees the work of the Department of Education of the State of New York, which plays a more practical role in the governance of education.

STATE UNIVERSITY OF NEW YORK (SUNY) is the coordinating center of the public institutions of higher learning in the state. This includes 4 university centers, 13 colleges of arts and sciences, 6 colleges and centers for the health sciences, 6 agricultural and technical colleges, 8 specialized colleges and 29 community colleges—64 campuses in all. These offices—called SUNY Central—provide administrative support for the single units and facilitate expanded cooperation between the various campuses.

STATE UNIVERSITY OF NEW YORK AT ALBANY (SUNYA) is the university center, the autonomous branch of the SUNY system, which has academic buildings and dormitories on its old and new campuses located in Albany.

Two Year Colleges

ALBANY BUSINESS COLLEGE, 130 Washington Ave Albany, 449-7163, is a two year college offering the associate degree in business. Founded in 1857 as a profit-making institution, the college currently enrolls men and women full-time and part time. It has been owned and run by one family, the Carnells, since 1885.

SUNYA
Michael Fredericks, Jr.

HUDSON VALLEY COMMUNITY COLLEGE, Vandenburgh Avenue Troy, 283-1100, sponsored by the County of Rensselaer under the program of the State University of New York, is a large multipurpose institution which serves a wide variety of needs. It provides AA and AS degrees for those bound for four year colleges, AAS and AOS degrees for those directly entering business, industry or trades, and courses and certificates for residents who need to acquire a specific skill or learn some specific information. A direct result of the recognition in the early 60's that education should not be available only for the intellectually elite, Hudson Valley states that, "The underachiever, the disadvantaged, as well as the ambitious, the financially able—these and others from the community—come to Hudson Valley to receive educational opportunities they might not otherwise attain."

JUNIOR COLLEGE OF ALBANY, 140 New Scotland Ave Albany, 445-1711, is a co-educational division of Russell Sage College. Its principal concern is preparation of students for transfer to four year colleges; to that end the college has established transfer agreements with over 30 colleges upon satisfactory completion of the requirements of J.C.A. The college also offers programs for those who seek full-time employment at the end of two years and for mature women wanting to embark on a career.

MARIA COLLEGE, 700 New Scotland Ave., Albany, 438-3111, is a private, independent, co-educational, two-year college sponsored by the Sisters of Mercy. It serves three different groups of students: those who intend to transfer to four year colleges; those who seek career training; and those who seek enrichment and personal development.

Maria, tailoring its programs to meet the needs of students, offers two options in addition to the traditional daily schedule—an evening degree, and the Weekend College. These allow working adults to integrate their studies with their other responsibilites but also to complete their degrees on schedule. The college consciously retains its small size to insure that the personal quality which has become its trademark continues.

MILDRED ELLEY SCHOOL, 227 Quail St., Albany 472-9227, is a small co-ed institution offering 2 year programs for Executive Secretary or court reporting and 1 year programs for a receptionist-typist or secretary-machine stenographer.

SCHENECTADY COUNTY COMMUNITY COLLEGE, Washington Ave, Schenectady, 346-6211, is a two year college which offers the Associate in Arts, the Associate in Science and the Associate in Applied Science to its graduates. Its objectives include two distinguishing features: full opportunity, an open admissions program supplemented by counseling, tutoring services and remedial laboratories; cooperative education, a commitment to alternate periods of full-time study and full-time work designed to aid in vocational selection and development. The college also offers a program in continuing education for those seeking part-time study.

SPENCER BUSINESS AND TECHNICAL INSTITUTE, 404 Union St Schenectady, 374-7619, offers programs in such areas as fashion merchandizing, national travel, electronics, accounting, and court reporting. Some programs run nine months; others are eighteen months.

Voorhees Computer Center, RPI
Michael Fredericks, Jr.

Hospital-Based Nursing Schools

In addition to nursing degrees offered at two and four year colleges in the area, there are four programs situated in hospitals. These are **ALBANY MEDICAL CENTER SCHOOL OF NURSING**, 445-4261; **ELLIS HOSPITAL SCHOOL OF NURSING**, 382-4471; **MEMORIAL HOSPITAL SCHOOL OF NURSING**, 471-3260; **SAMARITAN HOSPITAL SCHOOL OF NURSING**, 271-3285.

Four-Year Colleges and Graduate Schools

THE COLLEGE OF ST. ROSE, 432 Western Ave Albany, 454-5111, is a private, co-educational liberal arts college. The College takes pride in the personal quality created by the intimacy of the campus and the smallness of the student body. In addition to the liberal arts undergraduate program, the College presents Masters Degree programs in a variety of areas. It is particularly known for its offerings in Special Education, Communication Disorders, and Music.

THE NELSON A. ROCKEFELLER INSTITUTE OF GOVERNMENT, 411 State St Albany, 473-5328, was established in 1981 as a vehicle through which New York's academic community and governmental community could serve one another. Faculty from the 64 campuses of the State University work with citizens and officials on important issues of public affairs and policy. The Institute accomplishes its work through sponsoring fellowships, internships, and conferences and by supporting publications.

RENSSELAER POLYTECHNIC INSTITUTE, Troy, 266-6000, is a co-educational, non-sectarian, private university, known as RPI. It offers 117 under-graduate and graduate degree programs in five schools—Architecture, Engineering, Humanities-Social Sciences, Management and Science—as well as in several interdisciplinary areas. Forty-three hundred undergraduates and 1,700 graduate students attend this well established university long known for the rigor of its standards and the excellence of its programs, especially those in engineering and the sciences.

RUSSELL SAGE COLLEGE, Troy, 270-2000, is a private, women's liberal arts college founded seven decades ago to prepare "women who support themselves." Though its goals have broadened today and the fields for which it prepares its graduates have increased in number, its curriculum continues to emphasize field experience to supplement classroom learning. Its 1400 students choose from a variety of fields, taking advantage when they can of the proximity of RPI to share academic and social opportunities.

RUSSELL SAGE COLLEGE, THE EVENING DIVISION 140 New Scotland Avenue, Albany, 445-1717, was founded in 1949 to "provide high quality education for adults outside of work hours in the evening and on weekends." The division draws primarily on the expertise of the faculty of Russell Sage

College in Troy and its subdivision, the Junior College of Albany. It also enlists the services of a core of adjunct faculty drawn from the "unusual richness of abilities and experience found in the governmental, business, human services, and educational institutions of the Capital District." The division enrolls 2500 students per term; it also offers contract courses for government employees in the various state office buildings.

SIENA COLLEGE, Loudonville, 783-2307, is a private, coeducational, Catholic liberal arts college under the auspices of the Franciscan Order. Founded in 1937 as a small men's school, the college now enrolls 2500 undergraduates. In addition to its academic offerings, Siena takes pride in its athletic program and its series of guest lectures and personal appearances.

SKIDMORE COLLEGE, Saratoga Springs, 584-5000, is a private, co-educational liberal arts college enrolling 2000 undergraduates. Originally a women's college located in older buildings in Saratoga, Skidmore decided in the mid-sixties to construct a completely new facility on 600 acres of wooded land outside the city. The new campus contains some splendid adaptations of contemporary architecture. In summer the college cooperates with the New York City Ballet and the Philadelphia Orchestra to present workshops in dance and music.

STATE UNIVERSITY OF NEW YORK AT ALBANY (SUNYA), 1400 Washington Avenue Albany, 442-3300, founded in 1844, is the oldest unit of the state university system and one of its four university centers. The largest educational institution in the area, it enrolls 10,000 undergraduate students each year in 45 major fields as well as 6,000 graduate students in 47 fields. Admission to all these programs is highly competitive.

Although the University is supported by the allocation of funds by the legislature, students also pay tuition according to a scale adjusted to year of study and state of residence.

The University sponsors a well publicized Community University Day in October so that the public can become aware of its facilities and the resources it provides to the community.

The University cooperates with various cultural and educational agencies in the region in a program called Capital District Humanities Program to make programs more accessible to the general public.

The University offers credit courses to area residents through its School of Continuing Studies. Information is available at 442-5140.

UNION COLLEGE, Schenectady, 370-6000, describes itself as an "independent, primarily undergraduate, residential college for men and women of high academic promise and strong personal motivation." Established in 1795, Union was the first college chartered by the Regents of the State of New York. Until 1970 it admitted men only; today this seasoned institution enjoys a long-standing reputation of academic excellence and student and alumni loyalty. The excellent cultural enrichment program is often open to the public.

Professional Schools

UNION UNIVERSITY consists of four units: Union College and three professional schools—Albany College of Pharmacy, Albany Law School, and Albany Medical School.

ALBANY COLLEGE OF PHARMACY, 106 New Scotland Ave Albany, 445-7211, offers a rigorous five year program leading to a bachelor of science in pharmacy and an excellent four year program leading to a bachelor of science in medical technology. Numbered among its alumni are many of the practicing health professionals in the area. Graduates work in hospitals, clinics, laboratories and retail pharmacies, enter other areas of science or business, or go on to graduate school in dentistry, medicine or law.

ALBANY LAW SCHOOL, 80 New Scotland Ave Albany, 445-2311, is one of the oldest law schools in the United States. It offers a three year program leading to the J.D. degree and cooperates with Union College and RPI to

Campus Center, Junior College of Albany
Russell Sage

grant six year combined degrees in law and management or law and business administration.

ALBANY MEDICAL COLLEGE, New Scotland Ave Albany, 445-3125, was founded in 1839. It prepares physicians to serve in all forms of practice, using the facilities of the 800 bed Albany Medical Center Hospital, the 1,000 bed Veterans Administration Medical Center and the other affiliated hospitals in the Capital District to provide wide-ranging, in-depth clinical instruction.

CONTINUING EDUCATION

Continuing education is an important component in the offerings of many secondary, undergraduate, and professional institutions in the area. Some of the schools described in the earlier sections offer programs designed to help graduates keep their information up-to-date or to develop a new field of interest. Details and schedules are available through the main numbers. In addition, three free-standing groups organize educational opportunities for adults.

THE CAPITAL DISTRICT HUMANITIES PROGRAM is an educational program directed by SUNYA and community leaders to make high quality education in the humanities (the branches of learning concerned principally with human thought and human relations) available to adults in the community. Lectures, small group seminars and field trips are conducted by college faculty, area professionals and celebrated guest speakers in accessible locations at hours convenient to adults who are not full-time students. Information is available at CDHP, SUNYA, Humanities 361, Albany, 12222, 442-4240.

EMPIRE STATE COLLEGE CENTER FOR THE CAPITAL DISTRICT, 155 Washington Ave Albany, 447-6746, a part of the state university system, is an alternative approach to higher education. Students engage in contracts with tutors and arrange a schedule which fits into their other responsibilities and allows them to keep a pace they can manage.

THE KNOWLEDGE NETWORK, 478 Madison Ave., Albany, 465-0055, is the largest continuing education program in the Capital District. Established in 1981, the company publishes a monthly catalog with more than 100 courses in such areas as computers, cooking, business, careers, photography, self-hypnosis, stress management, writing, and sports.

The Knowledge Network has a practical approach: recruit talented practitioners and make their services accessible at reasonable times, places, and cost. There are two basic formats: the One Night Course (a three hour single session lesson) and the Four Night Course (a series of four two-hour sessions spread over four weeks).

OTHER EDUCATIONAL VENTURES

AMERICAN LYRIC THEATER is described in the music section of the chapter on The Arts.

ART instruction is described in the chapter The Arts.

EMPIRE STATE INSTITUTE FOR PERFORMING ARTS is described in the chapter The Arts.

HELDERBERG WORKSHOP is described in the chapter on summer activities for children.

JACOBS PILLOW SCHOOL OF DANCE is described in the chapter The Arts.

LUZERNE MUSIC CENTER is described in the chapter The Arts.

NEW YORK STATE SUMMER SCHOOL OF THE ARTS is described in the introduction to the chapter The Arts.

RENSSELAERVILLE INSTITUTE, known until 1983 as the Institute on Man and Science, is an independent, non-profit educational center which focuses on self-help as a solution to community decline. It is currently working with New York State on approaches to water and waste problems and on preventive help programs for rural residents. On its 100-acre campus it sponsors educational programs for area schools, hosts an annual inquiry into controversial technologies led by Isaac Asimov, and presents summer musical events. The Institute also serves as a conference center for groups needing a retreat setting for educational meetings. The Institute is located in Rensselaerville (a town on the National Register of Historic Sites), 25 miles southwest of Albany on Rte 85.

SAGAMORE INSTITUTE, SAGAMORE LODGE AND CONFERENCE CENTER, Raquette Lake, NY 13436, (315) 354-5311, is a non-profit educational organization which conducts workshops, conferences, institutes, and programs for a variety of youth and adult groups, using the Lodge originally built as the Vanderbilt Retreat. This historic "Adirondack Great Camp," intended as a site for simple but extensive entertaining, has 46 bedrooms, 26 stone fireplaces, and recreational facilities for all seasons. It stands by the shore of a mile-long lake.

SLAVIN HOUSE (THE RENSSELAER NEWMAN CHAPEL AND CULTURAL CENTER), 2125 Burdett Ave Troy, 274-7793, hosts lectures, films, conversations, discussions, art exhibits and other cultural events throughout the year. Situated in a flexible contemporary building, the center specifically serves the RPI community but welcomes participation by the general populace.

Siena College
Michael Fredericks, Jr.

TANGLEWOOD MUSIC CENTER is described in the music section of the chapter on The Arts.

LECTURES & DISCUSSIONS

ALBANY ROUND TABLE is an independent association of individuals and representatives of organizations who meet monthly, October to May, to hear speakers and discuss topics affecting the life of the center city. Information about meetings—always on the 2nd Wednesday of the month —is available at P.O. Box 7101, Albany 12224.

NEW YORK STATE WRITERS INSTITUTE was established in 1984 to acknowledge the importance of writers and writing for the well-being of society. The Institute has two major objectives: first, it creates opportunities for aspiring writers to meet with experienced writers; second, it makes it possible for the general public to hear eminent writers (Saul Bellow, Toni Morrison, and John Updike, for example) read their work and discuss their perception of the role of writing and the writer.

The Institute, conceived by William Kennedy, is centered at SUNYA, 442-5620.

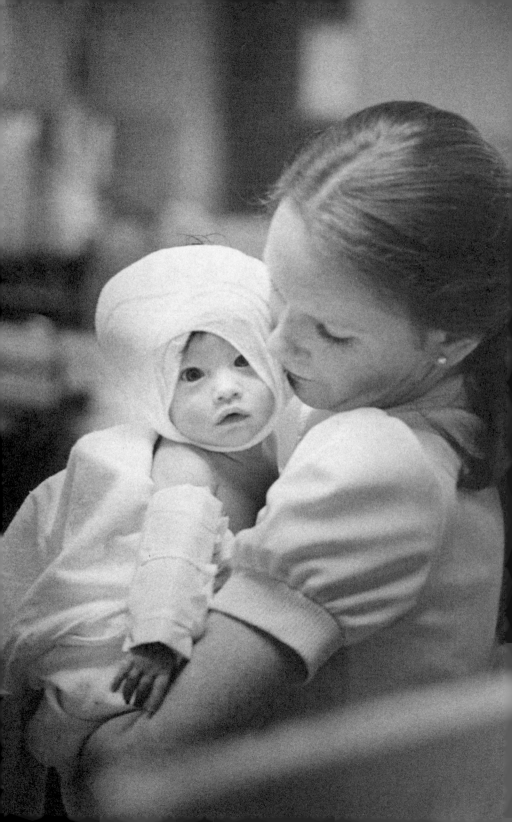

Health Care
and Related Services

The Capital District has an astonishing abundance of institutions and agencies dedicated to assisting people in need. It would not be possible to describe adequately all of the facilities and services to which residents of the region have access. (At last count there were over 650 social service agencies in the four county district.) What follows is, rather, a presentation of portraits of all the major hospitals and clinics and a description of a representative sample of some of the most active social service agencies in the region.

EMERGENCY NUMBERS

	Albany	Schenectady	Troy
Fire	463-1234	374-3311	272-3400
Police	463-4141	374-7744	270-4411
Poison Control	445-3131	382-4039	271-3424
Rape Crisis	445-7547	346-2266	271-3257

Child Abuse. 800-342-3720
Crisis Intervention
    Capital District Psychiatric Center 445-6675
    Refer Switchboard. 434-1200

Albany Medical Center

HOSPITALS

Albany

THE ALBANY MEDICAL CENTER, New Scotland Ave Albany, a major academic medical institution serving a 20-county region of northeastern New York and western New England, is made up of two entities, the Albany Medical College and the Albany Medical Center Hospital. They provide the most advanced forms of patient care, teaching and research.

The Albany Medical College is a part of Union University. It was founded in 1839 and is the only medical school between New York City and Montreal. The student population approximates 500 and there are more than 325 faculty members. Sponsored research programs account for approximately one third of the college's operating budget.

The Albany Medical Center Hospital is an 800-bed teaching hospital. It operates numerous specialty clinics and is the only provider of open heart surgery, kidney transplants, and intensive care of burn and trauma victims in this area. It was named in 1982 as New York State's first designated Regional Trauma Center.

```
General Information . . . . . . . . . . . . . . . . . 445-3125
Patient Information. . . . . . . . . . . . . . . . . 445-3791
Emergency Room . . . . . . . . . . . . . . . . . 445-3131
Clinic Appointments. . . . . . . . . . . . . . . 445-4343
TTY (for hearing impaired)
    Emergency . . . . . . . . . . . . . . . . . . . . 445-3438
    Non-emergency . . . . . . . . . . . . . . . . 445-3421
```

CHILD'S HOSPITAL, 25 Hackett Blvd Albany, is a small medical facility which functions under the auspices of the Episcopal Diocese of Albany. Although founded in 1874 as a hospital for children, it has emerged as a center for special surgery for both children and adults. The emphasis is on elective and outpatient surgery, with most work done in the areas of ophthalmology, enterology, and oral and plastic surgery.

```
General Information . . . . . . . . . . . . . . . . 462-4211
```

MEMORIAL HOSPITAL, Northern Blvd Albany is a 233-bed facility which offers care for surgical and medical patients. The hospital also staffs a general clinic.

```
General Information . . . . . . . . . . . . . . . . 471-3221
Emergency Room . . . . . . . . . . . . . . . . . 471-3111
Clinic . . . . . . . . . . . . . . . . . . . . . . . . . . 471-3171
```

ST. PETER'S HOSPITAL, 315 S. Manning Blvd Albany, was established in 1869 by the Sisters of Mercy. This 437-bed teaching hospital has a variety of special features including: St. Peter's Hospice; St. Peter's Alcohol Rehabilitation Center; South End Health Center; Mobile Meals; Emergency Care; and Home Care.

General Information 454-1550
Emergency Room 454-1318
South End Health Center 463-1160

VETERAN'S ADMINISTRATION MEDICAL CENTER HOSPITAL, Holland Ave Albany, with one thousand beds, is the largest hospital in the area. It provides medical and surgical services for short term and long term care of veterans of the armed forces.

General Information 462-3311

Schenectady

BELLEVUE MATERNITY HOSPITAL, 2210 Troy Rd Schenectady, is a 40-bed women's hospital which specializes in obstetrics, neonatology, gynecology, urology, perinatology, genetics, and infertility. The hospital serves an 18 county area, with half its patients coming from outside Schenectady County.

General Information 374-4561

ELLIS HOSPITAL, 1101 Nott St Schenectady, is a 455-bed teaching hospital serving Schenectady and surrounding counties. It is known for its active intensive care program and recently opened a Cardiac Catheterization unit. It operates a poison information center for the larger Capital District, a community medical service, and numerous specialty clinics.

General Information 382-4124
Emergency Room 382-4121
Poison Control 382-4039

ST. CLARE'S HOSPITAL, 600 McClellan St Schenectady, is a 296-bed multipurpose hospital supervised by the Sisters of the Poor of St. Francis. This relatively new hospital opened its doors in 1949. In addition to its medical and surgical care of inpatients and outpatients, St. Clare's offers a Family Health Center and a Family Practice Residency Program aimed at providing both comprehensive family health maintenance and general medical care.

General Information 382-2156

SUNNYVIEW HOSPITAL AND REHABILITATION CENTER, 1270 Belmont Ave Schenectady, specializes in comprehensive rehabilitation and treatment of orthopedic and neuromuscular diseases. It serves children and adults on an inpatient and outpatient basis. Sunnyview has its own physicians and therapists to whom area professionals may refer patients.

General Information 382-4500

Troy

LEONARD HOSPITAL, New Turnpike Rd Troy, is a 143-bed community hospital serving Troy, Mechanicville, Clifton Park-Half Moon, and Waterford. In addition to general medical-surgical care and outpatient services, Leonard offers a unique 28-day inpatient Alcoholism Rehabilitation Program and a hospital-based Home Health Care Agency.

General Information 235-0310
Emergency Room 235-6717

ST. MARY'S HOSPITAL, Oakwood and Massachusetts Avenues Troy, is a 200-bed community hospital supervised by the Daughters of Charity of St. Vincent de Paul. It is a general hospital with inpatient and outpatient services. It also operates a health center for children and adolescents.

General Information 272-5000
Poison Information 272-5792

SAMARITAN HOSPITAL, 2215 Burdett Ave Troy, is a 300-bed medical-surgical facility with full general service plus the following clinics: obstetrics-gynecology, oncology, family planning, pediatrics, hematology, mental health, and orthopedics. The new Louis and Hortense Rubin Dialysis Center is the only chronic dialysis facility in the Capital District.

General Information 271-3300
Emergency Room 371-3424
Rape Crisis 271-3257

CLINICS

In addition to the clinics associated with area hospitals, the region has independent clinics which serve the general community.

THE ALBANY COUNTY DEPARTMENT OF HEALTH, S. Ferry St Albany, provides comprehensive public health service including home nursing, x-ray, dental, and physical therapy. It operates programs on health education and offers a multiphasic screening program (comprehensive medical testing with the results being sent to the patient's personal physician) for a very low fee. The facility is open M-F 9-5. Information about the services and hours of the various clinics is available at the numbers listed below:

Pre-natal 445-7827
Chest 445-7833
Pediatric eye 445-7845
General pediatric
    Albany 445-7827
    Ravena 756-6914

Cohoes 235-4044
Sexually transmitted diseases 445-7862

ALBANY COUNTY MENTAL HEALTH CLINIC, 175 Green St Albany, is a community outpatient psychiatric facility. It is open M-F 9-5.

RENSSELAER COUNTY DEPARTMENT OF HEALTH, 1600 7th Ave Troy, is a combined public health-home health agency serving the entire county. It operates four clinics—Immunization, Child Health Conference, Chest Consultation, and Venereal Disease. It offers skilled nursing services plus physical therapy, speech therapy, and care by Home Health Aides. Anyone seeking information may call one of the three offices:

Troy 270-2660
Rensselaer 462-4256
Hoosick Falls. 686-7310

SCHENECTADY CITY HEALTH DEPARTMENT, City Hall, Schenectady is a combined public health and home health agency offering skilled nursing, physical therapy, speech therapy, occupational therapy, social work services, and home health aide services. It also supervises four clinics—Well Child, Adult Health, Comprehensive Health Screening, and Diabetes.

General Information 382-5039

WHITNEY M. YOUNG, JR HEALTH CENTER, INC., Lark and Arbor Drives in Albany, is a clinic that provides outpatient medical, dental, psychological, educational and rehabilitational services to adults and children. Methods of payment to this independent facility include a sliding scale fee, independent insurance, Medicaid, and Medicare. The staff also assist clients in obtaining financial support from the County Department of Social Services.

General Information 465-4771

SPECIAL CARE FACILITIES

CAPITAL DISTRICT PSYCHIATRIC CENTER, often called CDPC, offers inpatient and outpatient care for psychiatric patients from the entire area. It is located in a dramatic modern complex adjacent to the Albany Medical Center on New Scotland Avenue in Albany.

General Information 445-6601
Crisis Intervention 445-6675

CEREBRAL PALSY CENTER FOR THE DISABLED, 314 Manning Blvd Albany, has a twofold purpose—to provide a comprehensive range of services to the developmentally disabled of all ages and to create community awareness of the needs and promise of the disabled. The programs include center residences, a center school, day treatment, physical and occupational therapy, vocational development, speech therapy, home services, and out-client services. Currently the center serves approximately 900 clients from the surrounding 11-county area.

General Information 489-8336

CHILDREN'S HOME OF SCHENECTADY is described under **NORTHEAST PARENT AND CHILD SOCIETY** in the section on social agencies.

HOPE HOUSE, begun in 1966 by a young Roman Catholic priest, Howard Hubbard (now Bishop of Albany), was the first response to the need for drug treatment in Northeastern New York. The residency program, which provides comprehensive services for youth and adults experiencing difficulty with alcohol and chemicals, is located at 261 North Pearl St Albany in the former convent of St. Joseph.

General Information 465-2441

HOSPICE CARE is a service which exists to assist terminally ill patients and their families. A staff of nurses, physicians, therapists, social workers, and trained volunteers work together to provide care for outpatients (80% of the hospice caseload) and inpatients. Currently two hospice care programs—the Hospice at St. Peter's and The Hospice of Schenectady—serve the area.

General Information
Hospice at St. Peter's 454-1686
The Hospice of Schenectady 377-8846

(Information is also available at St. Clare's and Ellis Hospitals.)

MERCY HOUSE, 12 St. Joseph's Terrace Albany, is a shelter for women in crisis. Here the staff, under the direction of the Roman Catholic Diocese of Albany, provides three meals, room, and counseling to women who seek assistance.

General Information 434-3531

OSWALD D. HECK DEVELOPMENTAL CENTER, Balltown and Consaul Roads in Schenectady, serves the mentally retarded and developmentally disabled in the six-county area in a variety of ways. It offers assessment and program development for individual clients, and works in the community to improve the quality of opportunities in education, health care, and social and psychological adjustment available for those under its care. In addition, the Center provides residential units for approximately 250 severely multi-handicapped people of all ages. The full range of its program is generally referred to as the Eleanor Roosevelt Developmental Services. This use of two names and the fact that all services fall under the supervision of the State of New York Office of Mental Retardation and Developmental Disabilities has sometimes led to confusion.

General Information 370-7370

PARKHURST CHILDREN'S SHELTER is described under **NORTHEAST PARENT AND CHILD SOCIETY** in the section on Social Agencies.

PARSON'S CHILD AND FAMILY CENTER, 60 Academy Rd Albany, offers a wide variety of services for special children and their families. Included are two Special Education programs, one for children who exhibit autistic-like or atypical behavior, another for those who are not able to adjust to the community school. There are also two 24-hour care programs, one for emotionally disturbed, developmentally disabled, and surrendered children and youth for whom community living is not an option, the other for adolescents who are willing and able to live in a supervised group home in the community. Details on these and other programs is available at the center.

General Information 447-5211

RONALD McDONALD HOUSE, 139 S Lake Ave Albany, is part of a nationwide network of homes established with the help of the fast food chain foundation to serve as home-away-from-home for families of seriously ill children who are being cared for in major medical centers. The facility is staffed by one full and one part time person and operated with the help of many volunteers. It is funded by gifts in kind and monies raised within and without the Capital District. In this handsome house, families may sleep, cook, relax, and, if they wish, share their experiences with other families of ill children. Cost is nominal.

General Information 438-2655

ST. ANNE'S INSTITUTE, 160 N. Main Ave Albany, 489-7411, provides shelter, counseling, and education for children in crisis. The oldest and largest service is its residential treatment and prevention program for adolescent girls whom social agencies or the courts believe to be in need of supervision and counseling. In addition to these children, who come from throughout New York State, St. Anne's welcomes about 25-30 girls from surrounding counties into a day program of teaching and counseling. Newly added services include a sex abuse prevention program open to boys and girls aged 3-17 and a juvenile offender program for adolescent males. St. Anne's is supervised by a board of lay members and run by the Sisters of the Good Shepherd.

ST. MARGARET'S HOUSE AND HOSPITAL FOR BABIES, 27 Hackett Blvd. Albany, is a total nursing care facility for infants and children who are so ill or so developmentally disabled as to require skilled nursing care. As one of only two institutions in the State of New York dedicated to the care of these children, it receives patients referred from throughout the state. Sitting quietly on a hill behind Child's Hospital, St. Margaret's has served special children since its founding in 1883 as part of the Episcopal Diocese of Albany.

General Information 465-2461

ST. PETER'S ALCOHOL REHABILITATION CENTER, known by its acronym, **SPARC,** serves the entire area in the treatment of alcoholism and some forms of drug addiction. It operates a male community residence for patients seeking a full time recovery program as well as day treatment through an outpatient clinic. It receives patients referred through the courts and other social agencies as well as self-defined patients. It also offers programs dealing with alcoholism prevention. The Center is located at St. Peter's Hospital, 315 S. Manning Blvd Albany.

General Information 454-1307

WILDWOOD, a familiar word in the area, is the name used to describe programs run by the Capital District Chapter of the New York State Association for the Learning Disabled. These programs, which serve children, youth, and adults, attempt to teach, train, entertain, and supervise the residents of the area who have developmental disabilities of some form—usually a neurological impairment which limits one or more of the following areas: language, social and emotional development, cognitive-academic development, and physical development. Wildwood also works to aid families of those with disabilities. The programs for children include Wildwood School, Camp Wildwood, Follow-through Public School Consultation Program, and Parent-Child Home Training Program. The programs for adults include Community Residences, Vocational Services, and Recreational Services.

General Information
Children's services 783-1644
Adults' services 783-0147

SOCIAL SERVICES

Sources of Information

As noted in the beginning of this chapter, the Capital District has an astounding number of health care and social agencies to serve the needs of its people. In 1978, through a cooperative effort of coordinating bodies, a directory was published listing and describing over 650 social service units. This **FIVE COUNTY HUMAN SERVICES DIRECTORY,** revised in 1984, is indexed by type of service as well as by alphabetical order. Copies are available for purchase at **THE COUNCIL OF COMMUNITY SERVICES OF THE ALBANY AREA,** 877 Madison Ave in Albany, 489-4791, or for use without charge at the branches of the public libraries.

CATHOLIC CHARITIES of the Diocese of Albany, a vital part of the regional community in social services of all kinds, had compiled a **DIRECTORY OF HUMAN SERVICES OF THE ROMAN CATHOLIC DIOCESE OF ALBANY**. It is available through the central office at 39 Philip St Albany, 12207, 463-4411.

SARATOGA INSTITUTE, 110 Spring Street Saratoga, 587-8770, operates a mail order and walk-in bookstore featuring books related to human relations for teachers, counselors, and group leaders.

SENIOR'S DIRECTORY TO ALBANY AREA PHYSICIANS is a booklet published by the Senior Service Center, 25 Delaware Ave Albany. It is a concise and comprehensive listing of doctors in the Albany area, their specialties, those who accept Medicare and Medicaid, and those who accept new patients or make home visits. Copies are available upon request.

Information 465-3322

Some Social Agencies

This chapter does not pretend to be a comprehensive description of social services available to residents of the Capital District: that in itself would require several volumes. It does seem valuable, however, in addition to giving readers access to available directories, to present portraits of representative agencies as a way of demonstrating the remarkable variety of services available and of indicating the considerable number of people whose lives are devoted to easing human difficulties. Here, then, is a representative sample of social agencies.

THE CAPITAL DISTRICT TRAVELERS' AID SOCIETY, 225 Lark St Albany, was founded in 1924 to provide emergency services to stranded travelers. It has expanded its services to assist the homeless in the four county area. It functions 24 hours a day, seven days a week.

General Information 463-2124

CATHOLIC CHARITIES is a corporate name for a wide-ranging network of social agencies which serve over 100,000 persons each year. The central office, which coordinates the activities of the hundreds of health and human services personnel throughout the region, is located at 39 Philip St Albany, 463-4411.

CHARLEE is a national program sponsored by the Menninger Foundation and administered in the Capital District by SCAP (Schenectady Community Action Program.) The program's title (an acronym for "Children Have All Rights—Legal, Educational, Emotional") gives an indication of the scope of this organization for teens (persons aged 11-19) based on the concept of self-help. **CHARLEE** supervises small groups meeting in ten-week sessions to deal with problems members are facing—problems such as family conflicts, separation, divorce, or death of parents. It operates five homes, all located in well-established residential neighborhoods in the Capital District, in which a maximum of six children live with a married couple and experience a normal, unrestrictive, supportive family-like atmosphere. These homes are helpful particularly for children who have been placed in the custody of the Department of Social Services because they have been abused or rejected, or have demonstrated pre-problematic behavior. The main office for **CHARLEE** is at 148 Clinton St Schenectady.

General Information 374-9181

EQUINOX INC, with its center at 214 Lark St Albany, is a counseling agency with a variety of programs. Begun in 1969 with the founding of the REFER Switchboard, a crisis intervention telephone staffed by a professional coordinator who supervises volunteers, it has since added a permanent counseling center and a Youth Shelter. The counseling service offers out-patient support primarily concerning substance abuse. The youth shelter provides temporary quarters and counseling for runaway or homeless youth. One of the newer programs is a Youth Shelter designed to teach independent living for children who cannot go back home.

General Information 434-6135
REFER—helpline 434-1200

FIRST PLACE FOR DISPLACED HOMEMAKERS assists individuals who, as home-makers not employed outside the home, have been economically depend-ent and have lost or are in danger of losing financial support. The program assists by providing education and job skills, career counseling, job place-ment, and general encouragement to displaced homemakers searching for financial independence. The program is funded by the New York State Department of Labor and administered by the Schenectady Community Action Program. The office is located at 148 Clinton St in Schenectady.

General Information 374-9181

HUMAN RIGHTS COMMISSION is a community agency dedicated to the idea that all citizens should live in harmony and that the rights of individuals of all ethnic and all religious groups are inviolable. It serves on three levels: processing complaints of discrimination; assisting in counseling and place-ment to insure fair housing; intervening in group conflicts to prevent violation of individual rights and disruption of the community.

Information:
Albany 434-5184
Schenectady 382-3290
Troy 270-4520

INFOLINE is a free confidential information and referral service staffed by persons equipped to offer information or referral on the following topics:

adoption, aging, alcoholism, clothing, cultural opportunities, personal counseling, day care, education, employment, environmental concerns, family planning, financial problems, food, handicaps, health, housing, legal problems, recreation, transportation, and volunteer opportunities. In Albany the service is provided by the Albany County Department of Social Services and the County of Albany. In Schenectady it is supported by the Human Services Planning Council of Schenectady.

INFOLINE
Albany Area 447-4000
Schenectady Area 374-2244

JEWISH FAMILY SERVICES, 930 Madison Ave Albany, 482-8856, and 2565 Balltown Rd Schenectady, 382-5337, is a non-sectarian counseling and referral agency for families and individuals. Its professionals offer assistance in such areas as emotional adjustment, strained family relationships, marital problems, depression, unemployment, and childhood-adolescent issues. A special program provides supportive services for Jewish aged. Visits are by appointment.

MEALS FOR THE HOMEBOUND OVER 60 are provided under several programs functioning throughout the Capital District. In each case hot meals are delivered to the subscriber's home. Although there is no specific fee charged, there is a suggested donation requested. Information is available at the following four centers:

MEALS ON WHEELS
Ann Lee Home, Colonie 869-2231
MOBILE MEALS PROGRAM
St. Peter's Hospital, Albany 454-1536
CATHOLIC FAMILY AND
COMMUNITY SERVICES NUTRITION PROGRAM
34 Worden Rd Scotia 370-2161
HOME DELIVERED MEALS PROGRAM
County Office Building, Troy 270-2739

NORTHEAST PARENT AND CHILD SOCIETY, 120 Park Ave Schenectady, serves the abused and the troubled child and his or her family. It was formed in 1983 through the consolidation of Parkhurst Parent and Child Center and Children's Home of Schenectady with the goal of providing a variety of therapeutic, educational, and residential services. The services break into three categories: prevention programs designed to prevent out-of-home placement while youngsters and families work out difficulties; a special school designed to reach children whose learning disabilities or emotional handicaps limit their ability to perform in a public school setting; residential programs designed to shelter children temporarily or to teach those who will never be able to return home how to live independently.

General Information 346-1284

PLANNED PARENTHOOD provides professional medical counseling, medically supervised contraception, infertility counseling, abortion and adoption referrals, pregnancy tests, and general consultation and education about family planning and sexual responsibility. Information is available at the three area offices:

```
259 Lark St Albany . . . . . . . . . . . . . . . . . 434-2182
414 Union St Schenectady . . . . . . . . . . . 374-5353
5 Broadway Troy . . . . . . . . . . . . . . . . . . 274-5640
```

PROJECT HOPE is a non-residency program begun in 1976 under the auspices of Hope House to assist young people, ages 12-15, confront or avoid serious problems with alcohol, drugs, or general adjustment. The project has recently been expanded to include suburban communities as well and to offer assistance to adolescents who are not functioning appropriately at school, in the home, or in the community. The main office is located at 261 North Pearl St in Albany.

```
General Information . . . . . . . . . . . . . . . . 465-2441
```

PROJECT STRIVE, 135 Ontario St Albany, is a "brother program" to Project Hope. It assists young boys, aged 5-18, whom social service agencies, the courts, or the police believe need counseling, training, or shelter.

```
General Information . . . . . . . . . . . . . . . . 462-5366
```

SETON CENTER, established in 1899 to provide for the needs of young working women, offers day care for children of working parents. Seton has recently added a special program—Project Recess. This respite day care for abused or neglected children combines shelter with counseling for parents. The main center is at 240 2nd St Troy, 274-9245.

SCHENECTADY COUNTY ACTION PROGRAM (SCAP) provides a variety of services ranging from Head Start and Welfare Counseling to Weatherization of Homes. Several of its other programs—**CHARLEE** and **FIRST PLACE**— are described separately in this chapter. The office is at 148 Clinton St Schenectady.

```
General Information . . . . . . . . . . . . . . . . 374-9181
```

SUNNYSIDE CENTER, 9th at Engles, Troy, has as its major focus the prevention of and intervention in delinquency. This United Way/Catholic Charities sponsored agency operates a youth program for 5-16 year olds, offering them recreation and group counseling, as well as individual tutoring and homework assistance. Young people may learn cooking, dancing, ceramics, and arts and crafts after school. During the summer children may also engage in swimming and recreation.

```
General Information . . . . . . . . . . . . . . . . 274-5986
```

TRINITY INSTITUTION began in 1918 with the purpose of meeting the needs of the poor in Albany's South End, the city's port of entry for immigrants. It sought to help by improving the neighborhood as a setting for family life. Since that time, the area has built up a core of permanent residents through which flows a constant stream of newcomers; Trinity reaches out to both. Throughout the years, the Institution, a non-sectarian, multi-purpose social service agency, has modified its programs to serve its clientele regardless of race, color, creed, age, sex, or country of origin. Many of Trinity's programs are directed to the development of children and youth, with family counseling and intervention as well as with recreation. The Institution is located at 15 Trinity Place, Albany.

General Information 449-5155

UNITY HOUSE, 309 8th Street, Troy, was initiated in 1971 as a small program to supply basic support to families in low income neighborhoods. Since then, with the support of its founding agency, Catholic Charities, as well as funding from private and public sources, it has grown to have eight strong programs—a day care center for developmentally delayed children, an office of mental health with a three-step residency transition program, a Families in Crisis program with a 24 hour Hotline, a street ministry, a social club, and a transportation program.

General Information. . . . . . . 272-2672 or 274-2633
Families in Crisis Hot Line 272-2370

VISITING NURSE ASSOCIATION, with centers in Albany, Schenectady, and Troy, is much more than its name implies. Originally established to provide skilled nursing care to the sick, the aged and the poor, VNA now brings nursing, physical therapy, occupational therapy, speech therapy, nutritional guidance, medical social services, and nursing aide services to the homes of all people referred to them, regardless of age or income. Information is available at the three offices:

35 Colvin Ave Albany 489-2681
1520 Maxon Rd Schdy 382-7932
2212 Burdett Ave Troy 274-6200

VOLUNTEER SERVICES, which are crucial to the functioning of so many social service agencies, are coordinated by three groups in the Capital District. These agencies match the skills and interests of the volunteer to the needs of the community. Anyone wishing to volunteer, even a small amount of time, can call the offices below for advice and placement:

VOLUNTEER CENTER OF ALBANY
196 Morton Ave Albany 434-2061
VOLUNTARY ACTION CENTER
432 State St Schdy 372-3395
VOLUNTEER BUREAU OF THE TROY AREA
502 Broadway Troy. 274-7234

YMCA, 44 Washington Ave Schenectady, offers a variety of social service programs including a Families in Violence crisis program providing comprehensive services to battered women and their children. These services include a 24-hour Hot Line, sheltering, and counseling. Another service of note is that dedicated to the pregnant teen and young mother. The "Y" also maintains a residence and presents traditional recreational and developmental programs like a children's center, a job shop, a court advocacy service, general counseling, and classes in jazz, fitness, and aerobics.

General Information 374-3394

Families in Crisis Hot Line 374-3394

Index

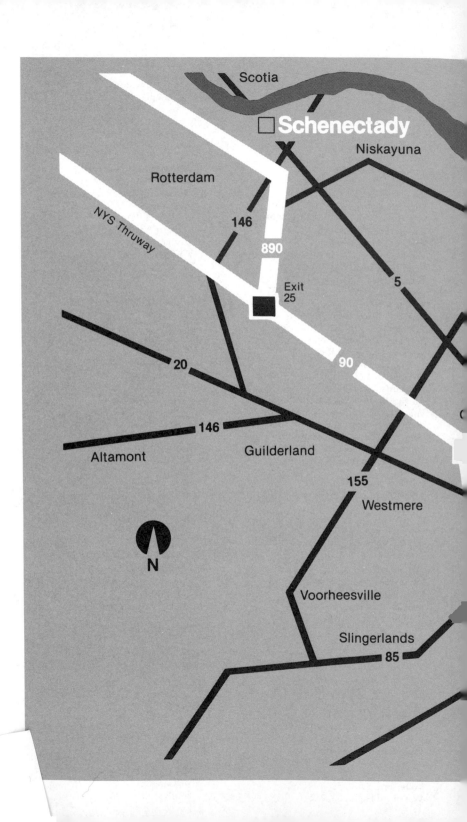

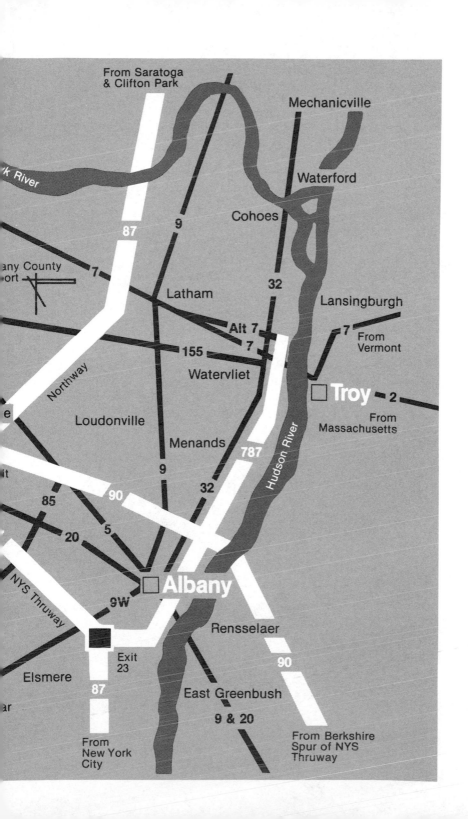

Notes